INEFFABLE UNION WITH CHRIST: LIVING IN THE KINGDOM

Selected Writings of J. Rufus Moseley, 1927-1937

Compiled and Edited By
Gregory S. Camp, Ph.D.

Copyright © 2016 Gregory S. Camp, Ph.D.

Cover image courtesy of the Middle Georgia Archives,
Washington Memorial Library, Macon, Georgia.

All rights reserved. No part of this book may be used or reproduced by any means, graphic, electronic, or mechanical, including photocopying, recording, taping or by any information storage retrieval system without the written permission of the author except in the case of brief quotations embodied in critical articles and reviews.

Scripture taken from the King James Version of the Bible.

This book is a work of non-fiction. Unless otherwise noted, the author and the publisher make no explicit guarantees as to the accuracy of the information contained in this book and in some cases, names of people and places have been altered to protect their privacy.

WestBow Press books may be ordered through booksellers or by contacting:

WestBow Press
A Division of Thomas Nelson & Zondervan
1663 Liberty Drive
Bloomington, IN 47403
www.westbowpress.com
1 (866) 928-1240

Because of the dynamic nature of the Internet, any web addresses or links contained in this book may have changed since publication and may no longer be valid. The views expressed in this work are solely those of the author and do not necessarily reflect the views of the publisher, and the publisher hereby disclaims any responsibility for them.

Any people depicted in stock imagery provided by Thinkstock are models,
and such images are being used for illustrative purposes only.
Certain stock imagery © Thinkstock.

ISBN: 978-1-5127-5410-0 (sc)

Library of Congress Control Number: 2016913797

Print information available on the last page.

WestBow Press rev. date: 08/25/2016

For Arlo, Aaron, and Abigail

CONTENTS

Acknowledgements xiii
Foreword xvii
Introduction xxi

Chapter 1 The Real Kingdom 1
           February 13, 1927

Chapter 2 The Ideal Kingdom 3
           August 21, 1927

Chapter 3 The Heart of Christianity 6
           September 4, 1927

Chapter 4 A Spiritual Autobiography (Charles G. Finney) 9
           November 27, 1927

Chapter 5 Two Sides of Christianity (St. Francis of Assisi) 13
           December 4, 1927

Chapter 6 St. Paul 17
           December 11, 1927

Chapter 7 Every Whit Wholeness 21
           June 3, 1928

Chapter 8 Christ in the Death Cell 24
           July 1, 1928

Chapter 9 The Overcomer and Conqueror 28
           August 26, 1928

Chapter 10	Keys to the Kingdom 32
	September 23, 1928

Chapter 11	Secret of Abiding in Christ 35
	September 30, 1928

Chapter 12	Grace Producing Grace 38
	November 18, 1928

Chapter 13	Going On to Perfection 42
	November 25, 1928

Chapter 14	Faith, Hope, Charity 46
	January 27, 1929

Chapter 15	Taught of the Lord 49
	March 24, 1929

Chapter 16	Putting on the New Man 53
	April 21, 1929

Chapter 17	Unity and Freedom in Christ 57
	August 11, 1929

Chapter 18	Appropriating Christ 61
	August 25, 1929

Chapter 19	Perpetuating Pentecost 65
	June 8, 1930

Chapter 20	Boundless Good Will 71
	July 13, 1930

Chapter 21	In Him Forever 74
	February 8, 1931

Chapter 22	Risen With Christ 78
	February 22, 1931

Chapter 23	Love to Everybody 82
	January 24, 1932

Chapter 24 Love to the Whole Creation 86
February 14, 1932

Chapter 25 Rejoice in Me Always 89
February 21, 1932

Chapter 26 All Taught of God 93
February 28, 1932

Chapter 27 Way into the Kingdom 96
April 17, 1932

Chapter 28 Living in the Kingdom 99
July 17, 1932

Chapter 29 Happy Days in the Kingdom 104
October 4, 1932

Chapter 30 His Great Love 109
January 8, 1933

Chapter 31 Creative Love 112
January 22, 1933

Chapter 32 Limitless Love For All 115
March 5, 1933

Chapter 33 The Quest for the Best Life 117
April 30, 1933

Chapter 34 Present and Coming Kingdom 122
May 7, 1933

Chapter 35 On the Universe's Throne 125
May 21, 1933

Chapter 36 Heart of Law and Gospel 130
May 28, 1933

Chapter 37 The Holy Presence 134
December 17, 1933

Chapter 38	Rare Wisdom	138
	January 21, 1934	
Chapter 39	The Resurrection: Love in Manifest Victory	142
	April 1, 1934	
Chapter 40	Keys or Secrets of Union with Him and His Kingdom ..	147
	April 29, 1934	
Chapter 41	His Great, Perfect Love	152
	May 6, 1934	
Chapter 42	Live Me Everywhere	158
	July 1, 1934	
Chapter 43	Put Up They Sword	162
	December 9, 1934	
Chapter 44	The Lord for the Body	167
	March 17, 1935	
Chapter 45	The Kingdom of Heaven	171
	May 19, 1935	
Chapter 46	Great Happy Days	176
	August 11, 1935	
Chapter 47	Glory Hill	181
	August 18, 1935	
Chapter 48	Vital Union with Jesus	186
	January 12, 1936	
Chapter 49	Overcome or be Overcome	190
	March 22, 1936	
Chapter 50	The Basis of Inexpressible Joy	194
	April 26, 1936	
Chapter 51	The Wonders of Love	200
	November 22, 1936	

Chapter 52   The Full Will of God 205
             January 3, 1937

Chapter 53   New Covenant Perfection 210
             August 22, 1937

Chapter 54   The Single Eye 214
             September 26, 1937

Appendix I 219
Appendix II 237
Endnotes 245
About the Author 247

ACKNOWLEDGEMENTS

In any endeavor of heart and mind, one invariably owes much to any number of people along the way: friends and family who through encouragement, prayer, constructive criticism, and in some cases needed financial help, were always there for support. I must begin by giving thanks to William Kroah for providing me with decades-old copies of dozens of already transcribed Rufus Moseley *Telegraph* articles between the years 1921 and approximately 1938. These formed the early base of this work. His generosity in making them available cannot be overstated and his good humor (and warnings) of what lie ahead were greatly appreciated. I also would like to thank Lisa Blackburn Wright of Mercer University's Tarver Special Collections for her efforts on my behalf. The same is true of Muriel Jackson and her staff at the Washington Memorial Library in Macon, Georgia. Their kindness and suggestions were gratefully received and saved me, on a number of occasions, considerable time in my limited schedule. Muriel also uncovered valuable information for me concerning historic Macon; her expertise is considerable and appreciated. A thank you also goes out to Sherrie Marshall, editor of *The Macon Telegraph*, for her time, efforts, and general helpfulness. I felt like I was a thorn in her side, but with gracious good humor she endured my persistent requests!

The encouragement of friends and family must also be stated here. I would like to thank the late Frank Vyzralek of Bismarck, North Dakota, a legend in the historical community of the upper Midwest, who always was available with council, humor, and wisdom. His passing in February, 2014 left a gaping hole in the profession and in the hearts of his friends who miss him so very much. Robert Barnett of Lee University (Cleveland, Tennessee), a friend since 1997, also has been generously supportive of my efforts, and more than anyone else I know embodies the Good Spirit that Rufus Moseley sought to follow and live.

Pastors Kurt Chaffee of New Song Fellowship of Bismarck, North Dakota and Aaron Schuler, now living in Ft. Collins, Colorado, were early encouragers of this work as well. Their example, teaching, and friendship have been greatly appreciated and always present. Indeed, New Song became my church home in December of 2013 and has been a great inspiration and support for me in sometimes trying times. In this regard, I would like to thank Dan Phillips, who moved to California that same month, for telling me about New Song and encouraging me to attend. It was wise and cogent advice, and I am forever grateful to him and his wife Kathy for their friendship and example. Also of great aid to me by their example and friendship are former and current New Song attendees Frank and Joni Johnson, Ben and Pauline Ehrmantraut, Jonathan and Sarah Stark, Mat and Erika Grade, Jessica Stramer, Giget Kelsh, Betty Erickson, Damian and Katy Schaefer, Elisha Scott (she who possesses the singing voice of an angel!), Bill and Karen Schneider, Doreen Quist, and last but most certainly not least, Joy Marimon, who was always available with friendship, words of encouragement, and sage advice all stemming from the deep spiritual well within her. There likewise have been people in my past who have been examples and encouragement to me then and over the years. These include Greg and Joy Maher, and Jay Bunker of Faith Fellowship in Elk River, Minnesota, as well as many of the people at Shiloh House in Anoka, Minnesota, most notably Betty Matthews, from those early to mid-1970's days.

Those people whom Rufus Moseley directly or indirectly influenced and who were of aid include the late Joyce Carole Carter, Vernon Tyson, Jack Taylor, and Kent and Brenda Littlejohn. These people have been a great help with stories of Mr. Moseley and how their parents and/or mentors were affected by him, and were of great inspiration to me and demonstrating the necessity that this work proceed. The Littlejohn's in particular have been stalwart moral, spiritual, and financial supporters of this project from very early on. Their friendship, fellowship, and financial assistance cannot be praised highly enough. The Littlejohn's had studied under Moseley protégé Tommy Tyson, so they were well familiar with the power of Rufus's work. I was blessed to spend a few nights at their country home, "Shalom in the Wilderness" in east Illinois, and share in watching videos of Tommy Tyson and Wayne McLain—and to sample Brenda's unbelievably good cooking! For a bachelor such as myself, that was a rare treat!

I was also blessed to meet and befriend the best of people in Macon, Georgia. Bobby and Joyce Covington, Caroline Harvey, Julie Morris, Donna Nye, Kathleen Dearmin, Fred Remick, Pastors Trey and Shannon Dickerson and Robert and Doreen Stumpf of High Point Church, Patrick and Velvet Cramer, and Matt Fabian, were all particularly welcoming and in a number of instances, helpful in the funding of this project. Above all, special thanks must be given to Kathie and David Walters. I first read Kathie's words on the on-line Elijah List and was moved by the depth of her revelation and love. Upon finding out she was from Macon, I contacted her and began an email friendship. Once I arrived in Macon in early October, 2015, she and husband David were overwhelmingly loving, friendly, and supportive, both spiritually and financially. Their mentoring of me is of value far beyond gold and silver; by merely being in their presence and witnessing the move of the Holy Spirit on a daily basis, I saw first-hand what it means to live in the Kingdom. I also need to fully thank the Byron, Georgia descendants of Rufus Moseley: Fran Williams, my initial Moseley family contact, as well as her parents, Emmett and Diana Vinson, all of whom proved the very picture and reality of what their uncle Rufus taught and lived. Their kindness and openness in discussing "Uncle Ruf," and making family records pertaining to him available to me was generous beyond words. Fran and her son even gave me a tour of their home, the same house that Rufus had lived in with his brother Millard and sister-in-law Effie from 1930 until his death in 1954.

My mother, Dolores B. Camp, has been perhaps my single greatest encouragement throughout this project, and always had a kind word and prayer support. From the time I was first impressed to take up this project and lacked even the most basic supplies and equipment to perform it, she was in sustained prayer for its outcome and watched with me in great joy as things came together in its proper timing. She never doubted me, although sometimes thought I may be pushing myself too hard to see its completion. Prayer warriors such as she are the very backbone of the Church today!

I also received great encouragement from people overseas who were familiar with Rufus Moseley's writings. One of these was Michael Basham, who as of this writing lives in Taiwan. His grandfather, Don Basham, personally knew J. Rufus Moseley and made his teachings a lifetime study. Like me, Michael holds Rufus in the highest regard and was a constant source of encouragement to me over these past years, and reinforced my sure conviction that Moseley's works need to come forth again to bless those who seek Him and hunger for a deeper walk in Christ.

There were times of great elation in this project and also times when I wondered if it would ever truly get if off the ground. To God be thanks for the strength and drive to continue on in what has been a truly inspiring journey. Anyone who becomes familiar with "Brother Rufus'" teachings will come to the same conclusion. I am honored to bring these early writings back to the Christian reading public!

Gregory S. Camp, June 2016

FOREWORD

My own contact with the works of J. Rufus Moseley began in June, 1974, at a Christian commune called Shiloh House, located in Anoka, Minnesota, a northwest suburb of Minneapolis. A friend of mine from Long Island and I were having a discussion on some spiritual matters when Rufus' name and autobiography, Manifest Victory, came up. Sitting along the banks of the Mississippi River that morning, I was asked if I had ever heard of him. I hadn't, and my friend then recommended purchasing a copy of the book in question. At the time, Manifest Victory, originally published by *Harpers and Brothers*, had been picked up by a then fledgling Christian publishing house of the times, *Logos*, and I was fortunate to find it in a local Christian bookstore.

So began a journey for me with a man who would, beginning decades later in 2013, come to mean more to me than any single Christian teacher or writer. For though Moseley wrote but two books, the autobiography already mentioned and a book on the ministry of the Holy Spirit entitled Perfect Everything, they were to have a profound impact on me and indeed, most anyone who read them. Over the decades since first hearing about and reading Manifest Victory, I went away to college where Bachelor's degree grew into a Master's, which in turn became a Ph.D. in American History. Despite the vicissitudes of life and personal decisions which resulted in many years away from Christianity, I nonetheless remembered Rufus Moseley and held to the secret hope that at least what I had read in his book years before was true—that there was a "Life as Love" as he described it, and a means of living in the Kingdom of God in the here and now in victory. I never forgot Rufus Moseley, nor the book that had such a profound impact on my life.

Relatively recently, in September of 2013, I had reached the point where the Holy Spirit wants all of us: willing to surrender, to leave off resistance, and to allow Him to live His life in and through me. Despite my many shortcomings—and they are legion—after that surrender I felt again that there was a purpose to life, although at age 56 at the time, I rather wondered what that could and would mean. Weeks after that reawakening, the memory of Rufus Moseley again came to me, leading me to seek out his two books. Long since out of print, I nonetheless was able to find them via interlibrary loan. When I received them, it was like meeting an old friend, and I quickly devoured them. This was sometime in late October of 2013, and as November arrived I found myself wishing that Moseley had written more. Thus began my search that was to last nearly three years as of this writing, and provide the basis for the book you have in your hands—the search and work proved an extremely rich spiritual blessing to me!

I began my search by looking for other works on this remarkable man of God. I came upon a book entitled <u>A Resurrection Encounter: The Rufus Moseley Story</u>, by the late Dr. Wayne McLain. This biography, itself a remarkable book, details some of Rufus' own spiritual journey and lays out for the reader the magnitude and importance of this singular life and ministry. McLain also provides expert analysis and knowledge of philosophical and theological trends during Moseley's life, and provides the reader with a thorough and reasonable account by one who knew Rufus well. Indeed, McLain spent a good deal of time with Moseley during the last years of his (Moseley's) life, 1945-1954. Along with the great Methodist evangelist, Tommy Tyson, McLain was a privileged companion of this inimitable man. In the early 1990's, he and Camps Farthest Out (CFO) representatives and research assistants William and Audra Kroah, compiled some articles Moseley had written for the Macon newspaper *The Telegraph and News* (the *Macon News* and the *Macon Telegraph* combined in 1930). The result was a book entitled <u>A Heavenly View: the Best of Rufus Moseley</u> (1993), which featured forty articles selected from the *Telegraph* as well as a few other pieces Moseley authored. Although McLain and Tyson are now in heaven, it is no exaggeration to say that I am but standing on the shoulders of those giants in this work. I did find and contact one of the researchers for that second book, William Kroah. It is difficult to imagine a more helpful and God-given contact than he. I connected with him via email through the website of Camps Farthest Out—North Carolina, and he generously provided me with some eighty articles that he and Dr.

McLain had collected from the Macon newspaper decades before, and set me on a path to obtain as many of these as I could.

Rufus Moseley wrote a near-weekly column for the *Telegraph* between 1921 and his passing in September, 1954. Rufus' submissions between the years 1921-26 were infrequent and spotty, and without a "by" line. Thereafter his writings were much more numerous and lengthy. While I had obtained some eighty articles from Bill Kroah several months earlier, I had reached the point where it became necessary for me to travel from my home at the time in Bismarck, North Dakota to Macon, Georgia where copies of these and other Moseley writings could be found. That initial trip to Georgia was accomplished in early April of 2015.

I returned to Bismarck two weeks later with some 600 articles, as well as a few lengthy talks taken from Rufus's frequent speaking engagements. I had hoped that I had obtained the vast majority of what he wrote, only to find out shortly thereafter that there were perhaps an additional 400! Nonetheless, I then began the long, arduous task of transcribing those articles for publication. The vast majority of the time Rufus would dictate his articles to a transcriber, which then would be put in the *Macon Telegraph (and News)* Sunday morning edition. The dictation made for sometimes difficult grammar, seen mostly in the form of run-on sentences, misplaced modifiers, frequent passive voice use, and some creative usage of commas and semi-colons. It became part of my task to rework the articles into a more readable form, something which itself was a very daunting task. In some cases I left the writing alone altogether—saving what those familiar with Rufus' writings call "Moseleyisms." By that I mean the sometimes homespun bent he would give to his words, and the humor and joy that peppered everything he wrote.

Moseley believed that when he dictated such things, it was done under inspiration of the Holy Spirit—and when you read these articles, I think you will understand why he felt that way. Besides, the manner in which the Spirit best spoke through Rufus in print was in the form of nuggets of truth which, in a few words or sentences, would capture great spiritual truth. Others, such as Rufus' great friend, the world-famous evangelist E. Stanley Jones, saw long before me this as one of Moseley's greatest gifts. As such, I took great pains when editing to not change the original meaning and intent of the author, but merely to ensure that it would be easier reading for the seeking soul. After all, I did not want to be in the ridiculous position of editing the Holy Spirit!

The task of collecting these articles—there could be around one thousand of them when it is all finished—and transcribing them will be a work of many months and perhaps even years. I believed and still believe, however, that it was time for this man's writings and revelation to bless another generation of Christians with a wisdom and insight that was decades ahead of its time.

It is no overstatement to say that the writings of J. Rufus Moseley read like new Epistles of John, as the centerpiece of his ministry was the Love way of Life and the tremendous power and revelation contained therein. Belonging to no denomination, Moseley has been considered by some to be the first Charismatic in that he spoke to many different groups about the New Birth experience and the Baptism of the Holy Spirit. Moseley shared this message far and wide between 1910 and 1954, and with great effect. Although he has been largely forgotten by the second generation after him, it is my hope that the message and the life he embodied will be known anew to hungry and thirsty seekers.

One will find topical repetition throughout these articles, albeit stated in different ways. It is not unlike the story of the Apostle John, who toward the end of his life constantly stated to those around him, "Little children, love one another!" When asked why he kept repeating this, he is said to have replied, "If this were accomplished, it would be enough." Moseley's writings, while presented chronologically, are by no means the sum total of Moseley's production during those years. While they may be read in any order the reader chooses, they do present a look at one man's spiritual growth over the period in question. Some articles have been shortened to deal with the specific topic intended: Living in ineffable union and in Kingdom of God in the here and now.

Gregory S. Camp, June, 2016

INTRODUCTION

Rufus Moseley was born in 1870 in the mountains of western North Carolina near the town of Elkin, the fourth of eight children born to James and Theresa Moseley. His father was a Confederate war veteran, serving in a North Carolina unit during that ghastly conflict. Moseley's memory of him is one of a man of great personal integrity who, despite injuries incurred during the Civil War, was a tremendous worker. Honest to a fault, his father when selling something would tell the prospective buyer exactly what he thought the item was worth—all after telling the faults of the item to be sold of which he was aware. Always interested in the well-being of his children and coinciding with his strong work ethic, he nonetheless wanted to ensure that his children did not "work too hard" in their daily tasks. Rufus's last conversation with his father in 1888 or 1889, prior to his leaving for Peabody College in Nashville, was most memorable for him. James "Cubby" Moseley told his son, "Rufus, I know nothing of the world you are to be in, I have no advice for you. I trust you."[1]

His mother, to hear Moseley and living relatives describe her, was something of a wonder in her own right. A woman of great prayer, she often would disappear into the woods when something pertaining to the family needed the consultation of the Holy Spirit, and she would not return until she felt she had an answer. Typical of many frontier wives and mothers of the period, Theresa made the family clothing at a loom, raised vegetables and fruit for their consumption, and saw to it that her children did their school work. Rufus describes reciting his lessons to her while she was busy with various daily tasks. In general, he described the mountain life he enjoyed as a youth as ideal "seed, soil, and climate" for his later ministry. When it came time for him to attend college, it was an ordeal for him to leave, so attached was he to his family and the rich life he experienced in the Blue Ridge Mountains.[2]

Paying college tuition for a large family was not something that was possible for Moseley family. It was agreed upon by the parents and their children that the oldest (Charles, who went on to become a noted physician) would first help pay the expenses for the next sibling to attend, with that one (Rufus) then agreeing to pay the tuition of the one below him (brother Millard). Rufus left for Nashville, Tennessee to attend Peabody College (before it was absorbed into Vanderbilt) where he immediately found a niche in academic life. He gravitated toward philosophy and history, thanks in part to the excellence of the professors he had in those areas. Two in particular whom he named were President W. H. Payne, and Wycliffe Rose; the former acted as something of a mentor before Rufus left for the University of Chicago—"wisdom fell from his lips"—Rufus said—and the latter became a life-long friend, and later a noted professor at the University of Tennessee in Knoxville.[3]

Other professors such as A. P. Bourland and Sam Jones introduced him to the writings of the great Transcendental and Victorian era writers such as Ralph Waldo Emerson, Henry David Thoreau, Macon, Georgia's own Sidney Lanier, Oliver Wendell Holmes, Nathaniel Hawthorne, and poets like Alfred Lord Tennyson. It was his study of the poets, particularly Tennyson, that introduced him to "the question mark." Moseley liked to quote Tennyson's statement that "there lives more faith in honest doubt, believe me, than in half the creeds." Despite his growing spiritual leanings, Rufus was never afraid to ask questions, to weigh assumptions whether political or religious, and to think for himself. His kind of Christian intellectualism is sadly lacking in 21st century America; indeed, in some instances it is downright discouraged!

Rufus also had a profound love of the ancient philosophers, especially Plato. It was while reading Plato that Moseley describes being so taken with what he read (Plato's <u>Dialogues</u>), that he said he "forgot my body" and was lost in pure intellectual delight. He strongly believed that both Socrates and Plato were excellent examples of pre-Christian wisdom that God had bestowed on the world. When Plato, for instance, watched in disgust at the manner in which 4th Century B.C. Athenian leadership treated the finest man he had ever known (Socrates) by sentencing him to death, he prophetically declared that when the Perfect Man arrived on the scene, He would be sent to the cross. Still, for Rufus, it would be a spiritual experience he had while a student at Peabody that was to set the stage for his later life and ministry.

In his sophomore year at Peabody College, Moseley attended a revival meeting held in a nearby church and in the presence of some of his classmates and professors. He felt inclined to come forward when asked, and fought an inner battle about doing so in the presence of his peers. He gave in and went forward to acknowledge his need for and acceptance of Christ's plan of salvation. It was a very difficult thing for him to do, the most difficult of his life according to his autobiography, but every step since then toward Christ had been made easier and easier. A couple of nights later he attended a service where there was a dedication ceremony held for those who had made the step at the revival meeting. The man leading the gathering perceptively stated that though they were few in number, he believed that Rufus in particular would mean far more in the Kingdom than he, the revivalist, had up to that point.[4] If anything, his born-again experience was to fire up his already voracious appetite for learning, and he was to leave Peabody with the support of his professors to begin graduate study in history, philosophy, and political science at the University of Chicago.

Rufus Moseley attended college and graduate school at some of the finest institutions of higher education of the day. As he had at Peabody College, he studied philosophy, history, and political science at the University of Chicago and Harvard University. He also attended Heidelberg University in Germany as a graduate student. At Chicago and Harvard, he was mentored by and counted among his friends some of the intellectual giants of late 19th and early 20th Century America: John Dewey, Josiah Royce, George Santayana, and William James, and later at Mercer, Edwin M. Poteat, Sr., and William Heard Kilpatrick. Through these contacts and still during his graduate training, he served as a professor of history and philosophy at Mercer (then College) University in Macon, Georgia between 1894 and 1900.

While there he quickly became recognized as one of the brightest minds on campus, and was greatly admired and loved by students and faculty alike.[5] Ever the spiritual seeker, his time at Mercer was cut short as a result of his interest in a relatively new spiritual movement of the time, Christian Science. Mercer, then a rather conservative Baptist school, did not view Christian Science in a positive light, and Moseley was aware of this. Nonetheless, the administration did their best to keep the young scholar on staff, so great were his contributions. It was Moseley himself who resigned to save Mercer any embarrassment his involvement with Christian Science might bring and, with great sadness, the school agreed to accept his departure. His leaving was a bittersweet one, but also one that was what Rufus would call a "love feast," in that there was no rancor or bad feelings on either side. Indeed, up until the time of Moseley's death in 1954, he maintained very good relations with Mercer and was a frequent speaker there at any number of events.

So began his time with Christian Science, and between 1900 and 1909, Moseley periodically served as an editorial consultant to the *Christian Science Sentinel* and *Christian Science Journal*, and himself submitted and published a number of articles in those journals. He was on somewhat close terms with its founder, Mary Baker Eddy, but as the first decade of the 20th century came to a close, Rufus became increasingly uncomfortable with what might be called a "cult of personality" that had grown up around her. The movement had also become more doctrinaire, something that a free-thinker like Moseley surely would have found stifling. That and the fact that he was a Bible-believing Christian necessitated that he hold Scripture at the forefront of any belief system, made it increasingly difficult for him to stay in that organization.[6] He realized that the next step in his spiritual walk was about to take him away from another group of people for whom he felt great kinship and love. The means of that break, however, would take him by surprise and was to again produce—as with his leaving Mercer—both a friendly parting of ways and entrance into a world of spiritual reality that was at the time quite controversial. Rufus Moseley had heard about and then himself sought after the Baptism of the Holy Spirit. His life would never be the same.

By early 1910, Moseley believed that his Christian walk was lacking. In Macon he had met and spoken with members of a new and controversial Christian group, the Pentecostals, about the experience they taught called the Baptism of the Holy Spirit. One must remember that at this point in American religious history, Pentecostalism was deemed a movement among the uneducated or the fanatic, or worse, the mentally unbalanced. Certainly members of Moseley's own family at the time considered it such. The great revivals in Wales in 1904 and 1905, and the fall of the Holy Spirit in Los Angeles at Azuza Street in 1906, were still quite recent and not widely known. To Moseley, it held such promise of unity with the Holy Spirit that it was something he believed he must investigate. He also had a friend who had participated in Pentecostal meetings in Macon's Moore Hall led by J. H. King, and successfully encouraged Moseley to attend.[7]

At one of these meetings, where English Pentecostal preacher Samuel Chadwick spoke on the Baptism of the Holy Spirit as a real, tangible experience, Moseley went forward and publicly announced, "I want God's best, and if the Baptism with the Holy Spirit is God's best, I want it." Not considered a conservative, one of the Moore's Hall group told Moseley that he would have to become more orthodox before he could expect the Baptism of the Holy Spirit. In typical Moseley fashion, he replied that "the promise was not the orthodox, but to those who hunger, thirst, and ask."[8] Rufus stated that after saying that, he felt an incredible sense of release that only comes when one abandons oneself to a higher purpose. He was to comment, "No one is ready for the freedom of the Spirit until he is ready to be led by the Spirit."[9] When the Holy Spirit did come upon him, it was to be the seminal event in his life, and would be the rudder directing his ministry thereafter.

On the evening of March 21, 1910, after walking home from a meeting where the Baptism of the Holy Spirit was talked about, sought, and prayed for, Moseley arrived at the Macon mansion located at the corner of Georgia and Orange streets where he was renting a room. He found that he had the house to himself, something he later attributed to Divine planning given what was about to transpire. Around 11:00 p.m. he prayed, "Jesus, if possible, come and live within me and be in me the life and principle of Your own good life and teaching that will enable me to go Your way." He then retired, sleeping for a few hours until waking around 3:00 a.m. He arose from bed and sat at a table with paper and pencil to record some thoughts he believed would be of benefit to a friend. Suddenly, the Spirit came upon him in power. Rufus found himself raised to his feet and placed in the form of a cross with his arms stretched outward. He became aware of a Person physically standing immediately in front of him of "barely concealed powers and immense sanctity."[10] He realized it was Jesus, whose Spirit then "infused Himself within" and filled him to overflowing. Moseley encountered what he referred to as the "Baptism with the Spirit, with Fire," and caused him to enter a place of love, joy, and bliss—an ineffable union that was more than he could contain. He fell at the feet of his Savior as though dead, but as he related, "more alive than I knew it possible to be."[11]

This was the beginning of a ministry for Rufus Moseley that would be to those "at the bottom of human need and suffering, as well as to those on top of human privilege." Intellectually brilliant as he was, it was his level of humility and sense of service to mankind, not to mention what he described as the "Life as Love," a term he used to describe the vital union with Christ, for which he was remembered. Indeed, it would be the clarion call of his ministry for Christians to live in moment-by-moment conscious union with Jesus, for a life of surrender, utter sincerity, and total yielding to Christ so that the risen Lord could live again through each of us. No one who ever met Rufus Moseley forgot him; he truly lived a life of love, peace, and bliss with the Holy Spirit that resulted in a ministry of unfettered joy. He liked to say, "We say we want to go to heaven; yet if we were to go there, we would find heaven anxious to come here!" In time he became known as "The Apostle of Love," and rarely has such a title been more aptly given.

Between that experience in 1910 until he began work as a religion writer for the *Macon Telegraph* eleven years later, Rufus engaged in a number of activities that gained him some notice—not to mention notoriety—in Macon. One of the first things that happened to him after his Baptism with the Holy Spirit was a strong negative reaction from his family. His mother (his father was deceased by this time) was fearful that her son had joined a new and dangerous group, and given that he was beginning to experience visions, had serious questions about his mental well-being. At her urging, Rufus did see a doctor, noted physician Dr. Henry Allen, who ran a private sanitarium in Milledgeville, Georgia. Dr. Allen recognized that his patient was not insane or delusional, merely in the midst of a very intense religious experience.[12] Indeed, Rufus found in the days immediately after the Baptism in the Holy Spirit that he saw natural things around him in a glorified state. He spoke of seeing Jesus in the faces of those around him, and even farm animals taking on a grace and beauty he had never seen before. Decades later, Dr. Wayne McLain shared how there would be times when Rufus, riding through an ordinary countryside or walking in a well-stocked grocery store, would suddenly erupt into thanksgiving for the beauty of the surroundings or the bounty on the shelves. As McLain stated, "I think it is safe to say that Rufus saw the earth as much more beautiful than that revealed to the natural eye."[13] A few weeks later, Rufus began a time of intense spiritual introspection about what had occurred, as well as dealing with some of his family's concerns.

It was during the first decade of the 20th Century, perhaps 1903, that one of Rufus' younger brothers, Millard, came to Georgia where he met and married a young teacher named Effie Crawford. Because of this marriage, Rufus released Millard from the responsibility of aiding the next youngest sibling in going to college, something for which his brother was grateful. Apparently in exchange for this, a few acres of land from the Crawford family were deeded to him and a room placed at his disposal in his brother's home. Millard, Effie, and Rufus moved into a house in nearby Byron, Georgia that year, and took care of the acreage of pecan trees outside of town. It was to be Rufus' home until his passing in 1954. It was not always a peaceful relationship, however, and Rufus himself spoke of "tension" with his family over his religious views.[14] One gets a better idea of this by what transpired shortly thereafter.

Rufus Moseley's religious views began to come to the notice of the city of Macon in 1911. He met and befriended two twin sisters from Macon, Suzie and Carro Davis, who had themselves experienced salvation and the Baptism of the Holy Spirit in 1910. In December 1911, the three of them apparently thought it a good idea to attend services at Macon's First Presbyterian Church on Mulberry Street--a church Suzie and Carro at one time attended--and there disrupted the service with boisterous worship. They were asked to leave. They took their worship to the street that day as well as other occasions, which garnered considerable attention from passers-by and then the press. On Christmas Day of 1911, despite the fact that they had obtained permission from law enforcement to hold street meetings, their group apparently got too big and when the police asked them to move, offered verbal resistance. Rufus reported years later that when asked to break up the meeting, he responded to the police officer by saying words to the effect that he was not in the business of stopping meetings, but of helping them along. The policeman to whom this was said was not amused, and took steps to arrest Moseley. Realizing that he had offended the officer, Rufus apologized and was released before a trip to the local station was made.[15]

These were part and parcel of his early post-Baptism days, in which the local population (and his family) considered Rufus at best something of an eccentric. An old friend of his, poet and scholar Professor George Herbert Clarke, even made it a point to visit Macon specifically to see Moseley. Clarke, perhaps at the behest of some of Rufus' friends, sought to get Moseley to tone down his very verbal and to some, erratic public religious pronunciations and demonstrations. Clarke failed, but did report to a third party about Moseley, "There is greatness there that you (meaning the friend to whom he was talking) and I can hardly begin to understand."[16] The amazingly redemptive thing about it all is that ten years later Rufus Moseley was one of the city's best-known and beloved citizens and was a frequent guest speaker at churches all over town, including the First Presbyterian Church. Those days were not in the least indicative of his anointing, but rather of his own early enthusiasm.

By the time of the First World War, Moseley became an increasingly active writer of editorials for the *Telegraph*, mostly dealing with the insanity of war, the needs of the poor and destitute at home and abroad, passionately speaking against the death penalty and visiting those on death row, the need to help the war-ravaged in Europe, and racial injustice. Indeed, in Jim Crow-era Macon, Georgia his stances against segregation and racial injustice were to cause many a raised eye-brow among the white population. On at least one occasion, he stopped the lynching of a young black man at the hands of an angry mob.[17] He also gained the positive notice of many aid and relief organizations during this time, and the editor of the *Macon Telegraph* even began to solicit his help in appeals for any number of worthwhile public programs.

His writings became identifiable and popular enough that W. T. Anderson, the *Telegraph*'s editor-in-chief, asked him to write religious articles beginning in 1921, something he continued to do until his death in 1954. He never took payment for this work and once, when the editor deposited money into his bank account, upon finding this out, Rufus rushed to the bank, withdrew some $2700 which had unbeknownst to him been accruing there, and with it paid off the mortgage of a woman being evicted from her home.[18] This story is typical of the man who would give away the last dime in his pocket to someone on the street, or give his coat away to a person without one. Indeed, in keeping with the scriptural mandate to keep one's good deeds secret, this story would not be known if a witness hadn't shared it decades later with Wayne McLain. Despite his remarkable personal generosity, Moseley's interests, besides local, were also cast over a wide philosophical and theological area.

Some readers may find Rufus' interaction with a few non-orthodox groups such as Christian Science with which he was affiliated between 1900 and 1910, "Jesus Name" or Oneness Pentecostals, and later Unity and New Thought proponents as somewhat odd, even cautionary. What you must keep in mind with Mr. Moseley was his calling to give the love of Jesus to each and all mandated to him that he fellowship and share with those with whom he might have theological differences. Moseley defined his calling as:

> "…to abide in Jesus all the time and give His love to everybody and to report as best I can the light that He makes clearest. What I have to give fits in everywhere there is belief in and love for Jesus and for His love-way of life. So I go among all groups; seeking to bless everywhere. I belong everywhere there is an open door and freedom of the Spirit, and yet I belong nowhere in a sectarian and denominational sense.[19]

Always at the core of his message was the born again experience, followed by the need to seek and ask for the Baptism of the Holy Spirit, and subsequent to those experiences, to walk in love was one he shared with everyone. It is safe to say that to Rufus Moseley, Salvation and Holy Spirit Baptism were on-going experiences; while both were remembered as specific events on specific dates, the manifestation of both were something that he experienced on a daily basis. He would happily share these spiritual truths with all who would listen. Still, all of this was not always understood by conservative Christians of the day, nor indeed in the years following his death in 1954. One thing is certain, however: whomever he met would be left with a most indelible impression.

To gain a personal perspective on what an encounter with Rufus Moseley was like, a young Agnes Sanford shares her first meeting with him in the late 1930's, and just how unforgettable he was:

> "There was a time when I made a trip alone to a church in the South and stopped to visit my brother, H.M., then surveying in Augusta, Georgia.
>
> 'Would you mind us going to visit an old man in Macon?' H.M. asked.
>
> 'What kind of an old man?'
>
> 'Well, I don't know, people say he is a very holy man, sort of a prophet. So we asked him to come with us to have a picnic lunch somewhere.'
>
> H.M. and Anne, the three children and I drove to Macon. We found Brother Rufus Moseley, took him into the car among the children and lunch baskets, and looked for a picnic place. The old man with the keen eyes and wizened face of an Old Testament prophet suggested a public park, not knowing that a fair had ended there the day before—and not caring. We wended our way through the torn newspapers and empty cardboard boxes and sat down on some wooden benches. We unpacked the lunch and chose sandwiches. Brother Rufus began to talk. Three hours later I came back to earth still sitting with the sandwich in my hand, listening to such as I had never heard before. For this old man had truly seen Jesus and had been filled with His Spirit…But here was a person who had seen—here was a man who had experienced in some measure that which the disciples experienced on the Day of Pentecost, and whose face shown with the joy of it, so that when he talked of the Lord, years fell away from him, and he was no longer an old man, but a youth, flaming with joy and love.

I cannot remember just what he said. But the man himself I will never forget."[20]

Sanford wasn't alone in her assessment of Rufus Moseley. Both before and after his death in 1954, newspaper religion columnists across the nation would offer stories about him. What follows is a good representation:

> "Our daughter, Anne, now a teacher in Raleigh, North Carolina, was fascinated by our friend, Rufus Moseley, when he would come for visits to our home. In her childish eyes she could not see the great Christian writer and speaker that he was; she saw only that he loved her and all children.
>
> 'You are born of the qualities you habitually give out,' Dr. Moseley said. 'If you give out hate, you become hateful; if you give out criticism, you become critical. If you give out love, you become lovely. So give out only love.'
>
> "Someone asked him in our congregation, 'But Dr. Moseley, suppose they don't return your love?' His answer: 'Increase the dose!'"[21]

Joel Rufus Moseley, over the years 1921 to 1954, became one the most respected religious leaders in the American South, and in time, nationally and internationally. His weekly *Macon Telegraph* articles contain some of the freshest, insightful, and anointed publications on Spirit-filled living that have ever appeared in print. Among the many topics he covered were first and foremost union with Christ, the salvation message, the Baptism of the Holy Spirit, the power of prayer, the surrendered life, utter sincerity, along with socially conscious topics such as labor, race, economics, the poor, and a smattering of local and national politics, philosophy and history. He also frequently recorded observations of his beloved Macon, Georgia. He was a Ralph Waldo Emerson scholar and frequently quoted him in his writings. He also wrote with passion about the tragedy of suicide, and though he never mentioned it in writing, knew of it first-hand when his youngest sibling, Maude, took her own life in 1911 at age 28.

The reader will also find a friendship established between Rufus Moseley and Glenn Clark, the Camps Farthest Out founder of St. Paul, Minnesota. The CFO movement of the 1930's and 1940's, was heavily New Thought influenced, and when Moseley and Clark met they immediately found a kinship, although it was clear that Rufus disagreed with some of the teachings. For instance, the effort to seek healing or any other spiritual benefit via the "Mind Sciences" was, to Moseley, a forlorn exercise. After all, Rufus himself had been a part of the Christian Science and knew first-hand something of the teachings of such groups. He believed the Clark and CFO were headed in the right direction, but that they needed to seek Christ and the Baptism of the Holy Spirit to obtain what it was they sought by other means.

Over the course of several years, the organization became solidly Pentecostal, with no small credit to Moseley's influence. In Rufus' articles you fill find a chronicle of his wide-spread travels from the 1930's until his death in 1954. He attended and taught at one CFO camp after another, and was a perennial favorite of the attendees—apparently especially so with the young people. Until recently, the history of Camps Farthest Out was largely unknown beyond the circle of those who participated in it. Prior to the Charismatic Movement in the 1960's, it was one of the few places a person could go to learn about the Baptism of the Holy Spirit outside of Pentecostal churches. Attendees were from all different denominations—a true precursor to the Charismatic Movement. In 2015, William DeArteaga published <u>Agnes Sanford and Her Companions: The Assault on Cessationism and the Coming of the Charismatic Renewal</u>, which details the changes the CFO underwent during this period, and how it helped form the groundwork for the later Charismatic Movement of the 1960's onward. I cannot recommend this book highly enough.

Rufus Moseley's interactions with those of different Christian beliefs were widespread and something he fully enjoyed. He had life-long friendships with Baptists, Methodists, Presbyterians, Catholics, Assemblies of God, Church of God, Pentecostal Holiness, and a host of others. His influence and friendship with the North Carolina Baptists was especially noteworthy. Every summer he would attend their meetings at Mars Hill, North Carolina where Baptist luminaries such as E. M. Poteat and Walter Johnson—Rufus called him" The Sage of Mars Hill"—would meet. In fact, that meeting in particular appears to be something of an annual highlight for him. Mars Hill College is located near Asheville, which was not far from his boyhood home up at Elkin, North Carolina. He would visit the old homestead at that time each year. In addition to such activities, Rufus, in his capacity as a reporter, would cover the annual conventions of some of the major denominations, as well as visit many churches and Christian schools. Wherever he went, he was welcomed as a friend and, even if they did not agree with his theology, loved him and appreciated the genuineness of his walk with Christ.

One will also find in these writings a good number of book reviews of Christian writers of the day. It is clear that Moseley's favorites were Henry Drummond, Samuel Gordon, F.F. Bosworth, A.P. Simpson, Frank Riale, and Oswald Chambers, although he reviewed many others whose writings he deemed worthy of support. Indeed, the Christian authors Rufus reviewed bear reading in our own time. Rufus met at one time or another and befriended all of these writers with the exception of Oswald Chambers. Indeed, he had on-going correspondence with these and other speakers and writers for several years. His opinion on spiritual matters was widely respected and even included brief correspondence with Mahatmas Gandhi, whom he encountered through a mutual friend, E. Stanley Jones.

What might surprise some Christians is that Moseley rarely wrote about the "end-times," a topic so wildly popular today as well in his own time. He was aware that in the 1930's many believers considered Mussolini, Hitler, or Stalin to be the antichrist. And, like today, there was no shortage of conspiracy theories around supporting a particular interpretation of any given end-times scenario. Moseley even made mention that FDR's "New Deal" was considered part of the antichrist system, and that the National Recovery Act's logo contained three sixes—making it the "mark of the beast" as proof. He brushed such nonsense aside, and like to say when considering the visible Second Coming—something he very definitely believed in—that gazing in the heavens (for Christ's return) does us no good; but great good is to be had in becoming heavenly. To Rufus, what was important is that whatever the times in which we live, living in first-hand ineffable union with Christ which produces His love, was the paramount concern. Moseley biographer, the late Dr. Wayne McLain, describes this personal spiritual dynamic as follows:

> "Some of us who knew Rufus Moseley were enabled to see beyond his humble appearance, his kindly and gentle good humor, his folksy parables, jokes, and frequent 'hallelujahs,' to the Greatness Who washed His friend's feet and Who is the eternal servant of all. For the greatness of Rufus Moseley consisted in the remarkable degree to which the Person of Jesus indwelt the person of Rufus."[22]

Rufus Moseley was a Christian mystic, although he did not like that term. He referred to himself as a "First-Hander," meaning that he had a first-hand intimate relationship with Jesus which produced a moment-by-moment conscious union with the Holy Spirit. Moseley never thought of himself as better than any other believer and strongly believed that such a vital union was available to all of Christ's followers if they would but ask, seek, knock, and believe. The Holy Spirit, he believed, is much more interested in His children having such a relationship than we as His children are in asking for it.

One of the things that made Rufus' ministry particularly effective with others, besides the depth of his walk in the Life as Love, was the discernment of spirits in individuals. Dr. McLain, while a young man at Duke University, witnessed this for himself:

> "The first experience I had of his gift to see beyond the natural was at Duke University in 1945. A group of us had gone with Rufus to the Oak Room for dinner. While sitting watching him at the table I noticed an unusual movement of his eyes looking at me and giving me the sensation that he was looking through me or beyond me. Still I had no sense of fear or condemnation. I learned later that this capacity of Rufus was what St. Paul had termed the gift of discernment of spirits, the ability to see beyond the natural to the spirit or spirits dwelling in a person..."[23]

Rufus Moseley met and influenced his contemporaries such as E. Stanley Jones, Rufus Jones, Olin T. Binkley, Edwin Poteat, Walter Johnson, Henry Sloan Coffin, and Frank Laubach, as well as up-and-coming religious leaders such as Oral Roberts, Tommy Tyson, Wayne McLain, Agnes Sanford, Glenn Clark, Starr Daily, and many, many others.

These in turn presumably shared "Brother Rufus" with their protégé's such as Kenneth and Gloria Copeland, and Mark Rutland, to name just a few. The impact of this diminutive yet giant of a man is beyond words. I would also highly recommend to those seeking a walk in the love of God obtain and read Moseley's autobiography, <u>Manifest Victory</u>, just recently back in print, and his writing on the ministry of the Holy Spirit, <u>Perfect Everything</u>. The latter, unfortunately, is out of print, but a Google search will show a few on-line sites with the complete work.

Rufus Moseley died in Oklahoma City, Oklahoma on September 26, 1954. He was there attending a meeting of a young Oral Roberts, and wrote positively of his experiences with him. Apparently suffering from some form of cancer, the disease began to noticeably incapacitate him. As a result, his weekly columns for the *Telegraph and News* became much shorter, and tended to deal mostly with his travels and his positive views of new up-and-coming preachers such as Billy Graham and the 'afore mentioned Oral Roberts. Despite declining health and family concerns about his travel, he continued to go to meetings and when asked, spoke to Christian groups. One of Rufus' much-loved young friends, Tommy Tyson, grew concerned with his mentor's declining health as well, and in September, 1954, wrote to Moseley and invited him to move to Greensboro, North Carolina, to live with his family. It is not certain that Rufus ever saw Tyson's letter. It is no exaggeration to state that both McLain and Tyson felt they lost a father figure with Moseley's passing; in messages decades later both would frequently quote Rufus with great affection and gratitude.[24]

Wayne McLain was in Oklahoma City visiting Rufus in the hospital in what turned out to be Moseley's last days and hours. McLain reported that he never heard a word of complaint, groan of pain, or anything else one would expect of someone dying of a painful disease. When McLain specifically asked him in the hospital if he was in pain, Rufus rolled over and said, "Wayne, I am so happy I don't know what in the world to do!"[25]

A prophetic word spoken about and for Rufus Moseley on May 22, 1954, around four months before his death, was recorded by a Margaret Fish of Lubbock, Texas, and found in Rufus' personal papers. This word was recorded on a single piece of paper and sums up the life of this remarkable man better than anything I could compose:

"Behold how great and glorious a witness for Me! Who can doubt My radiance expressed in a body so frail which could have no radiance, no glory, of its own. My servant has accomplished exceeding greatness! This is but for a moment...consider the power of the Light permeating such a body, already more spirit than mortal. The blacker the valley, the greater the glory!

Behold, no wavering in the testing, and for the unhealed to proclaim My healing power...How great a testimony! This is suffering for righteousness sake...little you know how My Kingdom has been enlarged because of My servant.

Behold the glory of sharing in the suffering of the Beloved Son. Can you not see the enabling Spirit? It is not always possible, because of the highest good for all to release from all suffering. Few have known such a ministry in Spirit and in Truth! Can you pray My Will to be done in perfect trust? Can you know My grace is sufficient? Can you not give Rufus to me unquestionably?

I have bestowed every gift of the Spirit upon Rufus. He bears the fruit. We have worked hand-in-hand for the Kingdom...Did not thee ask 'Why must the Sinless One suffer for the sins of others? It was for Salvation of All. I have proved Rufus willing to suffer all for My sake.'

Behold Mary at the foot of the Cross! Blessed is He that suffered for you...Blessed is Rufus. Greater is he in heaven than on earth. Rejoice that the victory has been won. For the manifestation be not anxious. Great, I say, is his reward. My peace I give unto you... not as the world giveth, give I unto you!" [26]

It is my great joy to be able to reintroduce J. Rufus Moseley to a seeking Christian audience again. You will find in him a man with a revelation of Jesus' Love Way of Life that is as timeless as it is relevant. Prepare to be blessed!

Gregory S. Camp, Ph.D.
June, 2016

CHAPTER 1

"The Real Kingdom"
February 13, 1927
Macon Telegraph

The publicity given the "Supreme Kingdom, Inc." makes especially timely a consideration of the real Kingdom which was the major hope of the prophets and the chief emphasis of Jesus Himself. Both John the Baptist and Jesus started their ministry with the proclamation that this Kingdom was at hand and with a call for the necessary repentance (change of mind, heart, and life) to enter.

The real Kingdom, or the Kingdom of God, unlike the kingdoms of this world, does not come with observation. It grows like things in nature grow; it starts like the mustard seed as something very small and almost imperceptible and grows until it becomes the largest tree. It starts like a leaven which the woman hid in three measures of meal and works quietly and incessantly until all the raw dough becomes leavened. While the Kingdom has its messengers and servants, it has no publicity agents. It is entirely free from all the advertising methods of the world. It is something that those who know about it pass on to those who do not know: it is the spreading of Good News.

The Kingdom from its very nature cannot be monopolized, cornered, or divided. It cannot even be commercialized. Men have divided over everything else, but can only be unified as the Kingdom is understood and entered into. In its beginning it was not of this world, but in the end all the other kingdoms come into it or go to pieces by not coming in. While all the organizations of men have sought for members of influence, honor, and wealth, the door to the real Kingdom has been wide open to everyone, especially to the poor, the despised, and the outcast.

The way one enters is by becoming humble like a little child, and the way that one becomes greatest in the Kingdom is by becoming the humblest of all and the best servant of all. In this Kingdom pre-eminence does not create rivalry. It is something that one enters or is born into and not something that one joins or pays to join. It has no fees of initiation, no assessments, and no dues. It requires, and only requires, that one leave on the outside everything that keeps him on the outside.

While Jesus Himself is not reported to have given a precise definition of the Kingdom, He makes unmistakably clear that it is simply the government and victory of righteousness, mercy, compassion, love, joy, peace, and life over all the forces of evil and death. It is the victory of God and His Good Spirit in men and in the creation, or as St. Paul puts it, it is righteousness, peace, and joy in the Holy Ghost.

CHAPTER 2

"The Ideal Kingdom"
August 21, 1927
Macon Telegraph

The feeling or perception that there is an ideal righteousness, justice, and friendship behind the scenes and function in the nature of things and especially in human life, which is partially yielded and conformed to and largely disregarded, dates back rather early in history.

Among the early Greek thinkers, the famous mathematician, Pythagoras, saw that without light (illumination or enlightenment) nothing could be uttered concerning God. He took the position that we have a direct intuition of the righteousness in the nature of things, functioning as a condition, a critic, and an ideal. Greek thought at its best took its stand upon this position. Socrates, the most interesting and likeable of the Greeks and the so-called "pagan saints," affirmed that he was guided and taught by a friendly spirit, and to this fact he ascribed whatever wisdom he might possess.

Plato, about the first mind in the history of human thought, not only dreamed and wrote of the possibility and conditions of an ideal state of society where temperance, justice, and wisdom were the reigning virtues, and where the truly wise returned good for evil. He also waged a war against the popular mythology in Greek literature and in Greek life that attributed evil qualities and evil deeds to the gods. He went so far as to argue that he would prefer children of his, if he had any, to say that they were fatherless than to attribute unworthy and unreal evils to him. While he believed that the true God was pure Mind, pure Idea, and pure Good, he believed that it would be better not to believe the gods at all than to believe that they did the things attributed to them by the Greek poets: acts of lust, human-like jealousy, anger, cruelty, and deception. While there were crudities even in such clear thinking as Plato's, it is interesting to note that some of the early Christian scholars had a feeling that Socrates and Plato were Christians born out of due season. The true Light lighteth every life coming into the world to the degree that one is receptive and obedient to the Light.

According to the Old Testament revelation, creation itself was the bringing of the cosmos out of chaos and of God doing His work and producing His work "good and very good." But since evil and disobedience and rebellion appeared, the work of God in history came to be the conquering of evil and the bringing forth a universe and Kingdom more wonderful than existed prior to the fall. Jewish prophets foresaw the complete victory of justice, goodness, and friendliness not only amongst men, but amongst the fiercest of animals, and the whole earth filled with the presence, government, peace, and knowledge of the Lord as the waters cover the sea. Daniel saw that the kingdom and government of God would not only be victorious over "the prince of all evil," but that all human governments and authorities would go to pieces before the coming Kingdom of God as the chaff before the summer threshing machine.

John the Baptist began his ministry with a proclamation that the long expected and hoped for Kingdom of God was at hand and called upon everyone to repent and get ready. Jesus commenced His ministry by the announcement that the Kingdom of God was at hand, and to repent and enter and by doing the works of blessedness that were to be the universal leaven and seed of the Kingdom. The Kingdom of God and the Kingdom of Heaven were the terms most often on His lips. He not only preached the gospel of the Kingdom and did the works of the Kingdom, but the seventy as well as the twelve of whom He sent out in His name were also to preach the Kingdom of God and the works thereof. While Jesus as reported in the Gospels does not precisely define the Kingdom, it is quite clear that by the Kingdom He meant the blessedness, peace, joy, love, healing, and transformation that came to those who believed in Him and who gave themselves over without reservation to doing the will of the Father in Heaven.

After the crucifixion, resurrection, and ascension of Jesus and the gift of the other Comforter, or the Holy Spirit that Jesus went away to send and to give, the term "Kingdom of God" is not used nearly as often as it was in the days of His time on earth. The Kingdom was then understood to be God's "righteousness, joy, and peace in the Holy Ghost" (Romans 14: 17) which was at hand and within those who were in union with Christ. The first Christians appear to have preached and to have written more about the King than the Kingdom. They knew that to be in union with the King and to be bearing the fruit of that union—love, joy, peace, meekness, goodness, and such like—was to be in the Spiritual Kingdom already at hand, and to be prepared for the coming King and Kingdom in great power, glory and dominion. St. John saw the victorious Kingdom as the holy city coming out of heaven to earth, and St. Peter saw it as the new heaven and the new earth wherein righteousness was triumphant.

Since the days of the Apostles, there have appeared books picturing the ideal Kingdom as the "City of God," and "Utopia" and so on. Recent spiritual history finds an increasing emphasis upon the Kingdom, not only as ideal righteousness, peace, joy, and love that one may have an increasing measure now, but the Kingdom as righteousness and just order of life in the affairs of men and in the affairs of nations. There is also the increasing expectation of the coming of the victorious Kingdom of God as promised by the prophets, the Apostles, and by Jesus Himself. The very conception of the Kingdom is unifying, and calls for God-likeness rather than discussions over matters of theological religion that have always tended to confuse and divide the household of God.

As Jesus said, speaking of the last things, the gospel of the Kingdom will be preached unto all nations, and then the end shall come. It is the last message, the transforming and reconciling message, bringing the things of God and the people of God together as one.

CHAPTER 3

"The Heart of Christianity"
September 4, 1927
Macon Telegraph

The side of Christianity represented in the preservation and by the handing down of the Bible is tremendously important. The letter apart from the Spirit kills and is too often used for stoning when it should also be used to give life and healing. Those fundamentalists in all ages who have stood upon and stood by the written Word, even when their spirit has appeared more belligerent and controversial than Christlike, have nevertheless played an important part of historical Christianity.

Today the controversy that is being waged over the best way to present Christ to an age like ours and especially in the mission fields appears to be, in part at least, a repetition of early Christian history. The first converts being Jews, did not find it easy to be reconciled to St. Paul and the way he presented the Gospel to the heathen world. St. Paul not only knew by revelation, but also by experience that faith in Christ opened the gates of heaven whereby salvation came through the Holy Spirit upon the Gentile world. It was made known to him that the Gentiles could become Christians directly without first becoming Jewish converts. And to the everlasting honor of the converts, disciples, and apostles who came out of Judaism to Christ, it seemed good to them to impose upon the Gentiles only the requirements that they abstained from fornication and from things offered to idols, and that they be charitable to the poor. As it was seen, if they would do these things to start and live in union with Christ and walk in the Spirit, they would not only fulfill the law, the righteousness which is fulfilled in love as one walks in the Spirit, but they would be changed from virtue to virtue, from love to love, and glory to glory, through the transforming power of the Lord the Spirit.

Since it is true that "those who have not the spirit of Christ are none of His," it is also true that those who do have His spirit are His. As understood by those who knew Him best when He was on earth and by St. Paul, who knew Him by immediate revelation and guidance, the spirit of Christ in the sense of the nature, attitude, and mind of Christ is humbleness of mind, compassion of the heart, and a rare combination of meekness, boldness, wisdom, and innocence. *"Put on therefore, as the elect of God, holy and beloved, the bowels of mercies, kindness, humbleness of mind, meekness, longsuffering, forbearing one another and forgiving one another, if any man has a quarrel against any, if as Christ forgave you, so also do ye. And above all of these things put on charity, which is the bond of perfectness."* (Colossians 3: 12-14)

In another of his epistles (to Timothy), St. Paul sums up the commandments to be *"charity out of a pure heart, and of good conscience, of faith unfeigned."* (1 Timothy 1: 5) St. Paul and St. John and other New Testament writers likewise interpret the attitude and mind, not only of Christ, but of real Christians to be best summed up in charity or love that is always believing, always hopeful, and that never fails. In II Peter the Christian characteristics, attitudes, and spiritual possessions start with faith and pass on with the additions of virtue, knowledge, temperance, patience, goodness, brotherly kindness, and cumulative charity or love.

St. John sums up the commandments as faith in Christ and love for one another as Jesus commanded—loving one another as Jesus loved and loves His little flock, disciples, or friends. This love for friends is to be extended to one's enemies, so the perfection of Christian character is the state of love that is boundless and a type of goodness that manifests only goodness as He manifests only light and warmth. Christianity conquers by faith, hope, and pure goodness. It overcomes evil with good and in its purest form fights with no carnal weapons.

From its inner source and inspiration, Christianity is Christ Himself, and the other Comforter that He went away to send. The fruit of Christ (the True Vine) is produced by abiding in Him. Approaching perfection from the outside and looking forward to its culmination in perfect charity or love, Christianity starts with faith, but from the side of union with the living Christ and His Holy Spirit, the fruit-bearing starts with love and flows out into joy, peace, goodness, and temperance in all its virtues. Its teaching here is pure spiritual biology—you cannot bear fruit unless you abide in the Vine, and you cannot abide in the Vine unless you bear fruit. The more fruit you bear the closer and more perfect the relationship with the Vine, and the closer the relationship with the Vine, the more and better fruit you bear.

The teachings of Jesus and of the Apostles are very simple, especially to those who want to live them. Christianity is only made complex and difficult to understand by those who are seeking to get its ultimate reward apart from entering the in "the straight gate" and walking in the "narrow way." The way is rich in reward, and gives the promise of everything as one moves on to full overcoming and likeness to and union with Christ Himself.

CHAPTER 4

"A Spiritual Autobiography"
November 27, 1927
Macon Telegraph

The years from 1792 to 1875, the period of history in which Charles G. Finney lived, were a most extraordinary 83 years of secular history. Finney's <u>Memoirs</u> that were copyrighted and published in 1876, and re-copyrighted again in 1903, gives a remarkable account of the moral and spiritual conditions that prevailed during this period. His <u>Memoirs</u> are also an especially rich source of material for understanding the opposition that existed in the North to the anti-slavery movement, a movement that Mr. Finney felt to be his religious duty to aid in the best ways open to him. However, his zeal for the abolition of slavery was in terms of his religious and humanitarian spirit and apparently free from any bitterness or prejudice towards Southern people. In fact, Mr. Finney's spirit was conspicuously charitable in dealing with all who differed from him or who even actively opposed him. But the high value of his <u>Memoirs</u> is the record they contain of his own spiritual experiences and labors which were so fruitful in bringing multitudes to an awakened life, and to at least the beginnings of genuine Christian experience.

Before Finney became a Christian, he was so outspoken about what he discerned to be the low moral and spiritual status of the church he attended, that he became a sore trial to the pastor. Young Finney told the praying members of this church that either they were just pretending to pray or that the Bible was untrue. Finney took pains to read every scripture he heard and came to the conviction that the Bible was true and that the religious people he knew were simply playing at Christianity instead of actually believing and practicing it. He came under deep conviction that he ought to be a Christian and went to the woods to pray. When he placed himself between some logs where he was not likely to be seen, he found himself looking up to see if anyone was near to hear him. This convicted him of false pride and cowardice by saying that he would pray as if every person in the world and every devil were present and listening to him. Very soon, the whole burden of guilt rolled away. At first he felt almost afraid to be so free. After he returned to the law office, he was very busy engaged with his law partner in rearranging books of their library. As soon as he was alone, Finney says, it appeared as if he "met the Lord Jesus Christ face-to-face." "It did not occur to me then," he says,

> "nor did it for some time afterwards, that He was in a mental state. On the contrary, it seemed to me that I would see Him as I would any other man. He said nothing but looked at me in such a manner to break me right down at His feet—I poured out my soul to Him. I wept aloud like a child and made such confessions as I could with my choked utterance. It seemed to me that I had bathed His feet with my tears; and yet I had no distinct impression that I touched Him, that I recollect."

Following this experience and during most of the night, Finney says, without having asked for it or expecting it,

> "The Holy Spirit descended upon me in a manner that seemed to go through me, body and soul. I could feel the impression, like a wave of electricity, going through and through me. Indeed, it seemed to come in waves of liquid love; but I could not express it in any other way. It seemed like the very breath of God...These waves came over me and over me, one after another, until I recollect I cried out, 'Lord, I cannot bear anymore,' yet I had no fear of death."

The next morning when a client came in and reminded him that his case had come up, Finney told him that he would have to get another lawyer, that he himself had accepted a retainer from Jesus Christ and was from then on at His service. The people that he talked to began to fall under conviction, and a revival started and followed him through all of his labors and travels. When his lectures on revivals were briefly reported to the editor of the *New York Evangelist* and published, everywhere they went and were read sympathetically, revivals broke out.

The whole story of his ministry as was conducted in this country, England, and Scotland either through him personally, through others who had come under the power of his preaching, or through his writings, is a remarkable story and in places reads like the history of early Christianity. Not only were people converted in great numbers, but those who had been stealing confessed and made restitution. Wherever sins had been committed in the darkness they were proclaimed from the housetops. A case in point is that of a young man who had tried to destroy his conscience and to drive away the workings of the Spirit. He had burned down the neighborhood school house to see if he could start a career of crime without condemnation. Under the preaching of Mr. Finney, he made open confession and was forgiven and became a good, practicing Christian. This is typical of the transformation wrought in the lives of thousands.

A distinguished lawyer who had charged a widow a considerable fee for his services insisted upon returning it, even over the protests of the widow, her relatives, and friends. A miser who had told God that he was willing to be damned if he could make another hundred thousand pounds was so convicted when Finney read to him the sixth chapter of Matthew, that he offered himself and his whole fortune to Christ. An Episcopal minister in London who heard him preach was so fired by his preaching that he started a revival in his own parish which resulted in 1500 conversions. Another man who heard Finney preach entered the Catholic fold and sought, with Mr. Finney's blessing upon him, to do among the Catholics what Mr. Finney was doing among sinners and orthodox church members. It is a remarkable story, one of the most engaging and heartening that has been told by anyone since the history of the first Christians.

At different periods in Finney's life he had other spiritual experiences almost as remarkable as those he reports that occurred in the beginning. One day when he was standing in front of a meeting place, he says that the "glory of God shown upon and around me in a manner most marvelous. The day was just beginning to dawn. But all at once a light perfectly ineffable shown in my soul that almost prostrated me to the ground. In this light it seemed as if I could see that all nature praised and worshipped God, except man. The light seemed to be like the brightness of the sun in every direction."

In 1842, when Mr. Finney was in Boston and praying four hours every morning before breakfast, he says that he came to the conviction that after all he might be deluded, and that possibly the Holy Spirit had only come in his feelings and emotions and that his will was yet unsurrendered. This led him to the deepest spiritual searching and to offer to God that if He could better use him by sending him to perdition, to send him there. With this breaking down and what seemed to him the fullest surrender of the will that he could make, there came the sweet light and assurance that a fully surrendered soul like his could not go anywhere but to Heaven, and that if it were to go perdition, hades would cease to be hades. With this surrender, he says, came a fresh Baptism of the Holy Spirit, and that he came into a fullness of unbroken peace, joy, and love that made his former experiences seem as only preparatory and introductory.

CHAPTER 5

"Two Sides of Christianity" (St. Francis)
December 4, 1927
Macon Telegraph

There are two sides of the Gospel of Jesus. There is the inner side which reveals the possibilities as well as the hunger for perfect union with Jesus and perfect union through Him with the Father; and there is the outer side, which is following in the footsteps of Jesus.

Last Sunday I made a study of Charles G. Finney, who perhaps more than any other well-known religious man of his time, lived in the Spirit, and wrought unusually well in bringing multitudes to an experience of salvation. Today, let us study St. Francis of Assisi, who also attained in an unusual way the consciousness of union with Christ and who dedicated his life to walk literally in the footsteps of Jesus.

After a period of youthful wanderings, he realized that the quest for glory, as well as for pleasure, was shot through with painful illusions. By rapid steps, he was then led to see that the true way of life is compassion, pity, and kindliness. Among the wealth of stories of his life that are handed down, this one is characteristic:

He was riding on horseback through the country and saw a leper. At first sight, his human sensibilities revolted so strongly that he turned his horse quickly and attempted to ride away. This brought him deep conviction that he was running away from the very life to which he was called. This inspired him to approach the leper and to kiss his hand and to give him all the money in his possession. He experienced the thrill of pure joy for doing so.

Francis read in the New Testament the call of Jesus to his first disciples to leave all and to follow Him, and to take with him neither purse nor scrip. A little later, as we remember his life story, he saw a portrayal of Jesus in a church where he was worshipping become a living and moving image. From then on, his life was not only miraculous in its loving kindness, but was attended by miracles after the manner of the early days of Christianity. But as Paul Sabatier, author of <u>Life of St. Francis</u> observed, living in the early 13th century was on the one hand straining itself after the miraculous, and on the other was in quest of knowledge; St. Francis saw the most excellent way—the way of perfect love, faith, and union with the Father.

The heart of St. Francis is revealed in a conversation he had one winter day as he and Brother Leo were on their way to visit some of the brothers of a new fellowship that was forming, a fellowship of brothers who possessed nothing, who labored with their hands, and who went about doing good. Said St. Francis, "Oh Brother Leo, may it please God that the Brothers Minor all over the world may give a great example of holiness and edification. Write, however, and note with care that not in this is the perfect joy." A little later on the journey, Francis said, "Oh, Brother Leo, if the Brothers Minor gave sight to the blind, healed the infirm, cast out demons, gave hearing to the deaf, or what is even more, if they raised the four day dead, write that not in this is the perfect joy." Going on a little further, he cried out, "Oh, Brother Leo, if the Brothers Minor knew all languages, all sciences, all scriptures, if they could prophesy, and reveal not only the future things but even the secrets of consciences and of souls, write that not in this consists the perfect joy."

As they proceeded on the journey, St. Francis continued in the same theme, making known to Brother Leo that if one knew all of the languages of heaven, could penetrate all the mysteries of heaven and earth, and could preach so well as to convert the infidels to the faith of Christ, that even then he might not know "perfect joy." While speaking in this manner Brother Leo finally said to him, "I pray in God's name, tell me in what consists the perfect joy?" To which St. Francis replied,

> "When we arrive in Santa Maria degli Angeli, soaked with rain, frozen and cold, covered with mud, dying of hunger, and we knock and the porter comes in rage and says, 'Who are you?' and we say, 'We are two of your brethren,' and he says, 'You lie, you are

two lewd fellows who go up and down corrupting the world and stealing alms from the poor. Go away from here!' And he does not open his door to us, but leaves us outside shivering in the snow and rain, frozen, starved, 'til night. Then, if thus maltreated and turned away, we patiently endure all without murmuring against him; if we think with humility and charity, that this porter really knows us truly and that God makes him speak thus to us, then, O Brother Leo, write that this is the perfect joy!'"

As Brother Francis goes on to say, "Above all the graces and all the gifts which the Holy Spirit gives to His friends, is the grace to conquer one's self, and willingly to suffer pain, outrages, disgraces, and evil treatment for the love of Christ."

St. Francis not only taught this, but lived it. In the early part of his Christian life when he made the great resolve to be as poor as Jesus and so far as possible, be as loving, kind, and compassionate as He who received the worst indignities that a son could receive from his father, and that a gentle soul could receive from the rough and cruel who do not understand. So far as the records tell the story, there is no indication but that he met everything except in the spirit of Him who commanded us to turn the other cheek, and to love and bless those who attempt to do the worst to us.

But, as Sabatier says, it was not very long until the best of humanity at that time "leaped to follow in his footsteps." While St. Francis received his inspiration direct from Heaven, and had for his inspiration none less than Jesus Himself, he sought nevertheless to be the obedient child of the church. So he and some of his brothers went on foot to Rome to get the sanction of the Pope, "for the strange privilege of possessing nothing." As Sabatier says, "the gifted Cardinal who listened to Francis for days, finally recommended him to the Pope, Innocent III, and must have felt the longing to be a Christian himself after the manner of St. Francis, but being headed toward the highest official position of the Roman Catholic church, did not answer the call."

It is deeply significant that the early days of St. Francis, when he received so much opposition and persecution, were his happiest. Later in life, when he had become popular, and popular against his own will, he saw that the ideal for which he strived was being compromised, and that in the future most likely would go the way that other ideals had gone, that is, it would be toned down so as not to go too much against the grain of selfishness and doubt that are all too regnant nearly everywhere. It was not what men did to him that made him sad, but what they would likely do to the true ideal of life. Then, too, St. Francis had profound sympathy which conquered the sorrows of the whole world, and yet radiated the joy of the Spirit and the bliss of heaven.

Few other lives in recorded history have lived in such rare simplicity, unselfishness and love as did St. Francis. His love went out not only to the whole race of men—especially to those in the most extreme need—but also to the whole creation. He even preached to the birds and the bears, and they somehow seemed to understand him.

St. Francis did not seek poverty for the sake of poverty, but for the sake of perfect Christian love and perfect Christian liberty. He saw that as long as one man gave himself to his acres, and another to his gold, that the highest in man is crowded out. Yet there must be a few men in the world who put everything on the altar of Christ, who gave everything to the poor and who follow Him as the lowest of all and as the servant of all. He did not establish an order of mendicants. As he himself put in his will:

> "We loved to live in poor and abandoned churches, and we were ignorant and submissive to all. I worked with my hands, and would continue to do so and will also that all other friars work in some honorable trade. Let those who have none learn one, not for the purpose of receiving the price of their toil, but for their good example, and to flee idleness. When they do not give us the price of the work, let us resort to the table of the Lord, begging our bread from door to door. The Lord revealed to me the salutation which we ought to give: 'God give you peace!'"

The brothers were not to receive hospitality anywhere, even in the churches, "except as strangers or pilgrims," and were to be espoused as he himself was to "Lady Poverty," who had been a widow since the days of Jesus.

St. Francis, with all his humility and deference to those in authority, sounds one of the finest notes as to the authority of the Spirit in Christian history: "No one showed me what I ought to do, but the Most High Himself revealed to me that I ought to live comfortably in the Holy Spirit."

CHAPTER 6

"St. Paul"
December 11, 1927
Macon Telegraph

Last Sunday we sought to give the readers a touch of the superlative beauty and compassion of St. Francis of Assisi, the most interesting and likeable 13th Century man we know about; the man who desired to be as poor as Jesus and went about doing good, finding the greatest joy in ministering to lepers and others in extreme need, and so loved the birds and wild beasts that he practiced and preached to them the gospel of love. Sunday before last we dealt with Charles Finney, whose spiritual power to bring sinners to repentance and to the beginning of a new life in Christ reminds one more of St. Paul than does any other well-known religious man of recent times.

Today we come to St. Paul, whom St. Peter refers to as "our beloved Brother Paul," who not only wrote of the things that Peter wrote about, "according to the wisdom given unto him," but who also wrote some things that were hard to understand. These things that are hard to understand have made St. Paul the storm center of Christian history, possibly the most misunderstood and most disliked of all of the friends of Jesus. He is also generally recognized as the most influential friend of Jesus of all the centuries, as the one who put Christianity into the current of world history. As Lyman Abbott has put it in his study of <u>Life and Letters of St. Paul</u>, that no matter what may be one's attitude towards him, "this much is at least undeniable, that no man of any era, except Him whom he delighted to call

Master, has done so much to mould the thoughts and pattern the characters of men and so shape the very framework of our modern civilization."

Paul is accorded the same high place in Christian history as is Moses in the history of Israel. He is held responsible for having laid the foundation for both Catholicism and Protestantism and for most of minor movements of historical Christianity. Most of the current discussions of religions by liberals point out what appears to be differences in the teachings of Jesus and of Paul, and most of the Fundamentalists turn to the Epistles of St. Paul for a statement of orthodox creed.

While it is only our purpose to dwell upon some of the great experiences and teachings of St. Paul that have in them the stamp and the carrying power of the everlasting, it is well to remember that Jesus was conscious that He was proclaiming everlasting truth and speaking words that would never pass away. On the other hand, St. Paul was seeking to be all things to all men that he might win as many as possible, not to himself, but to Christ. He had come into a great experience where all things become new and perhaps no other man ever gave himself more whole-heartedly than he to making this experience possible for the whole world.

Jesus never lowered his ideal, but held it up as a standard that we have to come to or respond to. He taught the most perfect love which, when responded to, will bring the Kingdom of God on earth. St. Paul, in addition to making the Gospel known to men, a Gospel he was so certain of that even angels from heaven could not change, was also seeking to help men to live it in its entirety. For example, Jesus taught that we should not go to law with anybody, that when sued at law to compel us to go a mile or to get one dollar that we should settle the matter by going two or giving two. St. Paul was so shocked that the early converts in Corinth were going to law among themselves, that he strongly urged them to settle their problems among themselves, and for brother to refuse to go to law against brother. Unfortunately, so-called brothers still go to law with so-called brothers, and the feeling is increasing that Christianity never will win even in the loves of so-called Christians until we turn to obey the Gospel in all of its perfection.

As Professor H. Weinel, in his enlightening book <u>St. Paul: The Man and His Work</u>, says, "Many are standing at the narrow window and gazing yearningly back across the years at the towering old cathedral church, in which our fathers found rest for their souls...but others who are fired by the ardor of youth that burned in the soul of Jesus, have dreams of future days when men will worship God in Spirit and in truth." Certainly no other disciple of Jesus that we know of longed more for the consummation when all shall know Him from the least to the greatest, and all worship Him in Spirit and in truth, and live in perfect love than did St. Paul. Whatever accommodations he made to the world in which he lived, he was looking to this consummation.

Perhaps in no other respects have St. Paul's teachings been more misunderstood and perverted than his teachings concerning justification by faith, not being under the law, election, and the Cross. To St. Paul, who came so suddenly into union with Christ and who found in Him everything beyond what he had known how to desire, it is perfectly manifest that his union with Christ and the gift of the Holy Spirit was the result of God's love and grace, and in no way the result of the deeds of his own life that had been performed in obedience to law—the highest system of law known to the world, and that St. Paul had sought to keep with great zeal and faithfulness. What he received cost him nothing but the readiness to receive it. The gift of God being free, all that was required on the part of anyone was simply faith or readiness to receive and respond. In Christian history, it appears too often that men have substituted a doctrine of faith for the kind of faith that St. Paul had and exalted as the condition for salvation, or the coming in union with Christ through the reception of the Spirit and through a life lived in the Spirit, bearing the fruits of love, joy, peace, goodness, and self-control. The faith that Paul had and exalted in was the faith that works by love and that opens one to all the fullness of God in Christ.

By not being under the law, St. Paul evidently meant that through union with Christ and through living in the Spirit one is lifted into a new world and given a new nature so that all of the virtues flow out from the union with the same kind of naturalness that flowers bloom. In his own experience, what he struggled after and could not attain to under legalism was given to him through union with Christ and a life lived in the Spirit. By making the tree good, the fruit became good. By the creation of a new heart, a heart that is tender and compassionate, pure and loving, one finds it easy and spiritually natural to fulfill all the righteousness of the law.

Those who are in union with Christ and led by the Spirit are not under the law. Of course, the abuse of this great truth is to claim to be free and at the same time be living in the desires of the flesh. St. Paul gives much attention to seeking to guard against this abuse.

By election, as Professor Wernle observes, St. Paul, out of experience, came to the consciousness that he had been called of God from the beginning for his mission to the world, and that all things worked together to this end. The consciousness of election, that one is predestined to be conformed to the likeness of Jesus and that all things are working together to this end, is one of the happiest attainments of Christian experience. Of course, its abuse is the feeling that one has to do nothing and can do nothing to aid in his own salvation and in the salvation of others.

While, as St. Paul said, the Cross was foolishness to the Greeks and a stumbling block to the Jews, it was to him and to believers the power of God. It was a revelation not only of the unspeakable love of Jesus, but also a revelation that God is just as loving as Jesus, that He not only gave His Son, but gives Himself to the utmost limits of love.

The revelation given in and through St. Paul in common with the revelation given to and through St. Peter and St. John, and all the others who have really known God as love, is that higher than all other gifts and the conditions of knowing God and abiding in God, is the gift of love. To use the Apostle Paul's own words, "Now the aim of the commandment is charity out of a pure heart, with a good conscience and with faith unfeigned." (I Timothy 1: 5)

Perfect love is the greatest and best of the gifts of God, because it works no ill to any and all possible good to all and fulfills both Law and Gospel.

CHAPTER 7

"Every Whit Wholeness"
June 3, 1928
Macon Telegraph

The superlative appeal of Jesus is that in Him we see not only the perfect love of God living for us, humbling Himself to the fullest and dying for us, but the perfect victory of God in the realm of the visible and the material, as well as the realm of the invisible and spiritual. He satisfies our sense of inner perfection and outer dominion. In Him, the All-Loving One is the All-Powerful One, too. In Him, God and man are seen to be one, God manifest in the realm of the human and man reigning on the throne of God. In Him and through union with Him, we also see the beginning of the new creation in His Likeness.

Initiatory Steps

According to the teaching of the Old and New Testaments, and confirmed by universal experience, the way for a lost life to return home and an enslaved soul to become free, is to yield to the awakening, drawing, quickening, and transforming power of the Spirit of God, who at every instant and every step gladly shows His will. To be hungry enough to obey or to do our best to obey opens the way for just the help needed. To hunger and thirst after righteousness puts everyone where he can and shall receive. To seek is to find, to knock is to have the door opened, and to open the door to His knockings is to have Him enter and sup with us. The hour anyone desires God and seeks Him with the whole heart He always reveals Himself, and where the desire exists, or is ready to be made manifest, He answers even before there is a conscious call.

Other terms used for our God-given ability to cooperate or co-work for our deliverance from every phase of evil and slavery-whether of desire or act- are of course, repentance, faith, confession, abandonment, restitution, prayer, and a whole-hearted turning to God and to Christ and the best we know.

Cases of Deliverance

I recall these cases here in Macon where men who had been slaves to tobacco and whiskey and other enslaving desires and habits, were set free. One man who had used tobacco for the better of his life and who was over 60 years old, was one day enough in the Spirit to have the revelation made to him that Jesus was the Christ. He realized that the use of tobacco did not belong in this new life that he was called to, but said that he did not have to power to give it up. A Voice, as it were, said, "Christ will give you the power," to which he answered, "That is true!" That was fully 20 years ago and from then until now he says that there has never been the slightest desire for tobacco. Two men from Macon who had been notorious drunkards as well as much given to the use of tobacco, were set free from the desire of both when they turned to Christ and sought and received the Baptism of the Holy Spirit. Since then, both have lived unusually devoted Christian lives and have been zealous for the salvation of others.

The Case of St. Paul

Of course, the best known case of struggle and victory is that of St. Paul, who describes the struggle in the seventh chapter of Romans—"O wretched man that I am, who shall deliver me from the body of this death?"(Romans 7: 24-25)—and who gives the secret and the testimony of victory in the eighth chapter. The victory comes through union with Christ, and through yielding to the spirit of life in Christ, which made him and makes us free from the law of sin and death. This brings one to where even the indwelling Christ and the Holy Ghost that raised Jesus from the dead is victorious not only in the inner life, but also brings the beginnings of quickening and redemption to the body.

In all of the marked instances of conversion, sanctification, new birth, the Baptism of the Holy Ghost, lives lived in fruit-bearing and transformative union with Christ (that are reported in the Scriptures and in religious literature), there has been the most complete possible surrender and submission to the call, will, and work of God. The key word on the human side has been "What will you have me to do?" This is a continuous as well as an initiatory attitude. The life seeking the highest will of God, and given to doing the things of the Spirit and to a life of benediction and helpfulness, neither has time nor desire for the things left behind. We look forward to the beholding of the glory of the Lord and the victory of good in the world, and the coming of the kingdoms of earth changing more and more into the likeness of the Kingdom of Heaven.

CHAPTER 8

"Christ in the Death Cell"
July 1, 1928
Macon Telegraph

Christ not only came in the flesh as Jesus, died, rose from the dead, ascended into glorification, and is coming again in His glorified body to change those prepared for it into His bodily as well as spiritual likeness. He also, after His resurrection and ascension and promised gift of the Holy Ghost, longs to come into everyone who opens to His knockings so that the miracle of the Incarnation, the heavenly birth, Baptism and life of the Spirit is made possible for everyone.

Christ's perfect identification with everyone who receives Him and allows Him to enter, and live and reign within, is among the most sublime manifestations of His infinite love. In His identification with us and our identification with Him, we become life of His Life, spirit of His Spirit, mind of His Mind, and members of His Body. He is made unto us love and life, wisdom, righteousness, sanctification and redemption. He so completely identifies Himself with even the least of His brethren that whatever anyone does or fails to do unto one of these, he does or fails to do unto Him. This applies to the worst as well as the best; to murderers, harlots, and outcasts, as well as to the moral and the eminently respectable. In fact, as Jesus said, those who are forgiven most love most, while those who are forgiven least, love least.

So in the references to Christ as being in the death cell, in the electric chair, in prison, before courts, the prison commission, the governor, and Christ and the lawyers and minister and so forth, I am referring to Christ as He now longs to come in each and every one. After I have known of this spiritual coming of Christ for our day and for all days, I have longed especially for someone who was condemned to die for a crime committed prior to his repentance and conversion to Christ to yield so fully to Him that he and Christ would become one. We could then see how Christ would lead and use him, and how Christ in such a one would react. I have witnessed this during the past months and days, and it is the most interesting history I have ever seen enacted.

Robert Jones

The one I refer to is Robert Jones, who was sentenced to be electrocuted last October and whose sentence was carried out last Thursday. *The Telegraph* has already had stories as to his remarkable conversion, spiritual anointing, and ministry in the Bibb county jail. It has also had an unusually well-written report by a staff writer of his electrocution. Today I wish to tell something of the way he spent his days in the death cell and especially speak of his last hours. The prison chaplain who was with him most of the time says that he never saw anything to compare with the spiritual elevation and the way that he spent his time. He ate nothing and when offered food, replied that he had meat and drink that men knew not of. He quoted more scripture, says the chaplain, while in the death cell (and quoted it with remarkable accuracy) than the average minister would quote in months. This is all the more unusual when we take into account that when he entered the Bibb county jail last October, he could only pronounce a very few words. But by putting these words together and by living the New Testament without human help, he soon found it possible to read.

Christ-Centered

The chaplain saw that he could be used to help the hardened criminals and instead of having the ministers come to see him, he used Robert to help the prisoners. The chaplain felt that if he were allowed to live and remain at Milledgeville, that a revival would break out. He also expressed the opinion that his spiritual and natural gifts and experiences were so extraordinary that he should become "the greatest black man who ever lived." A very bright high school graduate who heard him talk said that he had to be inspired to talk in that manner. He impressed the chaplain, myself, and others as the most Christ-centered and least self-centered person we had ever known. When a newspaper man came to see him for a feature story and asked him if he would be willing to talk to him, he said, "Yes, if you are willing to talk about Jesus Christ."

His face, when seen as he was in silent prayer, was in marvelous peace, reverence, and radiance. His spirit turned the death cell into one of the brightest and most wonderful of places. He was so free from gloom and fear that those about him were lifted somewhat into his own elevation.

Outside of Jewish and Christian history, there is nothing that has ever appealed to me as much as the way that Socrates is reported by Plato to have faced his accusers and to have spent his last hours discussing immortality, and the other great issues of the time and eternity. But Socrates was not absolutely certain whether it was immortality or profound sleep that he would enter into, but was certain that no evil could befall him anywhere. Robert, though humanly uneducated, but having the presence and certainty of Christ, appeared to have no thought that his death could mean anything but being in heavenly places with Christ in the task of eternity. When the news came that the governor would not commute his sentence, nor give a respite, instead of being disturbed it only seemed to add to his ecstasy.

Like the Rising of the Sun

While he came into his union with Christ through experiences similar to those of the early Christians, he explained that he did not get anywhere until he stopped desiring and praying that his life be spared. When he ceased seeking these things, the light began to break and he was brought to the place where he knew that one should have no fear of those who can only destroy the body, and that one's business here, after forgiveness, conversion, rebirth, and heavenly anointing, is to glorify Christ and to do all possible good. With all the time that I spent with him in jail, during the last hours in the death cell, and the minutes near the electric chair, there was no indication of the least fear. Instead, there was an out-flowing gratitude, radiance, kindness, and consideration for and in the interest of others that made him the most uniformly victorious in Christian faith that I have ever known.

Robert's last months, days, and minutes is a striking testimony of what Christ can do for anyone, no matter what he had done previously, and when one repents, surrenders, and makes an entire dedication to do His will.

CHAPTER 9

"The Overcomer and Conqueror"
August 26, 1928
Macon Telegraph

To be any kind of a real Christian, one must believe in the miracle of conversion and regeneration—the means by which people radically bad and miserable are forgiven and become clothed and filled with the righteousness, peace, joy, and love that is the start towards being Christlike. While I am somewhat familiar with the literature of doubt and the materialistic view of the world, the miracles of Jesus are so much like the God and Father that He revealed and reveals, that my spiritual wealth in Him rises with every increase of faith in His power to subdue all things unto Himself, as well as to bring us to His perfect nature, wisdom, and love.

The Full Overcomer

Jesus overcame all evil with good, all darkness with light, all error with truth, and all hate with love. He also exercised control over nature, quieting the storm, walking upon the water and making abundance where there was lack. If man had been as obedient to Jesus as nature was obedient, the Kingdom of God could have come at once. Jesus was never sick and never suffered except for others. He healed all who came to Him directly, or that believing friends asked to be healed. He raised the dead and at last died Himself to do away with sin and death. God raised Him from the dead.

His body could not see corruption. Even before the ascension, after the resurrection He had power to appear and disappear and to pass through closed doors as well as to be anywhere He chose to be.

Through His death and resurrection and complete victory over so-called matter as well as over all evil, He became the head of the new creation that is to be like Him. In Him is seen God as complete Master, Conqueror, Servant, and Friend. His nature, faith, assurance, wisdom, love, joy, peace, holiness, and glory give such a worth and wonder of life that after one has eaten of Him and tasted of the world to come, nothing else satisfies.

Inherit All Things

The marvel of God's goodness is that as we become overcomers and conquerors, we actually get in real experience, or inherit, all things. All enemies are put under our feet and what we call matter is to become as plastic to us as is was to Him, and best of all, we are to have His perfect everything with power to impart to others. We also become co-workers with Him in the task of time and eternity. As our inheritance is in Him, as we see Him aright through the revelation of the Holy Ghost, we also see ourselves-ourselves as we are to be. And beholding His Glory as in a mirror, the mirror being the Holy Ghost, we are changed from glory to glory until we arrive at the actual realization of our inheritance in and with Him.

How Brought About

It is easy to those willing to practice it, to see that the secret of overcoming evil is never to meet it with evil, but always to meet it with good. The secret of entering into His marvelous love in the Holy Ghost (which is the Kingdom of God to come universally) is to humble ourselves as little children and to enter into Him and abide in Him and open our whole being for Him to enter into, abide, and reign with us.

As to the mastery of nature and power over disease, limitation, devils, and death, Jesus taught that faith—faith in God and faith in Him, faith in His word, and faith in His faith—and a life lived in union with Him outflowing in joyful obedience and abundant fruit-bearing were the condition and the secret. By His life, example, teachings, and works, by His death and resurrection, by His ascension, by His gift of the Holy Ghost, He has opened the way for all of the works He did while on earth and even greater works to be done again and again until He and these works fill the earth. He longs for the same perfect love that the Father has for Him to be in us and for He Himself to be as fully in us and to reign as perfectly in us as the Father did in Him.

Keeping His Sayings

While on earth He made the promise with absolute assurance that anyone who kept His sayings would never see death. The doubters and those in opposition about Him interpreted Him literally and He did not correct them (see John 8: 51 to the end of the chapter). St. Paul compliments this teaching of Jesus with the revelation that when we come to have the humble mind of Christ and die to all that is outside of and contrary to Him, we come to be in the likeness of His death, and we shall come to His perfection and to be in the likeness of His resurrection. He saw that the Holy Ghost was already a pledge and promise that even the mortal body, instead of dying, could be clothed upon rather than unclothed, so that what was mortal would be swallowed up of life. Through the indwelling Holy Ghost that raised Jesus from the dead, the human body already feels the beginning of the divine quickening and translation. Still, St. Paul recognizes that he had not fully attained to Christlikeness and perfection, but knew that he was on the way to it.

The early Christians raised the dead for some time after the days of the Apostles. And all ages of faith and love, especially whenever the Holy Ghost has been yielded to, have had their miracles not only of conversion and regeneration and of overcoming of evil with good, but also their miracles of healing and victories over the flesh.

Present Day Miracles

In our day, there has been a partial revival of healings and renewed emphasis on holiness, the Second Coming of Christ, and the present power and willingness of the Lord to heal as well as to save and wholly sanctify. As to culmination of the revival, there has been the outpouring of the Holy Spirit over the earth with the primitive Christian sign of speaking with tongues and with a measure of the Apostolic gifts. The quickest and greatest miracles of healing I have witnessed have been in connection with this Pentecostal revival. The presence of the Holy Spirit not only brings in a marvelous way the healing power of God, but also greatly increases faith. According to the New Testament teachings, it is through being filled with the Holy Spirit and through being led by this Spirit and through much fruit-bearing, that we put on Christ and are prepared for His appearing and for resurrection and translation into His likeness.

CHAPTER 10

"Keys to the Kingdom"
September 23, 1928
Macon Telegraph

The emphasis of Jesus while on earth was upon the Kingdom of God. His life was given to bringing outcasts and outsiders into the Kingdom, doing the works of the Kingdom, and preaching the Gospel of the Kingdom, and is giving the secrets or the keys to the Kingdom. The Kingdom is of such supreme importance that we are foolish not to put and keep it first, not to sell all that we have and buy the field where this pearl of great price is found, not to let go everything that keeps us on the outside of it.

What is It?

As St. Paul puts it so simply and comprehensively, the Kingdom of God is not "Meat nor Drink," it is not anything physical or carnal, not anything over which there can be any strife or rivalry, or false pride, or selfish possession; but it is "righteousness, peace, and joy in the Holy Ghost." It is a life in the Good Spirit, flowing out in peace, rest, assurance, joy and bliss. It is the sweet holy meekness and boldness that Jesus had superlatively, and gives without limit as we humble ourselves at His feet and surrender to be made like Him, to know His will, and to do it. It is perfect love that believes all things, hopes all things, endures all things, and that never fails, nor grows old. It is innocence, desiring, willing no ill to anyone; but it longs, prays and works unspeakable good to all, even to those who most misunderstand, and make it hardest for us, or even hate us and despitefully use us. It is also the wisdom that is from above, that is gentle and pure, and full of kindness and good works. It is the state and place where all evil is met with good, all hate with love, all unkindness with kindness.

How to Enter

As Jesus explained to those about Him who were wanting to know who would be the greatest, and wanting to be greatest in the Kingdom, unless they repented and became as little children, they could not even enter. All false pride, all bondage to public opinion, all holding on to a life unlike God, and outside of God's nature, will and love has to go before we can enter into Christ, into God, and into His unspeakable Joy and Glory.

The call is to repent of and to leave on the outside everything that is keeping you on the outside, to surrender to His will, which is His perfect love, and to fall at the feet of Jesus. Here one enters in; here is found the secret place of the Most High; here is found the life hidden with Christ in God; here is Heaven on earth, and Heaven anywhere.

Righteous of the Kingdom

The righteousness that brings the assurance in the Holy Ghost is much more and better than the righteousness of the law, and of popular morality, and of popular religion. It is the righteousness that fulfills popular morality and religion and goes away above and beyond them. It not only does not kill, but it takes all of the hate out by putting in Perfect Love. It not only does not commit adultery, but it brings in the pure heart and mind where there is no desire and no imagination that is impure and unlawful. The righteousness of the Kingdom is in fact the love, nature, mind, and the life of God. The righteousness already exists for us and is at hand all the time and everywhere. It only has to be put on, and it is put on as we chose Christ and His will and way, his Spirit and teaching. In the first instance we must choose these once and for all, and ever afterwards. We choose

Him and the things of obedience of love or the faith that works by love. In doing so, we put on heavenly righteousness, or the wedding garment, the Christ nature, and thereby put on Christ Himself. This putting on not only brings Heaven within us and we within Heavenly peace, and the rest and joy in the Holy Ghost, but prepares us to be manifested with Christ on the plane of His resurrection and glorified body. This manifestation is the coming of Christ in His own Glory, and is the Glory of the Father.

The Witnesses

We have witnesses all along the way that we are submitting to or putting on the righteousness of God, or pleasing God, or doing God's will. They are that we have His peace, rest, joy, assurance, and love. By walking with Him and pleasing Him, by coming and abiding in the light we dwell where there is no darkness or evil at all. All that has defiled is washed away or burned up. His Spirit in this place bears witness that we are His. We have communion and fellowship with Him. He talks to us, and we talk to Him, and we are made white like snow. In this union there is no disturbance, all is sweet assurance, peace, and joy in the holy burning and the quickening of the Holy Ghost.

Since the Kingdom of God is all of the good fruit of the Spirit and life lived in Him, we must bear all of the good fruit thereof in order to have the Kingdom in power and in fullness. Of course, one must in the first instance repent of all that is keeping him out of God, and out of the life in the Spirit, and be born of the Spirit and Baptized with the Spirit, and then go on to the perfection and fullness that is in the Spirit and in the life lived in Christ.

All religious groups and all individuals need to humble themselves at the feet of Jesus, be baptized of Him, and enter into the union with Him, and into His kingdom, and never go out anymore. This is the way. There is no other way!

CHAPTER 11

"Secret of Abiding in Christ"
September 30, 1928
Macon Telegraph

I have been asked by an unusually enlightened professor in a university school of religion, and a preacher to preachers, to write out the secrets of entering and of living in union with the living Christ, of living in the Spirit, of continuous fellowship with God.

God being perfect love, perfect law, and the perfect Person and Father, is much more concerned that all His lost and prodigal children return home than the best of human parents. The only difficulty in getting to God and abiding in God is on our part. As our Father, He comes to meet us while we are yet afar off, and throws His arms of love about us. All that He asks is that we be willing and ready to receive Him, then everything is ours—the best robe (the righteousness and wholeness of Christ), the best ring (the sealing, the Baptism and the Gift of the Holy Spirit), the best food (the Bread, the Meat, the Water and the Wine of Life, a feast on Christ Himself), the best music (the peace, joy, bliss, and glory of Heaven in the Holy Ghost).

It requires only receptivity and response on our part to have God's best in actual experience. To hunger and thirst after righteousness and goodness is to be filled. To ask and really mean it is to receive. To knock and want to enter is to have the Door opened wide to us. And to open to His knocking brings the living Christ within to sup with us and to abide forever. Since God is perfect law as well as perfect Person, all that is required is that we conform to His perfection. Since He is merciful, we have to love mercy and practice mercy to abide in Him. Since He is grace, we have to come to love grace and practice grace. Since He is truth, we have to love truth and be truthful. All that He is as moral perfection we have to welcome and to rejoice in and manifest.

Christ Coming Within

The coming of Christ within may be as definite and certain as the outpouring and Gift of the Holy Ghost as supernatural power and glory, presence, and control. Indeed, the other Comforter Jesus went away to send, when received as promised and given to the first disciples, is an outpouring from Heaven, a definite incoming and abiding of the living Christ and a Baptism into Christ. The outpouring of the Spirit and in the incoming and indwelling of Christ come through invitation: our abiding in Christ depends upon our continually submitting ourselves in joy to do His will and to be like Him

In my own experience, I was brought to see and to acknowledge that Jesus lived right and taught right and that the Good Spirit leads us to go as He went. In going His way, we live the life of pure goodness and perfect love, even though we have of ourselves no power to perform a single miracle. I prayed for the Holy Spirit and for God's best for me and I felt the need of Christ within so greatly that I cried out, "Jesus, if it is possible, come and live within me and be the life and principle of Your own good life and teaching that I have found to be true." A little later, during the same night while I was alone, I decided to stop seeking and go to walking in the light that was clearest which was the most perfect sincerity, charity, and courage that I could give myself to: a life of love, pity, compassion, and Good Samaritan helpfulness.

After about an hour of heavenly clarification, revelation, and almost unthinkable happiness, the Holy Ghost came upon me as definite supernatural power, glory, and control and was accompanied with an ineffable love and bliss. Since the Holy Ghost Baptism in March 1910 until now, which has been over 18 years, the heavenly revelation and urge has been for me to abide in Him always and never to go out anymore. It has also been made known that the secrets of abiding life are always to live and go in love, and always to be consciously preferring and choosing to please Him, and keeping the heart and mind staid on Him and upon the increase and triumph of the Kingdom of God. No matter what alluring temptations come, to say and mean it, "I prefer and choose Christ and give myself to the bringing of God's best to all," is to be kept in the conscious and deepening union with Christ.

Love is All-important

It only requires right desire, hunger, thirst, and asking for the Holy Spirit and for Christ to come within in order to have these greatest of gifts as actual experiences. The entering into the Kingdom of God to abide and never go out requires a life rich in love and outflowing in love all the time. The Heavenly Power and Presence and Gift come to abide forever. The conscious abiding within Christ and in the conscious Kingdom of God is only possible as we live in His love, do His will of love and keep His commandments of love. Since God is the perfect law and principle of life, which is love, as well as the perfect Person and Father, it could not be otherwise. We have to consent and have to want to be and to co-work to be the thing we want, and the thing we must want above all else is to be like Him. To be like Him is to love even our enemies as He loves His and to do them good as He does them good. While God is everything that is good, excellent, and helpful, the essence of His being is perfect love. We have to love and yield ourselves to be like Him in all the perfection of His nature; the one thing that makes possible everything else is that we give ourselves to yielding to His love, and to manifesting His love. The abiding life in Christ is possible in no other way.

The failure of religion and life is from the lack of love and from substituting other things that are, after all, unloving, and choose instead His pure love. Only where there is pure and perfect love is there abundant life and pure and undefiled religion. To hate is to murder. Not to love is to be dead and to cause deadness. To love is to be alive and to impart life.

CHAPTER 12

"Grace Producing Grace"
November 18, 1928
Macon Telegraph

I have been asked to write on the grace of God in Christ. There appears to be three workings or states of the grace that results in perfect salvation or in Christlikeness: First, the grace of God, the "unmerited favor," the pity, compassion, and goodness of God towards even the evil and the unthankful; second, response to this grace in grateful and happy reception; third, the victory of this grace in us, making us gracious and loving, as God is gracious and loving to all, even to the ungracious and unloving. The work of love and grace starts with God, but it is not complete until we become not only partakers, but also channels and organs of His grace, that His co-workers act with Him in bringing the Kingdom, or realm, of love, grace, righteousness, peace, and joy in the Holy Ghost to all.

Love Begets Love

Love, by going to the utmost limits of love as was the case in the God-offering and in the Christ-offering, begets faith, grace, and love even in the unloving and unloveable. We are loved into loving Him, into loving one another, and into loving our active and seemingly dangerous enemies. He went out and goes out for lost lives as a housewife goes out for a lost coin and as the shepherd for the lost sheep. Where He sees us returning homeward, He runs to meet us. Even deeper than this is that the grace of God in Christ made and makes Him give all, including His very life, and this gift, in a special sense, was and is to His enemies to bring them home and to joint-heirship with Him in nature, blessing, dominion, and in service. As St. Paul says, *"For the grace of God that bringeth salvation hath appeared to all men, teaching us that, denying ungodliness and worldly lusts, we should live soberly, righteously, and godly, in this present world; looking for that blessed hope, and the glorious appearing of the great God and our Saviour Jesus Christ who gave himself for us, that he might redeem us from all iniquity, and purify unto himself a peculiar people, zealous of good works."* (Titus 2: 11-14)

Grace in Response to Grace

Our first work in the grace or love-way of life is to be gracious in response to grace. The returning prodigal must meekly, humbly, and gratefully receive the arms of love and grace offered by the Father: the robe, the ring, the feast, the music and dancing, before he is really to return and remain with the Father. No matter how bad we have been, the badness at least begins to go as we awaken, confess, and turn to God; it completely goes as we abide in God, as we walk in the Light, as we are born of the Spirit, and as we love in the Spirit.

Those who refuse the great welcome offered by the Father, who draw back from putting on His robe (being Christlike), who refuse the heavenly seal, Baptism, power and glory of the Holy Ghost and who dislike the rejoicing, music, and dancing that heaven seeks to bring to earth are not yet ready for even the receptive stage of God's grace. While it is more blessed to give than to receive, there is a rare grace in the receiving from God that opens the way to giving with and for God.

Grace Victorious

But as blessed as it is to be ready and open ourselves to receive in great joy, gratitude, love, and power of God in the Holy Ghost, and to receive Christ within, the culmination of blessedness comes on earth as we become co-workers with Christ in making His love and grace way of life victorious here and everywhere. Grace is not victorious until we become gracious and channels of boundless grace and love. Indeed, it is only as we give ourselves to His love and grace and holy way of life, and continue to increase that we become perfect in grace, truth and love. In this perfect way and life we love our enemies and do them all possible good; we return good for evil as well as good for good, grace for ungraciousness as well as for graciousness. There is no other way if we would enter and continue in the straight and narrow way of life of undisturbed peace, of unbroken joy, of continuous and increasing fellowship and union with Him.

Those who receive forgiveness and grace and refuse to extend the same grace to their fellows, fall from grace or refuse to walk and abide in the grace-way of life. It is the very perfection of God that if we refuse to forgive we cannot have the witness of being forgiven, that if we draw back from extending grace we get out of grace, that if we refuse to love we cannot abide in union with the All-Loving One. Christ is not only the perfect Person who forgives and saves to the uttermost, but He is also the perfect way that we have to walk in, the perfect truth that we have to be true to, and the perfect life that we have to live. While one may receive even the Holy Spirit and Christ within by asking and joyfully welcoming, in order to continue in the wonder of the reception of Him, and in the union with Him, we have to bear this fruit all the time.

Failures of Historic Christianity

The primary failures of historic Christianity have been the substitution of ritualism for the true life of worship of God in Spirit and in Truth, and in substitution of doctrines about faith and grace for the grace and faith that works by love, and the grace that is overflowing with compassion, mercy, and goodness. Those who feel that they can continue in grace, apart from becoming full of grace, seem to miss the way almost as much as those who feel they can substitute ritualism for the life of the Spirit.

It all comes back to restoring us and keeping us in union with Christ, and through the union making us like Him in nature, in spirit, and in active goodness. This work starts with God and ends with God, and its highest achievement with us is making us, through free choice and great joy, co-workers with Him in the tasks of time and eternity. While we have to be born of the Spirit before we can start to grow up in the likeness of Christ, while we have to be Baptized by the Holy Ghost into the church which is His Body, we have to live in the Spirit and in fruit-bearing union in order for God's loving purposes concerning us to be wrought out in experience.

CHAPTER 13

"Going On to Perfection"
November 25, 1928
Macon Telegraph

There seems to be two chief reasons why so few people live in the Spirit and go on to perfection—the perfection of love, faith, wisdom and dominion that are in Christ. The majority, it appears, do not get rightly started or initiated, and a majority of those who do get rightly initiated draw back from living in the Spirit and bearing the fruit thereof as their main life business. The entrance into the kingdom of God is, of course, through the new birth and the entrance into the church is through the Baptism and control of the Holy Spirit.

The emphasis of Jesus as reported in Matthew, Mark, and Luke is the Kingdom of God—the government and reign of God and the triumph of His righteousness and joy in the Holy Ghost. His emphasis as reported in John's gospel is union with Him and the bearing of perfect fruit of this union. Since the Kingdom of Heaven is righteousness, peace, and joy of God in the Holy Ghost, and since the union with Christ comes through a birth and Baptism and a life of the Spirit and abundant fruit-bearing, the life in the Kingdom and the life in Christ are very different sides of the same divine reality. Through entering into the Kingdom one enters into Christ, and through abiding in Christ one lives at the very heart of the Kingdom.

Both the Baptism and birth of the Spirit are essential for entering into deep conscious and satisfying union with Christ. The Baptism brings the power, glory and the control, the gifts and signs of the Heavenly realm.

The birth brings the nature and character of God into one's life. The Baptism gives the power and presence of God, and the birth give the Christlike Spirit and makes one a new creature in Him.

Jesus, it seems, performed no miracles prior to the descent of the Holy Ghost upon Him that clothed Him with God-power, authority, and dominion. His Holy Ghost conception made Him holy, loving, innocent, and God-like in nature.

Both the Heavenly Birth and the Heavenly Baptism are necessary if we are to have God's best. Each completes the other. If we are to go on to perfection we must get started right; that is, we must become new creatures in Christ and we must be placed by the Holy Ghost into God's will and Christ's body, or church, in terms of divine wisdom and divine love.

Jesus shifted the discussion with Nicodemus from theology to divine biology. As He told Nicodemus, even to see the Kingdom of Heaven, one must have a new birth. One gathers from what Jesus said on the conversation with Nicodemus, that there is no more sense in attempting to reveal the secrets of the Kingdom to one who is not born into it, than it would be to try to instruct an unborn child in the things of the visible world. Let one be born into the Kingdom of God and let him be led by the Spirit and he will be taught the whole truth concerning the Kingdom as fast as he is ready to receive it. There is nothing that is made clearer in the New Testament than that it is by the one Spirit, the Holy Ghost, that all who enter the real church of Christ are baptized into it.

Trying to Climb Up

It seems to be the prevailing mood of our time to try to make union with Christ a conscious reality, not by a definite birth and Baptism, but by believing and declaring that all are already in union with Him. In other words, the prevailing temptation is to substitute a mental process for a divine experience.

The Kingdom is a pearl of such great price that it has to be put and kept first. One does not drift into the highest. One reaches God's best by conscious and continuous choosing of His will and by the keeping of His commandments.

Gregory S. Camp, Ph.D.

Continuous and Perpetual Union

To go on to perfection there must be a constant denial of the flesh and the lower self, and a constant walking in the Spirit and a continuous and increasing fruit-bearing. We get started by faith and repentance, by asking, by knocking, and by receiving Christ through the Holy Ghost into our whole being to reign in the whole of our life. We continue and deepen in Christ as we continually look to Him for guidance, as we seek first the Kingdom of God, as we live and walk in the Spirit. Every time we are tempted or allured, we need to choose Christ and His will and Kingdom and love way of life. There is no abiding in Christ except through continuous fruit-bearing and through the deep preference to have Christ and His great peace, joy, and presence.

God has made it easy to get started right. Even the worst of the prodigals, by turning toward home, puts heaven into the greatest rejoicing. Anyone who knocks at the heavenly door and really wants to enter, finds the door swings open. God longs to bring everyone who desires it and who will consent to it into His Kingdom and into Christ. The Holy Ghost may be received simply by the hearing of faith, or by listening with faith, by asking, yielding, and responding to God. But the continuous union with Christ requires our constant preferring and choosing to abide in Christ and in God's Kingdom, and to bring forth the fruit of the union.

It seems that you can find 100 people who have received the Holy Ghost Baptism and in whom Christ has entered, to where you will find but one who lives in the Spirit and who is rejoicing in Christ Jesus all the time and going on from glory to ever greater glory. The temptation is that after having started in the Spirit to drop back more and more in the natural. Those who become full overcomers and the church that becomes glorious and spotless and victorious must live and worship increasingly in the Spirit. To live in great and undisturbed peace, joy, and in conscious love of Christ and in the power and glory of the Holy Ghost, requires deadness to public opinion, and a life of love and faith that is rare.

The Keys

When we actually desire, put, and keep first the will of God and His peace, joy, and love, we have the keys to the Kingdom and to everything. What we need to do is when anything tempts us that would decrease our deepening life in the Spirit, is simply to choose Christ and the things of His Kingdom. We lose His peace, joy, and glory because we do not prize them highly enough to gladly let go of all that decreases them.

CHAPTER 14

"Faith, Hope, Charity"
January 27, 1929
Macon Telegraph

A friend who lives on Willingham Street in East Macon, tells me that in a meeting in his home a few nights ago that he was slain by the Lord. and I infer from what he said, lost in the Spirit for a time. A supernatural fire touched his head and went over him. Three angels then appeared that were revealed to be "Faith, Hope, and Charity." Faith and Hope were very fat, but Charity was very lean.

As wonderful, creative and necessary as are faith and hope—the substance of things hoped for and the power by which all things that are according to the will of God created and brought forth in actuality of experience—greater than either faith or hope is charity. In fact, love, or charity, is the very essence and being of God Himself and of Jesus who is God revealed, manifested and victorious in the flesh. Nowhere is this better expressed than in 1 Corinthians 13. After all, love never fails!

The key to the Kingdom of God and the secret of abiding life in Jesus, the very heart of the Kingdom, is love. When one ceases to love he grows cold and dead, and one who has not been awakened or born into the realm of Divine love has never come to life, to the life of the Spirit. To be always in God, in Jesus, and in the Spirit, we have to be in a state of blessed love towards Jesus, toward the brethren and toward all men and all of creation. Even to hate an enemy is to be kept out of Jesus and the Kingdom until hate is repented of and love takes its place.

When love takes the place of all hate and all lust, and when Jesus and His perfect love, spirit, and nature that are knocking to come in are received and allowed to reign all the time, then paradise is regained. When we enter into Jesus never to go out any more, we eat of the Tree of Life and every enemy is put under our feet including the last enemy, death.

The Value of Experience

An unusually gifted and likeable friend who lives in Mitchell, Ontario writes me to the effect that experience is ephemeral, but he that does the will of God, abides in God, and gets God's best. Of course, it is true that there are no substitutes for doing the will of God and for choosing and doing His will happily and in great joy. But one who gives himself to doing God's will must from the very nature and riches of God's love and gifts be rich in Christian experience. And while some of the blessed spiritual experiences come gradually, like the rising of the sun and the blossoming of flowers, there are others that come suddenly—such as the overshadowing of the Holy Ghost, divine conception, entire sanctification, redemption, rapture, and glorification.

As the natural life is full of definite experiences, so is the spiritual and heavenly. Even conversion when it is genuine, real, and lasting, is a tremendous experience, such as the experience of a radically bad person becoming, sometimes suddenly and by manifest Divine miracle, a radically good person. The Baptism of the Holy Ghost, the incoming of Jesus, entire redemption or release from all of one's enemies are definite and certain experiences. But as the natural life is more fundamental than the experiences of the natural life, so the spiritual life is more rudimental and fundamental than the experiences that accompany it. Jesus comes to all ready to receive Him and to be and impart life. That is to say, His own Life, and that in full, rich, and everlasting measure.

Abiding in Christ

But the superlative importance of receiving the Holy Spirit and living in the Spirit and of receiving Jesus within and living in Him and manifesting

His love all the time, does not lessen the importance of keeping ourselves open to receive, nor from asking for every good gift and experience that He has for us. It seems as sanctification, healing, and the Baptism of the Holy Ghost has been the special gift of God in recent years, that today onward is in a special way the time for entering into the redemption or release that is in Jesus. This release, of course, means freedom from the enemies, worries and cares that have held us in bondage. While I have seen no one who gave the evidence of having as yet a redeemed body in the sense of a perfect body, it is perfectly clear that we may exchange the mind of the flesh that works lust, disease and death, for the mind of Christ that works peace and life not only to the soul, but also to the body. By the constant renewing that comes through being in union with Christ, and through having His mind and Spirit, bringing life even to our mortal bodies, we may go on and on until the body is ready to become like the Body of His resurrection.

CHAPTER 15

"Taught of the Lord"
March 24, 1929
Macon Telegraph

When I began to turn to the Lord for guidance, the two things that were made clearest were that the true life is the life of love and sincerity, and that we must be taught of the Lord and of His Good Spirit. Even before the Holy Spirit was given as a gift and as a Baptism of supernatural presence and power, and before the Lord came within definitely and consciously, it was revealed that the day would come when I would leave all religious group authority and leadership to be led and taught by the Good Spirit, the Spirit of truth and love. The Holy Spirit was not given in power and control, and the Lord did not come consciously and definitely within, until I consented to be led by the Spirit and to give my life to the bearing of the good fruit of the Spirit.

The Secret of Israel

Later, I found that the secret of Jacob and of the other great Jews of the Old Testament, notwithstanding manifest imperfections, was precisely that they turned to Jehovah for leadership and for guidance. As Moses said of Jacob, *"So the Lord alone did lead him, and there was no foreign god with him."* (Deuteronomy 32: 12). In all the desperately close places he found himself, he went to Jehovah for the help that he had to have, and Jehovah never failed him.

All the men of greatest spiritual power and worth reached the place where all teachers fail them but the Lord, where they had to be directly taught by God. As much help as we may receive from each other and as blessed as it is to give this help and to receive it, the greatest and sweetest peace never comes until we are taught directly by the Lord and know that we are being taught and led of Him. God even promised to write His laws in the heart and engrave them in the mind and bring forth the day when *"…they shall teach no more every man his neighbour, and every man his brother, saying, Know the LORD: for they shall all know me, from the least of them unto the greatest of them, saith the LORD: for I will forgive their iniquity, and I will remember their sin no more."* (Jeremiah 31: 34).

In addition to the great peace and certainty that comes through being taught directly of the Lord, there also comes a witness that all sins are forgiven and that all iniquity is taken away, along with the witness of being in continuous fellowship and union with Him (I John 1: 7). Indeed, all good opens to us as we turn directly and wholly unto the Lord and His Good Spirit to teach, guide, and transform us.

Jesus Approves and Fulfills

Jesus affirmed the prophecies that all shall be taught of God, and saw that as fast as men yielded to this teaching that He, God, would lead them Himself. (John 6: 45-46) He taught His disciples to call no man Rabbi (Teacher), for One is the teacher of all of his disciples, and He is that One.

While Jesus, as quoted in the New Testament, did not specifically forbid such terms as reverend and doctor (the modern Protestant counterparts of the greetings He did forbid), it seems perfectly clear that the custom of applying these terms as badges of religious honor and authority is directly contrary to the spirit and enlightenment of Jesus.

The Spirit of Truth

On the last night when Jesus so emptied His heart and mind to His friends who were so near and dear to Him, He made clear and certain to them that the Spirit of Truth, the Holy Ghost, the other Comforter, would be sent and would teach them all things. This Comforter would guide them into all truth, glorify Him, show them the things to come and would convict the world of sin, of righteousness, and judgment. He never referred to any other teacher or leader who would come after Him, but committed them to the Perfect Guide, to the wisdom of the Perfect Teacher. St. John, writing years afterward to one who had the anointing of the Holy Ghost that Jesus had given and gives to all open to receive, said, *"You need not that any man teach you: but the same anointing teaches concerning all things, and is truth."* (I John 2: 27) As St. John goes on to say, this teaching to everyone is to keep in union with Him and to love one another.

St. Paul's Letters

Of course until men are taught directly of the Lord, the closer they are to those who are thus taught and who are pointing them to the Lord as the Teacher, the better it is for them. As St. Paul says, the Holy Ghost set some in the church as apostles, teachers, prophets, evangelists, and pastors for the perfection of the saints until they are brought to the unity of faith and become like Jesus.

But it must be remembered that the appointment referred to by St. Paul was not according to man's selection, but an immediate appointment of the Lord Himself through the Holy Spirit. Where one is appointed or called of God, and speaks not his own words but the words that the Lord gives him, it is not the one through whom He speaks that is the source of the teaching. He is only the channel. The Lord Himself is the Teacher. The kind of teaching and leadership that impoverishes, divides, and scatters the sheep is of human origin no matter how pretentious be its claims. The more pretentious the claims, the worse it is in the sight of God and in its effect upon the sheep.

If we are all going to Atlanta and there is but one highway, the man who leaves Macon last follows the rest not because the rest have gone that way, but because it *is* the way. The way will be just as fresh and wonderful for the last man who travels it as it was for the first. It is the road of destruction that men rush into because others are traveling it. We travel the road that leads to life because it is the Way and the only Way of life.

Gregory S. Camp, Ph.D.

Love and Help One Another

This does not mean that travelers cannot and must not love one another, and be all possible help to each other. They must do this superlatively. It only means that if we are to go through to God's best and be the most help to each other, we must all learn to look to the Lord, refer all things to Him, be taught of Him, and keep in closest touch with Him. In this company that's taught of the Lord, the chief is the servant to the rest, and the greatest is a kind of slave of everybody.

Righteousness, Sanctification, Redemption

In one of the great sweeps of St. Paul, he refers to the fact that God has made Jesus our wisdom, righteousness, sanctification, and our redemption. (I Corinthians 1: 30) He is our everything, and the appropriation in experience comes as we take Him as our Teacher and our wisdom, and as we give ourselves to being taught and led of Him. As we follow Him, and walk in His light, we come into union with Him, and His blood cleanses us from all sin; and He becomes our redemption and victor even over death itself.

The Tragedy

The tragedy or dryness, division, lack of love, and lack of life that I have found in religions of our time has been due more to self-appointed and man-appointed religious leaders and teachers than any other cause. Every strong character, until the desire to be prominent and the desire to be first is taken out of him or her, and until filled with the spirit, love, and humility of Jesus, tends to create a sect of some kind, or group about him or her. So long as this occurs people are carnal, and the marvelous inheritance we have in Christ is only partially seen. The only remedy is for the Lord Himself to shepherd the sheep, and this is precisely what the prophets saw He would do in the last days. There will be one flock and one Shepherd. The sheep will be led unto green pastures and beside quiet waters. God's will will be done on earth as in heaven, and His glory, love, and peace will cover the earth as the waters cover the sea.

CHAPTER 16

"Putting on the New Man"
April 21, 1929
Macon Telegraph

The call of the Father, of Jesus, of the Spirit and of all enlightened children and obedient servants of God to all sinners and prodigals, is for them to repent and come to themselves and to come home. When they come, these sinners and prodigals are the only ones who make mention of their past alienation, state, and deeds of darkness. The Father and all who understand and co-work with Him, together with the whole heavenly host, give themselves to rejoicing, welcoming, and serving. All condemnation is unlike God. When we enter into union with Christ Jesus, there is not only no condemnation for us, but there is no condemnation for anybody.

Example of Jesus

As much as Jesus plead and interceded for us to be pure in heart and thought, as well as in life, He so loved those who had been captured by impurity that He gave the Water of Life and the Revelation that He is the Christ to a Samaritan woman who was badly mixed up with husbands. He welcomed her to the ministry not only of calling her husband who was not her husband, but to letting the whole town know about the Man who knew everything about their sinful lives and only had love and salvation for them. As much as Jesus hated impurity because it was such a blinding and deadly enemy of life, He did not condemn. He protected another woman from her accusers and would-be executioners when she was caught in the very act of adultery. She had been brought to Him to test out His doctrine of love for sinners as well as to expose and punish the woman. Here is revealed His loving feeling toward all sinners and His way of dealing with them. Where the self-righteous are punishing them, He gives protection. But He does not stop there. He tells them to sin no more, washing away their status and giving them His water and way of life that so completely satisfy that the desire for sin is taken away.

It is true that Jesus seemed severe to the self-righteous and cruel, and hard religious people; but this seeming severity was to open their eyes and to stop them from standing between sinners and the Kingdom of God. The way Jesus loved, drew, and won Saul of Tarsus, whom He made his special apostle and light-bearer to the Gentile world, is a revelation of the way He feels towards and deals with Pharisees. The difference between a self-righteous Pharisee who believes he is deeply religious, and an exposed and repentant person, is that it is much easier to save a sinner than to save the one who does not know he is one.

One who is going wrong and leading others into the ditch with him has to have the light turned on and turned on in love whether it seems to be love or not. It is just here that Jesus to accomplish God's fullest will of redemption had to do the very things that led up to His death, resurrection, ascension, Gift of the Holy Ghost and His coming within. Since then, it has been possible to be in such union with Christ and to so lift Him up in love, mercy, and drawing power that the Holy Ghost could convict of sin so as to draw all men unto Him. The first followers of Christ had to share very deeply of His sufferings and persecutions, many of them having been put to death almost as cruelly as He was. But most so-called Christians today are not suffering on account of Christlikeness, but because of their failure to enter into the peace, rest, love, health, and victory that are in Him. It is also true if we were more Christlike, we might be severely persecuted. It is also true that we might be among those who would glorify Christ by getting victories over all His enemies rather than be put to death by them.

I know of one very zealous Christian, who seemingly had much more zeal than wisdom or love, who was told of the Lord that charity was the most excellent way. He sought for this and later was persecuted by Muslims in Persia at the time of the [First] World War. He was given such grace and wisdom that the Lord preserved him through everything. Many about him suffered martyrdom, but no harm came to him or the group of Christians that went with him under Muslim protection to the American consulate.

Appeal of the Epistles

It should be remembered that the epistles of the New Testament and Revelation are addressed to believers, to called-to-be saints, and to the churches of Christ. Take for example, Paul's epistles. They were addressed to individuals and the churches that had believed in Christ, received the Holy Ghost and the gifts of the Spirit. St. Paul, under divine anointing and inspiration, urged those who had already been begotten of and Baptized with the Holy Ghost to become Christlike. In many ways he makes this call an appeal and command. In what scholars believe to be his first letter (the first epistle to the Thessalonians), Paul urges that these members of Christ's body who were made members by being baptized into Christ by the Holy Ghost, be at peace amongst themselves, to admonish the disorderly, to encourage the faint-hearted, and to support the weak. He also called for them to be long-suffering to all, to never render evil for evil, not only among themselves but to outsiders, to rejoice always, to pray without ceasing, to give thanks in everything, and to quench not the Spirit. He further commanded them to despise not prophesying, to prove all things, to hold fast to all that stand the test, and of course to abstain from all appearance of evil, and to be wholly sanctified. He prays that their spirits and bodies be preserved blameless unto the coming of the Lord, speaks of when the dead would be raised in incorruptible bodies, and how the bodies of the living changed into the very likeness of the body of the Lord of Glory.

Putting On Christ

In Ephesians, Galatians, and other epistles, St. Paul exhorts that "the old man," the old self and old manner of life be put to death, put off and away. Moreover, he stresses that those who have the first fruits of the Spirit be renewed in the spirit of their minds and put on the new man, that after God hath been created in righteousness, holiness, and truth. All insincerity, all falseness, all ungodly lusts, hardness and impurity of heart, selfishness, and pride and desire to lord it over others has to go. We must put on bowels of mercy, a heart of love and compassion, a humble mind, a truthful and kind tongue, and a charitable spirit. In his letter to the saints at Philippi, St. Paul emphasizes the necessity of being completely clothed in the righteousness of Christ that we may know Christ in the power of His resurrection and in the fellowship of His suffering, being conformed unto His death. So if by any means we may attain unto the resurrection of the dead, and be conformed to the likeness of the body of His glory.

Light for Today

Not only our inner lives but also our bodies can and must be brought into the Kingdom of God. This is redemption. The taking of the whole being out of the hands of the enemy and bringing it into the nature, spirit, and hands of Christ is the kind of redemption that is open to us now. With this redemption we can go on from experience to experience, from glory to glory.

There is little progress until the dragon's seed and nature are destroyed, as the dragon attempts to devour the man-child or keeps him from coming forth. But when the seed, nature, and power of the beast, the serpent, the dragon, and the destroyer are put to death and eradicated from our nature, the growth of Christlikeness can be rapid. We must grow up in Him and overcome every enemy, the last being death, and become joint-heirs with Him. Then Jesus takes His place with us as the First Born and Elder Brother of the household of God, and God the Father becomes all in all. But until this consummation, everything that is in God's will must be in the name of Jesus, to whom every heart must yield and every knee bow. This is the perfect way of God to bring about His most loving purpose, which is not only our full redemption, but also the redemption of the whole creation.

CHAPTER 17

"Unity and Freedom in Christ"
August 11, 1929
Macon Telegraph

It should be self-evident to everyone who has a measure of the mind of Christ and heart of Christ that He desires and wills that all of His disciples to be one. He also desires and wills that each and every one at every step of the way should receive whatever experience and enrichment for which they are ready. In Christ is perfect unity and perfect freedom. In Christ there is one fold and one Shepherd, one body and one head, one church or bride, or wife, and one Lord or Husband. Yet within the Lord and His church everyone may freely receive everything of the Lord as fast as he is ready to receive.

Jesus is known by many descriptive titles: the Son of the Living God, the Son of Man, the Lily of the Valley, the Bright and Morning Store, God-with-us, Wonderful, Counselor, the Mighty God, the Everlasting Father, the Prince of Peace, the King of Kings, the Lord of Lords, the Word of God, the Way, the Truth, and the Life, the Light of the World, the Bread of Life, the One among us that Serves, the Savior, the Redeemer, and the All in All. So too are His people and His church known by many names: sheep of His pasture, dear little flock, disciples, servants, friends, called-to-be-saints, saints, the Church, the Church of God, the Church of the Living God, the Church of the First Born, the Churches of Christ, the Churches of God in Christ, the Bride and the Lamb of Life. But just as there is but one Lord who has many designations, so there is but one body or church, so loved that it has name after name of endearment and enrichment.

One who is Baptized by Jesus into His body or Church, and this is the way we enter His Church (I Corinthians 12: 13), and one who is living in fellowship with His people, can rightly be called a Christian, a disciple, a friend, and a member of every designation that belongs to those who belong to Christ. Through belonging to Christ, one has all the things of God.

Tragedy of the Carnal

One of the tragedies of being yet carnal is that it causes one to have a sect-sense instead of the love and universal sense of the things of Christ. Even the early Christians soon yielded to the carnal temptation, because they had not given up all their carnality, of thinking of themselves belonging to either Paul, or Apollos, or Peter, or Christ, in a sectarian way. And, as St. Paul reminded them, so we should be reminded that as we belong to Christ we also belong to God, and through this union with God in Christ all things are ours. Since Paul and every apostle, saint, church and everything of God is ours, how blind and carnal it is for us to make a sect of any name or of any part of God. God being One and being Spirit, cannot be divided. He belongs to everyone who belongs to Him, and all the things of God belong to each child of God.

Not long after the days of the apostles a rivalry arose between the bishop of Rome and the bishop of Constantinople, and this rivalry, based on the carnality of those who were not fully Christianized, led to the division into the Roman Catholic and the Greek Orthodox church; of course there were many minor rivalries and oppositions to the Spirit of Christ who wills and works for all of His people to be one. Later when the Protestant Reformation emerged, it divided into sect after sect. Even so highly an organized movement as the Methodists has divided up into about fourteen different kinds of Methodists, and there are about as many kinds of Baptists as there are Methodists.

Even people who have in our time tarried for and obeyed and received the Holy Ghost, have not been spiritual enough to escape division after division. Some are known as Pentecostal, some as Apostolic, some as Church of God, some as the Church of the First Born, and so on and so forth. In fact, there seems to be no remedy for division except a complete yielding to the Lord.

As this yielding is made, the Lord takes out the carnality and the sect-sense and lifts one to see that all His people are one, and one at the same time, being in union with Him, has everything that is His. He may not belong to the Methodists, but the Methodists belong to Him. In fact, he may not belong to the Church of God in a sectarian sense, or to the Church of Christ, or to the Church of the First Born, or any other name however blessed that is held by anybody as an exclusive term, but all of these belong to Him.

The True Sense

It is blessed to be a Baptist, a Catholic, a Christian, or a member of the Church of Christ in the same sense. We'll have to come to this sense before the church can see itself as one and become one. Since all things are ours through union with Christ, how little, blind, and selfish it is to make a sect or division of any of the things of Christ.

Jesus took Peter, James, and John with Him to witness His transfiguration. But quickly after these experiences that they were ready for and the rest were not, He took them back to the common life and the common service. In the same way, Jesus is ready to lead any of us to any experiences and transformations that we are ready for, but if we obey Him, we will not allow any of these to separate us from any of those who have been baptized into Him. It's just the opposite of the true Christian spirit, vision, and life to form a sect or division over the gifts or blessings and Holy Name of the Lord.

Variety is Unity

The gifts of the Spirit are distributed as is the best for each and all, as it pleases God. As we enter into the experiences of God as we are prepared for them, every one of those experiences should make us more loving to each other and more at one with every other child of God, no matter how little or how much experience he may have had.

The only divisions that God stands for and causes is the division between the sheep and the goats, the wheat and the tares, the children of God and the children that are not His. Even the wheat and the tares grow together until the judgment and the harvest. There's no conflict between the things and the names of God. There's only conflict between the good and the evil, the spiritual and the carnal, Christ and Satan. When we really have Christ and understand and do His will, we will not only love but we will also fellowship with everyone who is begotten of Him. When all come to His Spirit, mind, and love all will be Baptists (we will be Baptized with His Holy Spirit), all will be Church of God, and so on. At that point, we will be fully of each other as we are in Him, and all divisions over the things of God and Christ will disappear. All of the names that are not Biblical and beautiful, such as the Holy Rollers, Quakers, Shakers, and Methodists, that have been given in derision, will disappear. But God's people may be called by new names that will express the marvels of His love.

Unity in the Spirit

But until we arrive at a unity of understanding, or a unity of the faith in perfection, we can have and must have the unity of the Spirit in the bonds of peace and love. By this unity of the Spirit and by meekness, and by each child of God esteeming other children of God better than himself, each will be led on to perfect unity with each other and with the Lord, and this perfect unity will bring to the light also perfect likeness. First, there will be the likeness of spirit, mind, and life and in the end, likeness of body.

CHAPTER 18

"Appropriating Christ"
August 25, 1929
Macon Telegraph

Whatever we really believe (*really* believe), we act upon. One who believes in Jesus vitally is receptive and responsive to Him, His Spirit, and way of life; and by being receptive and responsive the way is open for Jesus to make him like Himself. Whatever we will and do, we become; and whatever the heart and mind feed upon, they appropriate and become like. The spiritual food that we eat when we feed upon Christ, being greater than ourselves, makes us in His likeness.

One is kept in perfect peace as his heart and mind are stayed upon the Lord. To behold the glory of the Lord as in a mirror, is to be changed from glory to glory into His Likeness. In fact, it is a universal law that whatever the mind, heart, and innermost nature feed upon they become like, and for the likeness to be brought about quickly, the spiritual feeding must be continuous. Even when one sleeps, when his heart is set upon the highest, the deeper recesses of his being are responding to the highest. One can do any work that's good to be done and yet keep the depths of his being feeding upon the highest, provided his leading and dominant love is from the highest.

When one loves the Lord well enough to keep His commandments and keep his heart and mind upon Him, he is sure to receive the Holy Ghost, and Christ and the Father manifest themselves and take up their abode with and within Him. As the Holy Ghost is yielded to, He takes the things of Christ and reveals them. This revealing glorifies Christ and changes the one who yields and responds to the revealing into His nature, character, and likeness. The commandments of the Lord are not grievous but simply the leadings, revealing, and perfect way of love.

The perpetual working of the power, presence, and glory of the Lord will not only redeem and transform the spirit, soul, and mind, but also the body. The body being the effect and agent, is transformed, renewed, and redeemed through the transformation and redemption of the heart, mind, and life activities. If one were to get his body redeemed in advance of the redemption of his spirit, soul, and mind, he would at best be a hypocrite and at worst an antichrist. So the divine order is, of necessity, first the inner salvation, transformation, and redemption; then the outer, or rather the outer comes through and with the redemption of the inner.

"For whom he did foreknow, he also did predestinate to be conformed to the image of his Son, that he might be the firstborn among many brethren. Moreover whom he did predestinate, them he also called: and whom he called, them he also justified: and whom he justified, them he also glorified." (Romans 8: 29-30) On the way to glorification (to be made like the glorified Christ even bodily) everything works together for our good. Even the afflictions, persecutions, and the worst that we are permitted to suffer are light and easy and work to a greater weight of glory. As St. Paul further develops, if one loses his body or his "tent," he has a heavenly body prepared for him and enters into this, but at the same time we prefer and live in the hope of not being unclothed, but clothed upon that all that's mortal may be swallowed up in life.

Our Meat and Drink

Jesus said His meat was to do the will of His Father and to finish His work. Our meat, if we are real Christians, is to do the will of Jesus, which is the will of God, and help finish the work of redemption of putting under His feet every enemy and of bringing the Kingdom of God on earth. As St. Paul says, we have been made to drink of the One Spirit. So as we do His will, we eat of the heavenly meat; and as we yield to, receive, and live in the heavenly Spirit, we drink of the heavenly water, wine and blood. This should make more real to us how it is that we may eat of the flesh of

Jesus and drink His blood. Moses did not give the true bread from heaven; Jesus, by giving Himself and His Spirit, gives this bread and heavenly meat. The words that He gives us are Spirit and life. His commandments, Spirit, and love are life. Everything of Jesus is life, while everything contrary to Him is death.

The True Worship

The true worship as well as the true life is in Spirit and truth. Every time we yield to this Spirit and do His will we are in the true worship and the true life. As we yield and obey all the time we are in the true worship and the true life all the time. It's not in this place or that place, but by being in the Spirit and in the will of God that we offer a worship that pleases Him and transforms us.

The value of the sacraments that those who are spiritual can all understand is the spiritual reality that they symbolize. Baptism symbolizes the immersion and life in God, the death of the old life and the resurrection with Christ in the Spirit to walk in the newness of life. The Lord's table symbolizes the broken body and the spilt blood of Jesus; and as we partake of His table in deep humility and great gratitude, letting the Holy Spirit make real to us that His suffering was for us, that His death was for us, and that everything of Him was and is for us, we somehow drink of His Spiritual blood and eat of His Spiritual body. Deeper than this, His blood and life through the Spirit are appropriated even by our bodies. We realize the literal through the spiritual. It must be done in memory of Him and in gratitude to Him. As the heart and mind feed on Him, the body also feeds. This is the truth of transubstantiation. It is not ritualistic; it is biological.

Experiences of Life

A child has to be begotten and born before it can grow up in the likeness of its parents, and all epoch-making and initiatory experiences, the special gifts and blessings, are tremendously important. But along with these great experiences and gifts, life itself must be continuous, growing, and healthy. It is so with the natural, it is also true with the spiritual.

It is not experiences opposed to life, nor life opposed to experiences, but experiences initiating and advancing life, and life holding together, utilizing, and glorifying all gifts and particular experiences with God. The life of Jesus was rich in great experiences, and these experiences are glorified by His perfect life.

But the special emphasis of this article is that we must continually feed on the Lord, eat of His heavenly bread and meat, drink of His heavenly Spirit, and do His will. This perpetual feeding, drinking, and obedience keeps one in peace, joy, and in the continuous quickening and transforming power of the Lord. Whatever we love, think about, and do, we become like. God has made it so that His will concerning us is fulfilled as we believe in and feed upon Jesus. As we have seen, by continuing meditating on Him, communing with Him, and rejoicing in Him and doing His will, we feed upon Him, and are transformed into His likeness. The way is to be filled with the Spirit, to live in the Spirit, and bear the fruit of the Spirit. As we do this, we show forth the Lord, fulfill His will, and are made ever more and more like Him. As long as we think of the Lord, yield to the Spirit, and do God's will only part of the time, we will only have blessed seasons of peace, joy, and transformation. When we make the entire consecration and dedication to live in His will and in His Spirit, and keep ourselves in constant communion and obedience, His peace, presence, and transforming power will be continued. Then, perhaps sooner than anyone realizes, all that's mortal will be swallowed up in His life.

CHAPTER 19

"Perpetuating Pentecost"
June 8, 1930
Macon Telegraph

Today is set aside by the various Christian communions of the world for the celebration of the nineteenth hundredth anniversary of the Gift of the Holy Ghost and the beginning of the church as the body of Christ Jesus on earth. The Federal Council Commission on Evangelism suggests that the sermon subject for today throughout Christendom be "Perpetuating Pentecost," indicating, as the *Christian Century* says, "that the celebration of this historic day should not close with June, but that the spirit of the celebration be perpetuated through the months and years."

The Methodist bishops recent address to the conference at Dallas, Texas and to Methodism at large, said: "The Spirit of God seems to be brooding over His church, and awakening unutterable longings. Let us respond to the wooing!" The report on the spiritual condition of the church which was read by Paul B. Bern, who was later made a bishop, urged not only the preaching of Christ as Lord, but prayer for a Baptism of the Holy Ghost that shall light a flame of radiant power upon every altar and in every heart in Methodism.

As quoted in previous article, E. Stanley Jones closes his recent book, The Christ of Every Road, which is a study of Pentecost, with this striking statement:

> "The world ground is being prepared for a spiritual awakening on a wide-spread scale. We are on the verge of something big. We

cannot capture these latent yearnings for Christ, unless Christ captures us more completely. Materialism and inertia will close in on these spiritual yearnings and smother them unless we meet them with a Gospel adequate in breadth and depth. Pentecost gives both. We are, therefore, shut up to the alternative of Pentecost or failure. We cannot go further until we go deeper."

John M Versteeg has written a widely-hailed book on <u>The Perpetuating of Pentecost</u>, and this is only another of many of the recent books dealing with the meaning and necessity of the Baptism of the Holy Ghost. There's the feeling generally among the spiritually-minded that the superlative need of the church is the Holy Ghost Baptism, presence, and leadership.

Jesus and the Apostles

Jesus went away from His glorious ministry of doing the works of the Kingdom of God, healing the sick, casting out devils, forgiving sins, feeding the hungry, bringing God's dominion over nature, setting at liberty the captives and even raising the dead—and of preaching the gospel of the kingdom for the express purpose that He might send the other Comforter, the Spirit of Truth, the power and the glory of the Father; that is, the Holy Ghost. As He said on the last night addressing the disciples, who were so grieved at the thought of His going: *"Nevertheless I tell you the truth; It is expedient for you that I go away: for if I go not away, the Comforter will not come unto you; but if I depart, I will send him unto you."* (John 16: 7)

The first disciples, obedient to Jesus' instructions, did not leave Jerusalem until they had received the Holy Ghost and the power, gifts, love, and certitude that He gives. The early church was a Holy Ghost church, filled with the Spirit, and doing His mighty works. Wherever the full Gospel of Jesus went, the Holy Ghost fell upon obedient believers. When the apostles found believers in Jesus who had not received the Holy Ghost, they prayed for them to receive Him, laid hands on them and it appears that where they had not been baptized in Jesus' name, that they were subsequently so baptized. With the apostles, everything else was to wait until the Holy Ghost was received. In fact, there is in reality no New

Testament Christian church apart from the baptism, inspiration, guidance, gifts, fruit, and control of the Holy Ghost.

What Occurred at Pentecost

The disciples, after the ascension of Jesus, returned to Jerusalem in great joy and remained there worshipping and praising God for the promised gift of the Holy Ghost. There were fourteen different nationalities present and each not only saw the glory, wonder, and love that those who had received the Holy Ghost were in, but all the foreigners were amazed to hear some of the 120 speaking to them in their own tongues. In other words, the Holy Ghost had not only come and brought the love, power, and glory of God upon the 120, but was speaking to every man in his own language. With the gift of the Holy Ghost the bodies of the 120 became literally, in experience, the temples of the living God, of the Holy Ghost, and of the Christ of Glory. They were not only given power, spiritual gifts, love, and guidance for their work, but were sealed until the day of redemption. Christ also came within them as the promise of glorification.

Think of it! Heaven's power and glory upon us, and Christ within us as Companion, Teacher, and All in all, and being in heavenly places with Him and in Him and being made ready to be resurrected or translated into His bodily likeness! This is just part of the present privilege we have in Christ if we will receive the Holy Ghost He went away to send, and receive Him within and live in the Spirit and move on to the full purpose of God concerning us.

As the inner side of Pentecost is the living union with the living Christ through the power, gift, and life of the Spirit, leading us on to full Christlikeness and glorification; the outer side is a life of love and service to the whole of creation. The first fruit of the Spirit, including all the other fruit, is perfect love and this love not only makes abiding union with God possible, but it also makes union with one another inevitable. As Jesus said on the last night when His disciples received the other Comforter, they would know that He was in the Father and the Father in Him, and that He was in them and they in Him. He prayed not only for the little group around Him, but for all who would believe on Him later, to be one as He and the Father were One, that the love wherewith the Father had loved Him might be in them and He in them.

For a time the early church had so much love that all things were held in common, and when the church again comes to this much love and then moves on to the fullness of Christ's love, everything we have will be at the service not only of Christians, but of all.

The Offense of Tongues

I am glad that Bishop Mouzon in his remarks at Dallas upon the report on the spiritual state and needs of the church, went far enough to say that "we should leave the manner of the coming of the Holy Ghost in the hands of God." I am also glad that he gave recognition to the fact that wherever there is such high reality as that which came at Pentecost, that there will also be high emotionalism. For it seems that the excuse that some churchman are offering against receiving the Holy Ghost as early Christians received Him and as He is being received at least in a measure today throughout Christendom, is that we must avoid emotionalism and that there is no need for tongues.

The prejudice against speaking in tongues appears to especially unreasonable. Not only did the 120 speak in tongues, but all the early Christian groups reported in the Book of Acts, except the group in Samaria, also spoke on tongues. The report about the Samaritan group does not say whether they spoke with tongues or not, but the fact that Simon the magician saw something so miraculous about it that he wanted to buy the gift, and that the Holy Ghost's gift and control was and is accompanied with the "speaking in tongues as the Spirit gives utterance," points to the conclusion that the Samaritans as well as Jews and Gentiles who received the Holy Ghost, spoke with tongues.

St. Paul, in the 14th chapter of I Corinthians, appears to be speaking of the gift of tongues which one may use at will rather than the full control of the Holy Ghost with the sign speaking in tongues as the spirit gives utterance. Paul himself spoke in tongues more than all the rest and told the Corinthian brethren not to forsake this speaking, but to use it with interpretation for the edification of the church. Of course, tongues as a gift, if willed by everybody in the assembly at the same time would bring confusion. But God taking entire control, and speaking Himself, longs to bring perfect order.

As I have stated before, when I sought for the Holy Ghost Baptism, I had a measure of the general popular prejudice against tongues, and told the Lord that if He could give me the Baptism without the tongues I would prefer it, but if not to give me the Baptism with the tongues. With the great visitation, control, and glory that came, the speaking and singing was in English. In this glory and control the Lord definitely came within. The Holy Ghost then took control of my lips and tongue and I began to speak, or the Spirit began to speak through me, foreign words and phrases. Since then, the speaking has been both in English and in tongues.

The tongue of Isaiah had to be cleansed and made holy by the fire from heaven, and the tongues of all of us have to be made holy, pure, and loving and be brought under control and inspiration of the Holy Ghost before we can be best used of God. While out of the heart are the issues of life, the tongue is the member of the body that has to submit to the love and control of the Holy Ghost presence and Baptism.

How to Receive

The New Testament gives many instructions as to how to receive the Holy Ghost: Hunger and thirst, ask and tarry, obey and yield. The Holy Ghost as St. Paul and St. John unite in emphasizing, is for everyone who believes in Jesus, for everyone who will receive. Some of the early Christians received the Holy Ghost by listening with faith. They heard the good news about Jesus with great joy; and wherever there is great joy in Jesus, one is being made ready to receive the Holy Ghost. The early believers at Pentecost rejoiced and tarried. People are receiving today by tarrying, and by asking for the Holy Ghost. Some of the early Christians received the Holy Ghost in connection with the baptism in the name of Jesus.

The instruction that Jesus gave on the last night to the disciples was that if they loved Him, they would keep His commandments, and that He would pray to the Father and the Father would give them the other

Comforter. This always brings the Spirit: the dedication to obey Jesus, to be led by Jesus, and to be led by the Spirit.

In my own case, I had tried everything that I knew to do and without remembering Jesus' promise in John 14: 15, I decided that whether I received anything more from Heaven or not, I was going to seek to be led by the Lord's Good Spirit, that I was going to seek to be loving, sincere, and brave. Quickly the revelation and glory commenced that led up to the descent of the power, control, and bliss from On High, and to the appearing and incoming of the Lord. The Lord not only wants to Baptize and to come within, but He has His own best way for doing it. As we seek, we find; as we open the door, He comes in; as we surrender, he takes control; if we want Him to, He will be All and in all.

How to Abide and Increase

The secret of abiding and increasing is to live in the love and joy of God and in perpetual thanksgiving. We are to behold and rejoice in the glory of the Lord, and as we do this we are changed from glory to glory into His likeness. This is to continue until we have put on the wedding garment, until we are prepared for the full manifestation of Christ, which will change us into the likeness of the body of His glory.

CHAPTER 20

Boundless Good Will"
July 13, 1930
Macon Telegraph and News

A friend writes me and asks how one can attain to the boundless good will that works good to everyone; how one can battle with enemies and if necessary rebuke and expose their darkness and yet love them? The first thing to see is that it is possible, and the next is to desire it enough to pray for it and to do the things and only the things that increase it.

Jesus not only attained to the love that desired and worked the greatest possible good, even to his worst enemies, but His disciples also attained it. Even the wise men of India, Greece, and China saw that the only way that evil is successfully overcome is by goodness. If they did not attain unto the vision, they nevertheless saw that it was possible and that it was the true way of life.

When Stephen was being stoned for his faith in Christ and for his bold testimony concerning Him, he prayed for those who did the stoning, and the scriptural account says that the heavens opened to him and he saw Jesus at the right-hand of God. As I read the New Testament, Stephen, the layman and deacon, is the first one who is reported to have reached that perfection of Christian love which makes martyrdom really for Christ's sake and wholly in the Spirit of Christ. The heart of the Christian spirit is pure love which cannot do otherwise than manifest pity and compassion and employ only the weapons of love and good will.

As impetuous as was Peter in his early discipleship, in one of the last things we have from him he counsels us when we are reviled never to revile again, but to do as Jesus did: commit ourselves to God who judges righteously. St. Paul, in one of his epistles, specifically commands us not to be overcome with evil, but to overcome evil with good. In this same epistle, the Epistle to the Romans, as well as the Epistle to the Galatians, he declares that love fulfills the law and works no ill, and that he who loves his neighbor as himself has by this love fulfilled the whole law. Love not only fulfills the law, but is the very substance of the Gospel itself. It is the fruit of the Spirit that inspires and includes all the rest. Where perfect love is, there God is, and there all of the virtues are manifested.

Perfect love is not only a gift of the Spirit, it is also an attainment. As Peter puts it in his second epistle, we are to add to our faith, knowledge; and to knowledge, virtue; and to virtue, temperance; and to temperance, godliness; and to godliness, brotherly kindliness; and to brotherly kindliness, charity, which is perfect love. When we desire perfect love enough to pray, resist the enemy, and to work for it, we find it flowing in as a gift from God, and we also find that God gives the ability to manifest as much love as we choose to.

The Method of Jesus

The instructions given by Jesus in the eighteenth chapter of Matthew and in the Sermon on the Mount are the clearest possible revelations of the way love works, and the way that we must work if we are to attain and increase in love. One of the great temptations of life is to talk about people, rather than first talking to them. To yield to this temptation invariably produces alienation and a decrease in love. But to carry out the instructions of Jesus, first go alone, and of course one must go in love with the superlative desire to help and get things right. If the one we go to hears, we have won him. If we fail to win alone, the next step is to take one or two more; if these should fail, we can take the matter to the church for the help of the whole church.

I take it that in dealing with those who are not Christians that we can carry out steps one and two, and if we have failed after taking these steps we could then carry the matter to the best moral sense of people generally. Until we go in love and go in wisdom, and follow out the steps that love requires and wisdom supports, the whole tendency is in the direction of misunderstanding and feelings that are not Christ-like.

I know no temptations more subtle than those which would cause us to excuse ourselves as being less than entirely loving in spirit and in method. The spirit must come first but the method of Jesus brings the greatest reinforcement to His Spirit. When one starts with a purpose to have His Spirit and apply His methods, then no temptation will arise where the Spirit does not put before us the right word and scripture. Those who desire right guidance will always receive it; those who desire to overcome will be given the ability to overcome. In the way to full overcoming everything works together for one's good.

CHAPTER 21

"In Him Forever"
February 8, 1931
Macon Telegraph and News

Sets Captive Free

My friend, A. P. Peterman of Reynolds, Georgia, who left the jail this morning, was so happy over being set free, not from jail, but from sin and desires of the old life, that he wants everyone to know about it and be helped by it. He told me yesterday the jail life had not been what people call a prison to him; at first it worried him, but it soon came to be a "straight-out blessing." A few days ago he said substantially this: "I came here a sinner and am going home a Christian. I came here so miserable that I wanted to end my life, I am now going away happy. I came here all run down in health and am going away well. I came here a slave to tobacco, I am going away with even the desire for it taken away." He has come to see that the true way to love everybody and help everybody the best you can is to give thanks for everything. The orphan boy of 19, who pleaded guilty to three felony charges and left jail this afternoon on parole, was so determined to have another chance to make good that he reached the hearts of enough of the right people to get the chance.

An old lawyer friend when told today of the fine spirit that Solicitor Garrett and Judge Matthews had shown in dealing with the boy said, "People are more merciful now than they have ever been before." This is true of many, and I wish it were true of all.

Going into the Kingdom to Abide

Since the Lord Baptized me with the Holy Ghost and came within me nearly 21 years ago, the most persistent urge and my own greatest conscious need have been to abide in Christ and in the Kingdom of God all the time as He abides in me. It is wonderful that He will come and abide forever in any of us who want Him enough to invite and welcome Him to come and abide and reign. It is so unwise and ungrateful for us not to prize Him enough to make it our chief concern all the time to have Him enter, increase in us, and triumph fully and for us to enter and abide perpetually in Him.

I have looked forward to the day when I would enter into Him and into the Kingdom of God deeply enough that I would never go out anymore. About a month ago the witness came that I had at least the beginnings of perfect love. For the past 21 years I have been seeking the Spirit to guide my prayers and my whole life and for God to write His laws, His will, and His nature so fully in my heart, mind, will, and nature that I would do His will even unconsciously and divinely naturally and with keen joy. It only required eight days of definite seeking for me to receive the supernatural Baptism and control of the Holy Ghost, and in the midst of this seeking, I had only to ask once for Jesus to come within.

This last seeking to enter in deeply enough never to go out again has required more time and dedication. It is strange to say that He so willingly comes with the asking and we are so slow to surrender and die to the old nature, and be born anew to Him and be ready to enter into Him and abide forever. Pray, pray, pray to be in Him in the wonder of the revelation of the Kingdom never to go out again. It is far better to be even the least in the Kingdom than to be the greatest on the outside of it.

How to Enter the Kingdom

We enter the Kingdom by desiring to enter greatly enough, by desiring the Kingdom more than anything and everything else. We enter by asking and knocking to enter. We enter by repenting, by humbling ourselves as a little child. We enter by leaving on the outside everything that keeps us on the outside—everything that will not come in with us, and everything that would keep Heaven from being Heaven. The gate is very straight and the way narrow—just straight enough and narrow enough to keep out everything that has any evil, harm, and misery in it. There is plenty of room for all that is heavenly, all that is Christ-like, all that gives rest, peace, joy, bliss, and glory in the Holy Ghost.

How to Abide In the Kingdom

1) Live in love. Nothing that is not love can abide in Christ and in the Kingdom of God.
2) Meet all evil with good.
3) Prize Christ and the Kingdom above all else. Choose to think of Him in preference to everything else. As you do this your heart and mind will be kept centered on Him, and you will be kept in His peace, rest and joy.
4) Watch and pray without ceasing. Watch the desires and the thoughts and the imaginations as well as the words and deeds. Reject every suggestion that leads out of love and kindness and peace, out of Christ and out of His Kingdom.
5) Choose not to come out, but choose to abide forever.
6) Live in perpetual thanksgiving and never complain of anything that the Lord permits to come to you.
7) Ask to go ever deeper and deeper in Jesus and in His love, peace, rest and joy.
8) Ask to be led by the Spirit in everything. Just as the Spirit convicts of sin, of righteousness, and of judgment, and leads to Christ and reveals and glorifies Him and makes us His habitation, so the Spirit also leads us into Christ and keeps us in Christ and is ever seeking to lead us deeper and deeper in Him.

There are other secrets of the Kingdom, but as we are led by the Spirit we will be guided into all of them. One who has the laws, nature, and will of God written in his inmost parts is led by the Spirit. He is brought into the place where he needs no man to teach him. When this has been achieved in all of the children of God, and it is to be achieved in all of them from the least to the greatest, the whole earth will become filled with a knowledge and love and peace and glory of the Lord.

CHAPTER 22

"Risen With Christ"
February 22, 1931
Macon Telegraph and News

About 25 years ago a glimpse given by the Spirit of the wonder and glory of being identified with the risen, living Christ Jesus, not only lifted and blessed me greatly, but was associated with two cases of marked release and healing. One of these was a friend I had been seeking to help for some time, apparently with no success at all; the other, a previously unknown person, had been healed years before, but had become ill again and had failed to receive the healing that she was looking for, and was healed while reading something I wrote on the wonder and blessedness of union or identification with the living Christ.

The friend who was released at the time the glimpse was given me that identification with Christ is just what we need, and that this identification opens the way for us to receive abundantly from Him, was at the time of the release several hundred miles from Macon. This friend was under severe and almost mentally unbalancing condemnation. I made a trip to try to help, but all I could say or do seemed to be of no avail. Shortly after my return to Macon, a letter came from the friend indicating continued and possibly deeper gloom and even more severe condemnation.

While seeking light as to what to write the friend, this came with authority and the witness of the Spirit: "The trouble with you," the Light said through me, "is that you are identifying yourself with your past sins and mistakes, your nerves and your body. Instead of this now identify yourself with Christ Jesus, with your ideal self and with the good that you can do."

We Are Like Our Identifications

It was made known that we are always like whoever or whatever we identify ourselves with, and that if we identify ourselves with Christ we become like Him and that we appropriate not only His spiritual and moral virtue, but also receive from Him His abundant life and healing. It was also made known that it is not the length of time of the identification, but the thoroughness of the identification that counts. Those who come in last may be paid off first. As one who falls in a river may get wetter in a second than one in an all-day's drizzling rain, so one who thoroughly trusts, yields, and responds to Christ may receive a great deal more in an instant of time than one who has been for a long time in an attitude of only partial trust and obedience.

For about two weeks the light continued to shine as to the wonder and transforming power of being identified with Christ, and on the second or third day after the light came, I received a letter from the friend saying that she was set free the very morning that the light was given to me. The One who gave the light that so lifted and blessed me also released and healed the friend.

He In Us And Us In Him

Some time after this I was reading the words of Jesus as reported in John 14: 15-20, where Jesus said if we love Him we will keep His commandments, He will pray the Father to give us the other Comforter, and in that day we will know that we are in Him, and He in us. While I was reading I had a spiritual experience prophesying of the Baptism of the Holy Ghost and of the incoming and indwelling of the Risen Christ. After this experience the urge of the Spirit has been to abide in Christ all the time with the same faithfulness that He took His abode and abides in me. It has also been made clear—and clearer—that one has to live and do everything in a loving spirit, willing and working good to everyone, in order to have sweet fellowship with Christ and to be conscious of being in Him and in the Kingdom of God now at hand.

During all these years there has always been a spiritual quickening and unusual blessedness every time I have thought about the wonder of being identified with the risen, living Christ. A few days ago when I was inwardly groaning for something, I asked the Holy Spirit to give me and to lead me into just what He saw as best. A day or two previous to this I had cried out to the Lord that my lack was the tender and compassionate love that He had in such marvelous perfection. The answer came, "You lack everything, but I supply where you lack." After the prayer to the Holy Spirit to give what was needed, it was made a glorious reality that through the Spirit I am identified with both the death and resurrection of Jesus. In the Spirit, I am dead with Him and risen with Him and in heavenly places with Him.

Opening of the Spiritual Eyes

Later it seemed that my spiritual eyes were opened wider and that new views were given of the heights, depths, and glories of being dead with Christ and alive in and with Him. It was made alive in a new way that Jesus is the Living Bread and that by believing Him, meditating on Him, loving Him, rejoicing in Him, obeying Him, that we eat of His flesh and drink of His blood and become consciously flesh of His flesh and bone of His bone. He means for us to live by and through Him. As we do this we are supernaturally sustained and the whole of our being, including the body, feels His marvelous presence, quickening, abundant life, and healing.

The Witness of St. Paul

St. Paul has told all this, it seems, better than anyone else, but any of us who will identify ourselves with Christ—the Christ of the Cross, the Cross of the Resurrection, the Christ who is alive forever more, and the Christ who is to be manifested in bodily glory and to change us into the likeness of this glory—may be going through the spiritual experience symbolized by water immersion baptism, and share in the same revelation and experience that St. Paul had so richly experienced.

In, But not of the World

Even to do our natural work best, we have to be in the world, but not of it. We have to be dead to lust, sin, bondage of this life and of this world and live unto God—alive unto Christ and His purity, holiness, love, and glory. Our citizenship is in Heaven when in union with the Risen Christ and when crucified to the things that crucified Him. Christ died for the lusts and sins of the world; we have to die through the cleansing, healing, and transforming power and glory that is to raise the dead and translate the living into the bodily likeness of Jesus. It's our privilege to live all the time in the abundant life of the living Christ. In union with His death and resurrection, we can be right now be in the beginning life of Jesus, in the power and glory of the Holy Ghost, and we can literally be filled with Christ. As we do this, we can be married to Him and bring forth fruit unto God. Through identification to and with the glorious hope of being manifested with Him, we can enjoy the glory and reign with Him.

CHAPTER 23

"Love to Everybody"
January 24, 1932
Macon Telegraph and News

Since the preparation of last week's article, there have been given a few days filled with such light, abundant life, and happiness that they seemed to be at least the beginnings of Heaven on earth. I have never been able to keep all the time in the witness of being in Heaven on earth, but these rare days create such a hunger that they must be leading up to the Kingdom of Heaven, as a present, abiding and increasing experience.

On Sunday morning (January 17) when I asked the Lord what work He had for me, the answer came, "Give My Love to Everybody." With this answer came a wonderful sense of the Kingdom of Heaven at hand. During the whole of Sunday and most of the time since, it has seemed easy to abide in heavenly places in Jesus Christ. In this realm, to think of anyone there comes also the revelation "The Lord Loves You," and one of the best things about it is that it makes it easy to love. In the flow of the Lord's love it seems unthinkable that we were so blind as ever to have had any other feeling towards anyone except a feeling of good will and love.

During Sunday and Sunday night, the way was opened for me tell possibly 1500 people "The Lord Loves You." I have for a long time known this, but the constant witness of the Spirit to it makes it so real that it now seems the easiest and quickest way for Heaven to come to earth is for everyone to begin to feel, think, speak, and act upon the Commandment of the Lord to give His love to all.

The Lord is here in the Spirit knocking to come in everywhere that He has not been received, and inviting everyone to enter and abide in Him. This entrance of the Lord in us and our entering and abiding in Him brings the marvelous love, joy, peace, and happiness of God which is the Kingdom of Heaven at hand.

We have to strive to enter into the Kingdom. Most humans are too large in self esteem, in so many false possessions, that they have to become very humble and glad to turn loose their enemies and false possessions, before they enter into the Way that is so narrow that nothing but the things that bring Heaven can enter and abide. You just have to leave on the outside everything that is keeping you on the outside, and humble yourself at the feet of the Blessed One. Here is the Door and the Key that unlocks it all: love.

The way is just right. It is narrow enough to keep out everything that if you carried it along would keep any place from being heaven, and it is just wide enough to admit everything that is good and blessed. The very Way keeps out all that has evil in it and admits all that leads to Heaven and that is good enough to be in Heaven.

Should be the Sole Quest

Jesus did not define the Kingdom of Heaven, but did tell what it was like. In Canon Charles H. Raven's newest book, <u>Jesus and the Gospel of Love</u>, he says, "For Him the Kingdom is indeed at hand, subordinating all else to itself. Membership in it is the chief, indeed, the sole quest for mankind, the sole condition for blessedness, the sole reason for the attainment of every blessing."

River's book contains many other things that are so excellent that one would like to pass them along. He sees that the most orthodox person is the one who has the most love, joy, and peace, and that the best interpretation of Christianity is found in the lives of its saints. He also sees that the whole childhood of the church is represented by the apostleship of St. Peter and its youth by the apostleship of St. Paul, that its maturity is best represented by the apostleship of St. John, the apostle of "light, life, and love." In Jesus perfect light and love are incarnated and made flesh.

When we see what we need and what everybody needs is this perfect light, life, and love and that union with the Lord makes this life and love not only possible, but necessary and inevitable, there is nothing left for us but to seek perfect union with Him and to be His incarnations and channels. In perfect light and love there is nothing to differ about or divide over. Here all who see the light and life are one.

No Pain in Glory of Christ

Jesus said in the world we would have tribulation, but He also said, "be of good cheer, for I have overcome the world." As Raven reminds us, there were Christians who knew so well how to live in Christ that they only had to say "I am a Christian" to be set free from their enemies—the enemies of the body as well as the soul. They knew by experience that nothing is fearful where the love of the Father is, and that there is no pain in the glory of Christ.

Better to Give than to Receive

One of the finest enlightenments of Raven's book is that everything we do or give in love and joy becomes an eternal possession. But it has to be in love and joy, and when we do an act of real charity we must not tell it in order to get glory for it. The true way is to do it in love and joy and not let the one hand know what the other is doing. When people go to giving in this manner, they will get so much joy out of it that they will have to put on the brakes rather heavily to keep from giving everything they have.

John Wesley's rule and advice "make all you can, save all you can, and give all you can" is splendid. If it had been practiced it would have prevented the Depression. It would quickly relieve it and do away with future depressions.

I am frequently asked what the times in which we live mean, and the only answer I am sure of is that it is going to be better and better in Christ and in the Kingdom of Heaven on earth, and worse and worse on the outside. The world is in its present trouble because it has put self and mammon first, instead of putting the Kingdom of God and being upright before Him and goodness, love, and brotherhood first. As soon as we turn around in repentance as did the Prodigal Son, we will be led away from the swine feeding to the Father's House.

If we could be happy away from God and God's best for us, we might stay away. But since nothing can satisfy us but God and God's best for us, we are led on to this not only by the drawings of God's love, but also His chastisements. He made it so that everything works together for our good. When we co-work with Him with gladness and joy, we are led on without being chastised.

CHAPTER 24

"Love to the Whole Creation"
February 14, 1932
Macon Telegraph and News

We have but two great needs: The entering into and abiding, increasing, and perfecting union with the living Lord, the reception, birth, Baptism, and living in the Spirit and the Kingdom of God; and the outflow from this union with the Lord of perfect love, love for brethren, love for one's enemies, and love for and to the whole of creation. Of course, there must be superlative love for the Lord Himself, but we cannot love Him without loving one another.

With the continuous and increasing urge "Give My Love to Everybody," is also the urge to "Give My Love all the time to everybody" and "Give My Love to the whole creation." The Lord not only urges us to think and speak to everyone, and to deal with everyone as one whom He greatly loves and wants us to love, but also to think and deal with every creature as an object of His love, concern, and care. Indeed, to be greatly pleasing to the Lord and to be in happiest fellowship and deepest union with Him, to be great in the Kingdom we have to be in a state of outgoing goodwill and love to everybody and to everything. To hate or to be cruel to an animal or to anything, even though it may seem inanimate, is to experience a touch of evil. The opposite is to experience Heaven. The only thing that we are allowed to hate is iniquity or evil, and we must hate this first of all in ourselves. To hate it in others before we hate it in ourselves enough to cast it away, is to miss the way.

To hate, fear, and abuse even an animal only makes it worse. The Lord of love and the spirit of love and the practice of love is the only way.

It is by loving people who are evil and unthankful, by intelligently loving even those who hate us that we ourselves are delivered from evil and enter into heavenly places in the Lord. It is also the way by which the victims of evil and hate are brought to repentance and into the true way—the way of Jesus, the way of the cross, and the way of the Holy Spirit. It is also by love and kindness that the wildest things are tamed and the fiercest things made gentle.

So long as you have in you anything unloving and unmerciful even in feeling, it is going to torment you until you resist it and overcome it. There's no heaven here or anywhere except the Heaven of perfect love. To give yourself without reserve to the Lord of love and to the life of love is to enter into this Heaven. To live a life of pure love all the time is to abide in this Heaven.

Early this morning (February 6) in a dream, I was given a terrible warning as to the subtle blinding of our eyes through cruelty and murder in the name of patriotism and war. In the dream I had in my hand a stick and was being urged to use it in a deadly way. Even in the first stupor of the dream, I felt the awfulness of it and when I approached a group of fine boys, the kind that are made fodder for war, Heavenly love for them swept through me and the stick disappeared. In love there are no weapons except those of kindness and blessedness. Love is to end all war, to bring Heaven on earth, redeem the whole creation, and to make everything friendly, innocent, and blessedly helpful.

Not only did the Lord reveal His victory of righteous and holy love, and peace to His prophets and apostles, but He is revealing it now in a special way to everyone ready to receive it. As Alfred Lord Whitehead, professor of philosophy at Harvard puts it, only the God of love, the religion of love, and the life of love is acceptable to us. We are seeing that where there is no love there is no God, no real religion, and no real life. You cannot pick up a good book that does not sound this note. It is the only note of life. People are being shown through the spirit that nothing but love is acceptable to God. Just the other day a letter came written in pencil from some obscure place in Georgia that said in prayer it had recently been revealed to the writer that the Lord called him to "abide in His Love.' The Lord said on the night he was betrayed to keep His commandments, which enables us to abide in His love. As He said twice on the last night, "This is

My commandment, that ye love one another, as I have loved you." (John 15: 12) This commandment includes and fulfills all other commandments.

Let go of everything that is not loving in thought, feeling, deed, words, and will. Begin to see everyone as one the Lord greatly loves and do your best to get everyone you can to do the same thing. In doing so, you will quickly enter and abide in heavenly places in Christ and in the Kingdom of Heaven; you will also be great in the joy and services of the Kingdom.

The most spiritual people that I meet make it known that what they need most is precisely that blessed love and charity that Jesus gives, that St. Paul so marvelously writes about in the thirteenth chapter of I Corinthians—the love that suffers long and is kind, that is always patient, that is always humble, that is always gracious, the love that never fails, the love that is only success.

This morning it was given to me to pray not only for the Lord's will to be done about everything, but also for us to have His thoughts and feelings, and almost instantly even my body felt a new infusion of life, power, and peace. He wants to fill our whole being and to bless our whole being beyond thought. We must get rid of our thoughts and get into His, out of our feelings and into His, out of our realm or kingdom into His.

Put first the Kingdom of God which is the mind, spirit, and love of the Lord Jesus. Desire this above all else, pray for this above all else, work for this above all else! As you do this, your whole being enters into abundant life, peace, joy, blessedness, and all you will need of food, clothes, shelter, and everything else necessary will be added. This is absolutely sure.

The Lord has employment for all the unemployed, with the best of wages. He has far better employment for those who believe they are already well employed. The Kingdom of Heaven is at hand. Enter! Work for it! Don't continue in fear and doubt and misery. Don't sin anymore. Give yourself to the Lord of Love, the Life of Love, and the Heaven of Love!

CHAPTER 25

"Rejoice in Me Always"
February 21, 1932
Macon Telegraph and News

Always Give Love

To the continued inspirations and urges "Give My Love to Everybody," "Give My Love All the Time to Everybody," "Give My Love to the Whole Creation," and "Always go in Love," are added the instructions to "Rejoice in Me Always," "Live in My Peace Always," "Give My Peace to All Men," and "Give My Keys to all Men."

To think of everyone and to speak and deal with everyone as being greatly loved of the Lord and to be seeking and delighting to give this love to everyone in thought, word, and act, and to be always looking to and rejoicing in the Lord, is to be lifted above the world. Though we are seemingly in the world, we are to abide in sweet blessed places in Jesus Christ and in the Kingdom of Heaven at hand. In the world there is trouble-plenty of it-and tribulations, too. But in Him there is an everlasting blessedness. All we have to do is change our residences or abiding places. As long as we live in the wrong place, in the realm of false desire, pride, and effort, in the realm scripture designates as the flesh, things will of right and wise necessity get worse and worse. If they did not, we might never be driven out of them. God leads us on to His best and also drives us out of our false positions so that we have nowhere to go but to Him and His best appointments for us.

Gregory S. Camp, Ph.D.

The Keys of the Lord

Every secret of the Lord is a key of the Lord, unlocking the doors of life and of all of the things of the Lord. The Key of keys is love. This key unlocks the Kingdom and all the doors of life. By love we enter into and abide in God, know God, and are known of God. By love we enter into joy and peace and fulfill all the laws of God and of man. When we love God and love everybody and do nothing but loving blessed things, every door opens to us. God opens to us and man also begins to open. Even the animals find it out and become unafraid and friendly. We are no longer bound by anything that fetters. We are free. We have the very essence of everything, and the beginnings of everything of God that are yet to be unfolded here and hereafter.

Another Key is Prayer

Prayer begins as desire, hunger, thirst, and longing after the things of God. God Himself being the author of this desire and thirst, its existence is the sure promise that we are to have all things of God, and even better things than we desire and are hungry for. Desire passes on into asking, and when it reaches this stage of sincere asking, we are made ready to receive. We may even receive before we ask, but we are absolutely sure to receive good things and even receive the Lord within and the Baptism of the Holy Ghost and the other very great things of God when we reach the place of asking. "Ask and you shall receive." You are absolutely sure to receive when you really ask and ask in God's will, and everything good for you and for others is in God's will. If you don't know what is God's very best, ask the Holy Spirit to take charge of your desires and to show you what to ask for.

Years ago when I was praying for the Lord to Baptize me with the Holy Ghost, I also asked Him to give me His best, whether I knew how to ask for it or not. Among other things, He led me to ask Jesus to come within. Quickly this prayer was answered in a way that I had no conception was possible. With His coming within there has been revealed the need of asking a death to everything that keeps us from keeping Him first and from abiding in Him as a perpetual and increasing experience.

A little over a year ago I asked the Holy Spirit definitely what I was to pray for at that time. The answer came, "Ask to enter into Christ and the Kingdom never to go out anymore." The next time I prayed I asked, and it was given to pray for the burning up and the death of the things that keep the heart and mind from being always centered and stayed on the Lord. The next time it was to ask for His laws, nature, spirit, and desires to be written in the depths of my heart, mind, and life so that it would be divinely natural and happy to do His will, and so that I would do it even unconsciously. Something happened in the depths of my being, and later there came the witness of everlasting union with Him.

Every ray of light, every virtue, everything of God is a key into more of God. But love, the prayer of faith, rejoicing in the Lord and thankfulness for all of the good of life, purity of heart, humility, forgiveness, the meeting of all evil with good, and happy yielding and joyous obedience to the Spirit and inspirations of the living Lord unlock the doors of life. It also locks the doors against the evil one, sin, sickness, death, iniquity and every enemy and destroyer of life.

Secrets of Loving and Rejoicing

Since God is love and Spirit, every yielding to Him and His Spirit bring us into His love, joy, and rejoicing. To desire this love, to ask for this love, and to offer ourselves to be a channel for this love is to have it in as great measure as we are willing to receive it.

Every touch of His Spirit is also a touch of His love. To be born of His Spirit is to be born of His love, joy, peace, and everything of His nature and blessedness. To be Baptized with His Spirit and to live in His Spirit is to have a baptism and life of love and of all of the things of God. If we want the God of love and the life of love, every door is open to us. Of course, we must also be willing and glad to die to all the enemies of love, and to everything that is unloving.

We first receive because of the Lord's love and grace and because of our great need, but we are to go on to a life of perfect giving as well as of receiving. We are to become like our Father in heaven and our Elder Brother, Savior and Redeemer. While we are saved because of His great love for us, we are created in Christ Jesus for a life of perfect love and good works.

Everything is working together to make us loving and perfect like our Father in Heaven. When we happily consent and rejoice to yield to God and to co-work with Him, His chastening is no longer necessary, and we can always be at a feast of fellowship and move on to the consummation of the present dispensation, which the resurrection or translation even unto the bodily likeness of Jesus.

CHAPTER 26

"All Taught of God"
February 28, 1932
Macon Telegraph and News

Love-The Best Way of All

Last Saturday afternoon (February 20) when I visited the Earl of Manchester, he told me among other things, "I have found your teaching (not mine, but the love teaching of Jesus) about the best of all. You have to conquer everything with love." Previous to this, he told me that he had tried meeting evil with good and it made him feel "mighty good." It will make anyone feel "mighty good," and the meeting of evil and meanness with evil and meanness will make anyone feel mighty mean, dirty, and miserable.

Friends widely scattered are increasing my joy by letting me know that the Lord has been putting upon them the urge to "give His love to everybody." A friend from Allentown, Pennsylvania writes that "our own release comes by giving His love to everybody." When we repent, when we let go of everything unloving, and go to thinking, feeling, doing, in the spirit of good will and boundless love, we are released from all of our enemies and come into God's kingdom of marvelous light, life, love, joy, peace, and transforming glory in the Holy Ghost.

Release and you shall be released. Refuse to love and to forgive and to release and you remain bound. Even to try and bind others binds the one who tries it. What you give, you get, "good measure, pressed down and running over." Therefore give love and forgiveness and release everywhere and to everyone, and do it all the time and you will receive it in great and increasing measure every good of God and life. You will always be baffled and defeated until you stop trying to have your own will and way that is contrary to God's perfectly good will and way. Release and success and happiness will come to you when you fall in line with God's loving will and efforts in behalf of all. There is no defeat for one who wills and seeks to do good to everyone and who refuses to do evil to anyone. If you want joy, gladness, sweet contentment and for everything you do to prosper, forgive everybody and love everybody and serve everyone you can.

In the kingdom of Heaven, in the family of God, in the brotherhood of Jesus, all are taught of the Lord and the teaching is not from the greatest to the least, but from the least to the greatest. In the fullness of the New Covenant, where the laws, nature, and Spirit of God are written in our inmost parts, and the Lord is seeking to bring all of His children to this, no one is allowed or desires to come between any soul and the Lord.

The Whole Gospel

A friend from St. Louis writes that she has been reading many good things of late, but that the clipping sent her from the *Telegraph*, giving the urge of the Lord to give His love to everybody and to the whole creation, "contains the whole Gospel." The gospel is a pure love message calling us to the love life, the love life of Jesus. God so loved and loves the world that He gave His Son and gives His Spirit and gives His all. The Spirit gives all. Our call and predestination is to receive all and to give all.

"My Holy Ghost People"

With the inspiration and urges of the Spirit, "Give My Love to Everybody," "Give My Love to the whole creation (this is the great secret)," "Give My Love all the time to everybody," and "to all of creation," there has been the special urge, "Give My Love to My Holy Ghost people."

This seems deeply significant. Since Jesus was glorified and gave the other Comforter or the Holy Ghost, the Holy Ghost birth, the Holy Ghost Baptism, the Holy Ghost life, the Holy Ghost revelation, power, glory, manifestations, and fruit have been and are for every believer and disciple of Jesus.

Jesus went away and went by the way of Gethsemane, the judgment hall, Calvary, and the tomb that all of us may be His Holy Ghost people. The same Spirit, power, and glory that raised Him from the dead to the Most Holy Place may be poured out upon us and dwell and triumph within us. It will even quicken and heal, and give abundant life to our human bodies and change us from glory to glory into His likeness.

Not to receive the Spirit, not to live in the Spirit, not to be filled with Holy Ghost power, love, comfort, revelation, glory, and victory is a tragedy of lack—of failure to have what Jesus has for us and longs to give us.

I am glad that the Spirit uses "My Holy Ghost People" and that His people are not called by any separating and denominational names. Even such precious names as Pentecostal, Church of God, Church of God in Christ, and Church of the First Born should never be used in a sectarian sense. "My people," and "My Holy Ghost People" happily include all of the disciples of Jesus who are born to the Spirit, Baptized of the Spirit, led by the Spirit, live in the Spirit, and bear the fruit of the Spirit.

Christ All in All

Of late the witness and the fruit that the Risen, Living Jesus Christ is our safe dwelling place, our Life and Life-Giver, our Health and Health-Giver, our Wisdom and Teacher, our Redemption and Redeemer, and our All-in-All are increasingly real and precious. He wants us to enter into Him and abide in Him and find in Him our safety from every danger and fear.

When we come into Jesus and abide in Him, He sets us free from both the fear and the sense of failure, lack, sickness, and death which are fundamental human fears. He makes Himself real as our every good in God. By receiving Jesus within, by entering into Him, by abiding in Him, by giving ourselves to receive fully from Him and to co-work happily with Him, all things are ours.

CHAPTER 27

"Way into the Kingdom"
April 17, 1932
Macon Telegraph and News

Frank Riale, a Ph.D. of Harvard, one of the most earnest, eloquent, and enlightened proponents of the healing ministry of Jesus today, begins a several days mission at the Vineville Methodist Church in Macon next Sunday morning, April 24. I have never met him face to face, but estimating him from his letters, his books, and the impression he makes upon those who hear him and come in personal touch with him, his visit and ministry here should mean increasing faith, deepening of spiritual life, and healing for many. His conviction is that there is no more reason for being sick than for being a sinner; Christ saves from both sin and sickness.

Jesus and Socrates

Socrates believed that knowledge is virtue, that virtue is so beautiful and vice so ugly that to know the good, really know it, is to fall in love with it, and to see in evil its ugliness and to turn away from it. But the deeper truth, as Jesus announced it, is that by being willing to do, and then doing the will of God that we come to know the truth and become free. Jesus came first of all practicing or doing the will of Him who sent Him, and He told His disciples if they continued in His word, if they did what He told them to do, they would know the truth, the truth that makes one free. As we give ourselves to doing what is right and good according to the true light that lights every life coming into the world, we find the light grows brighter and brighter until the day of perfect enlightenment when we shall know even as we are known.

It is not by study apart from practice, but by obedience and love that we attain to real knowledge, truth, and insight. One can study and study and never come to know the truth. As Jesus said in closing the Sermon on the Mount, the inaugural address of the Kingdom of God on earth, that he who came to Him and listened and did not obey was like the foolish man who built his house upon the sand, while he who comes and listens and does builds upon the Rock.

Tragedy and the Kingdom

During the past week I have read and reread, and thought much about, and been spiritually enriched by the communication in the *Christian Century* of April 6, "The Only Way to the Kingdom of God," by H. Richard Niebuhr of the Divinity School of Yale University. As I understand Niebuhr, he sees that the chastisements, tragedy, and tribulations are only the preludes to the coming of the Kingdom of God. These trying experiences are necessary because of the stubbornness and blindness of human nature. If we were ready to see and enter into the Kingdom and let it come happily, we could avoid the suffering. Children of the Kingdom may be born without travail and the Kingdom of God should come with great rejoicing. But as Niebuhr sees, come it must. Whether we shall see it or not depends on our recognition of His presence and our acceptance of the only kind of life which enables us to enter into the life of repentance and forgiveness.

This is profound yet very simple truth: that the kingdom of God, the reign of love is here, and only has to be recognized as here and entered into by repentance, forgiveness, and the love to God and love to the whole creation. Without this recognition of the presence of the Kingdom and supreme desire for it, one may think he is religious and Christian, and give himself to religious work yet live on the outside of the Kingdom and be ignorant of what it really is. To be religious and not enter into the Kingdom is a double tragedy. It is a personal and social tragedy in that it keeps others out who would enter. Even harlots and other outcasts are not so far from the Kingdom as are religious workers who have substituted anything else for the Kingdom and for a life in vital union with Christ Jesus.

As the Kingdom of God is love, righteousness, joy, peace, self-control, temperance, and goodness in the Holy Ghost and in union with the living Christ, if we are to have the Kingdom life here and now we must receive the Spirit, live in the Spirit, worship in the Spirit, and work and do everything in the Spirit. We must have the new birth, the Pentecostal seal, Baptism, power, peace, glory and love. We must increase in the Spirit and in vital union with Jesus more and more.

As we come into vital union with the Living Lord, we begin to share His victory over the world, the flesh, the devil, the grave, and everything and enter into our inheritance of joint-heirship with Jesus. In the Baptism and control of the Holy Ghost, we are baptized not only into the church which is His body, but also Baptized into Christ Himself: but after this Baptism and union everything of us unlike Him must be put off and everything of Him put on.

After vital union is established with Jesus of the resurrection and glorification, every time we think of Him and rejoice in Him, seek to be in union with Him above all else, we feel His presence within and feel ourselves in Him in increasing preciousness. All yielding to His love, kindness, holiness, meekness, and goodness makes Him and union with Him increasingly real, precious, and glorious.

It is all summed up as follows: We must desire, seek, and prize first of all the Kingdom of God and vital union with the risen, glorified, and glorious Jesus. We must bear the blessed fruit of the union in getting out all the love, healing, and helpfulness we can to everybody we can and in every way we can. We must also meet and overcome all evil and injuries with love.

So long as we meet any evil with evil it obscures or breaks vital and happy union with the Lord. When we meet all good with good and evil with good, everything in the realm of human experience is just opportunity to glorify Christ Jesus and His love way of life.

CHAPTER 28

"Living in the Kingdom"
July 17, 1932
Macon Telegraph and News

Last night, July 8, it was made clear, emphatic, and glorious, in a new way that what we need to seek and prize above all else is entrance into abiding and increasing in the Kingdom of God. In the Kingdom, in Christ, in the Holy Spirit, we have everything added—healing, health, abundant life, the best services, and all food and clothing and the best means to do good and live the best life. What shielding and guidance in the presence of God!

Years ago it was made known to me that the ministry as well as the life that we must have is to be vital, free, victorious, and pleasing to God in order to escape dryness, deadness, and being overwhelmed. It must be through being within Christ and being directed by Him. We cannot minister the things of the Kingdom outside of the Kingdom; they must be ministered from within the Kingdom. We enter by child-like humility and happy yielding, that we enter at the feet of Jesus, and the key that unlocks the Door and all doors is love. If you are on the outside, nothing is worthwhile except entering or re-entering and abiding.

The Spirit Leads Us In

As we turn to the Holy Spirit to direct our desires, thoughts, prayers and everything, He leads us to Christ, into Christ, and into the Kingdom.

As we ask Him to lead us in, never to go out anymore, He is faithful not only to lead us in, but to keep us in.

Over a year and a half ago this was brought to me with authority and witness of the Spirit. I had read something from Samuel D. Gordon that recommended when we pray, that we ask the Holy Spirit to direct our prayers. The first time that I asked Him to take charge of my desires and cause me to pray according to His Highest will, He led me to pray to enter into Jesus and into the Kingdom of God, never to go out anymore. The next time He led me to ask for the burning up of all desires, thoughts and everything in my nature that separates from perfect fellowship and union. The next time He led me to pray for the writing of His law and nature and Spirit within, so that it would be divinely natural and happy to keep the heart and mind centered on Him to do His will and to abide and increase in Him.

A little later, January 31, 1931, while I was in the courthouse waiting for the judge and solicitor to parole an orphan boy instead of sending him to the chain gang, this song and witness started and continues to this day: "He's in me and I'm in Him, forevermore, forevermore!" While I must go much deeper and abide much more gloriously, since then there has been a witness and conscious guidance and victory not known before. "Ask, and ye shall receive," and ask the Holy Spirit to direct your desires and prayers and the whole of life.

God's Wills our Perfect Good

As S.D. Gordon says in another of his books, <u>Quiet Talks On Prayer</u>, the main reason many do not turn wholeheartedly to God to do and know His will about everything is the fear that "He might put something bitter in the cup or something rough in the road." This is because God is not really known; for when we know Him aright, and Jesus Christ, whom He sent, we find Him so wise and loveable and with such a wise, loving and blessed way for us that His will is just what we would have chosen for ourselves, had we been wise and free enough to have chosen perfectly. God gives us not only just what we need, but just what we really desire. There's nothing wiser than surrendering to perfect wisdom, and nothing wiser than surrendering to perfect love. God's all this as well as our perfect

Father, Mother, Friend, Lover, Husband, Healer, Teacher and Everything. All that stands between us and Heaven on earth is perfect trusting and yielding so that He can bring us into His best use for us.

As Gordon says, "God's will for us includes body, health and strength, the family and home matters, money and business matters, friendship including the choice of life's best friends; it includes service, what service and where, and constant guidance; it includes the whole of life and the world of lives." It includes the whole of life and every detail of life.

When we turn to the Spirit to guide our prayers--and we should always be doing this--the Spirit makes clear for what we should pray. He gives witness that what we are praying for has been heard, we must believe not only that the prayer will be answered, but also believe that what we have prayed for has been given. *"Therefore I say unto you, What things soever ye desire, when ye pray, believe that ye receive them, and ye shall have them."* (Mark 11: 24) Then Gordon says "dispute every inch of ground with the enemy; and by faith and holding on in the Spirit, the enemy has to go."

When I pray, the Spirit so often says, "I give you the whole of creation," and I find by holding on to this and by claiming all things for Christ, I am always lifted into heavenly places and always have the witness of the Spirit. While we seem to need very little for ourselves, everything must be claimed for Christ. The wonder is that it is through union with Christ, everything of His also becomes ours.

Manner of Intercession

I have been interested to see the manner of intercessions that Mr. Gordon has been led to make. Here are some of them:

> "Blessed Holy Spirit, thou knowest this man (the one interceded for), and what in him is lacking. There is trouble here. Thou knowest this sick woman, and what the difficulty is there; this problem, and what the hindrance is in it. Blessed Spirit, pray in me the prayer thou art praying for this man, and this thing and that. The prayer Thou are praying I pray in Jesus' name. Thy will be done here under all circumstances."

He says often times the prayer that he is led to pray is after this manner: "Holy Spirit, be praying in me the things that the Father wants done. Father, what the Spirit within me is praying, that is my prayer in Jesus' name."

The Spirit will lead you to pray and just what to pray for, and the prayer will always be after the manner of the prayer that the Lord taught His first disciples to pray. The heart of this prayer is that the Father's will be done everywhere on earth as it is done in Heaven, and to deliver us and the whole of creation from the influence of and the yielding to the evil one. The whole creation is to be brought out of the hands of the enemy into the Kingdom of God.

Prayer is joining hands with God to bring this about. As Gordon says, while the Holy Spirit is the inlet of God's power and of Christ in our lives, that the Holy Ghost comes within us to do in us what Christ has done for us. There are these outlets for God's power: A good and holy life that radiates God and Godliness and health and everything blessed; the spoken word that enables us to speak God's word and for God to speak His words through us; all kinds of loving services and ministries; the right use of money; the prayer of communion, petition and intercession. Fine as all the others are, it is by prayer under the guidance of the Holy Spirit that we must have the most world-wide and powerful outlook for the co-working of God. The prayer of faith in God's will links us with God's omnipotence and is the earth side for the accomplishment of what God longs to accomplish.

Make Room for Prayer

As Gordon urges, since prayer is co-working with God to rout the enemy and to bring God's Kingdom, we must make room for it. We must not only pray without ceasing, but we should give at least the first half an hour of the day to offering ourselves to intercede with the Spirit and for getting the inspiration and guidance God wants to give and that we need.

The secrets of prayer are: interceding under the leading of the Spirit, according to the will of God; abiding in Christ; freely forgiving everyone from the heart and letting the love and compassion of God flow out freely to all; praying in the God-given faith that He will answer and that we have the thing we ask for; refusing to believe the testimony of the senses and the enemy if they deny the witnesses of the Spirit and witness of faith, and holding on to God's promises and God's revelation, until the claims of the enemy disappear; and asking in His name. There is a wonder in His name that those who do not pray in the name of Jesus know nothing about. It is all Christ and through Christ and therefore all in His name. To miss this is to miss everything.

CHAPTER 29

"Happy Days in the Kingdom"
October 4, 1932
Macon Telegraph and News

These are very happy days for me and get happier as I and others enjoy the Kingdom of God, the life of the Spirit, vital union with Jesus, and the good fruit and activities of this union. It will always be better and better in this union and worse and worse outside of it.

When I travel and keep these first things first, life is so happy and blessed that it seems that it might be best of all to travel and carry the good news everywhere possible; and when I am here in Macon it seems so good to be here that it doesn't seem that it would be quite so well anywhere else. After all, the Kingdom of Heaven at hand is not a fact of geography, but the life and fruit of the Spirit. In the consummation the Kingdom will be both the most blessed state and the most blessed place. Now it is the most blessed state under existing conditions, preparing the way for both the most perfect state and the most perfect place of all.

Can't Afford to Die

I heard something this summer at the conference of ministers at Mars Hill College near Asheville, North Carolina that I should have shared at once. A brave young fellow, who in the midst of unusual difficulties and handicaps, worked his way through Mars Hill College, and had a pastorate or two near Asheville. A member in one of those circles was almost dead with dropsy (edema). The man so afflicted said to his young pastor, "Pastor, you must get busy. I can't afford to die. I have too much to live for. I have a wife and children who need me and there's so much good to be done." The pastor went on to say that this man commenced getting better at once and soon got entirely well. One of the Asheville pastors present who knew the man confirmed the truth of the testimony.

This case reminds me of one of the early experiences of Mrs. A. Scott of Lakeside, Macon, who was then Miss Minnie Davis. When she was a very young woman, her brother Henry died leaving his widow with five children: Mack, Ethel, Carro, Susie, and Henry. The mother in turn became so sick unto death and was disturbed in her mind as to what would become of her children. She not only wanted them well educated, but also wanted them to be kept together. Mrs. Scott and her sister told the mother that they would take care of the children and do their best for them. Later, the sister, Miss Carro Davis, became ill and died. A little later, Mrs. Scott was stricken with the same disease that had so quickly taken the lives of her brother, his wife, and her sister. She ran a high temperature and became too weak to even raise her hands and arms. But she held fast to her promise that she would keep the children together and educate them. Against the advice of her doctor and friends, she kept one of the children in her room to remind her that she must live and carry out her promise. Her love for the children was greater than the disease.

The God of love, life, and health lifted her up to health, and she did wonderfully by the children. How could God have been God and not lifted her up? He will lift you up when you dedicate to live for Him by living to do your best by His children. Love and faith, faith that works by love, and love that produces true faith, are stronger than disease and death and all other obstacles and hindrances to life.

No matter how sick you are, or how hopeless your situation may appear, don't despair; don't give up, but dedicate yourself to the God of love and life. Enough dedication and enough of His love and faith will bring you in touch with His abundant life and health and healing that you will be given sufficient health to do all the fine things He sent you here to do. As Emerson says in effect, "A man's work is his life preserver." This is especially true when our will and work is to do the will and work of Him who sent us here; He is ever ready to help us to the utmost to do the fullness of His will and work.

When Zion cares greatly enough really to intercede, dedicate and travail, she brings forth. And the day comes-and is here-when she can be so happy to yield and to obey that she will bring forth even before she travails.

Need of Sincerity

When one really and wholly turns to the Lord for guidance and to get out of his sins, errors, and even out of his dryness, deadness, and barrenness, and to get in His will and Kingdom, the fetters that have bound break. The door then opens, and he enters into the Kingdom, into abundant life, joy, peace, and services in the Holy Ghost. Timid and conventional conformity even to good religious conventions is death. There is only life in the Quest—in the Quest to be as perfect as He is perfect, loving, clean, holy, and victorious over every enemy even as He is loving, holy, and victorious. Don't settle down anywhere, even in a good state. If you settle down in it, it won't stay good unless we keep in the Quest for the perfect.

Don't binder your growth or the growth of others. Do not lead by trying to boss them or dominate them. Lead them by goodness and by being a light and the greatest possible help to all. The only way one you can lead in the right way is by becoming the most humble, kindest, holiest, and best servant and example to the rest. This is true leadership, and the only kind that won't hurt both you and those whom you attempt to lead. It is terrible for the blind to lead the blind. They not only get in the ditch together, but the leaders get in first and get the worst place in the ditch-at the bottom. Anyone who is not seeking to get under the immediate leadership, guidance, control and transformation of the Perfect One, and is trying to lead on the basis of his present imperfections, is blind to a degree greater than he realizes.

All Taught of the Lord

All of God's children, from the very least to the very greatest are to be taught and led by Him. Until every member of His body is directly connected with Him as his or her Head, Teacher, Guide, and Everything, there is paralysis in the spiritual body. It is the same as if the hand or foot or any other member of the natural body that does not respond to its head (intelligence and will), but has to be moved mechanically, is diseased or paralyzed.

I am impressed every time I meet members of the First Century Christian Fellowship (Oxford Group) of people who are reading, rejoicing in, and appropriate their teaching, particularly those who practice surrender and are actively seeking guidance, as well as confessing their sins and errors, and seeking Jesus and His transforming spirit and power. Their splendid and vital method of entering into and maintaining their spiritual life on the plane of the faith and experience they have attained is admirable.

I told the good medical doctor who heads the Asheville, North Carolina Fellowship group, that they seemed to have the best method and that the Pentecostal people the richest and deepest order of first-hand spiritual experience. He replied, "Then we need their experience and they need our method."

Why is this method so excellent? Because they not only offer themselves in the beginning to be taught and led of the Lord and begin to confess the barrenness of their lives as well as the sinfulness prior to this offering of themselves to Him, but they keep it up as a daily practice. It is in only by keeping up the surrender and the confession, and by looking for continuous guidance that comes from looking to the Lord and trusting Him, that one can continue in the freshness and increase in the vitality of the experience with which they start.

They have an excellent method of going alone the first thing every morning to find out the most important things the Lord would have them do that day. They are also given to the confessing of their faults one to another. No one can get his faults anymore than his sins behind him, except as he confesses them and does his best to forsake them. As (William) James of Harvard used to say, it takes the fresh and open air of confession for anyone to get free from rottenness.

There must first be the deepest experience of repentance, surrender, dedication, and divine birth from above, the Baptism of the Holy Spirit, and the entering into vital union with Jesus. The people whom we call Pentecostal, if they are really Pentecostal, seek for and surrender and receive these experiences. Their need is to go on to perfection, to live continually in the Spirit, to bear the fruit of the Spirit, and go on to the full overcoming that is wholeness, holiness, and inward perfection. This will make them ready for the Lord to be manifest to them in His glory, and for them to be manifested with Him in the likeness of the body of His glorification.

CHAPTER 30

"His Great Love"
January 8, 1933
Macon Telegraph and News

Love is Key

When I asked this morning what I should write about, the answer came, "Write about My great love, My great love, My great love." About fourteen months ago the urge came to give His love to everybody and the whole creation and to give this love all the time. It was many years earlier that it was made known that the secret of abiding in Him was going in love and keeping in His Spirit of love.

He is love and loves to the utmost limits of love. He gave and gives all in perfect love. He, the King of Kings and Lord of Lords and the richest of the rich, became the poorest of the poor that He might make us eternally rich. He loved us, even while we were His enemies, so greatly that He gave Himself in death as well as in life in our behalf. Because He is perfect love, His love goes out to all and especially to those who need it most. But it is also as we yield to His love and become channels of His love and go to loving one another as He loves us, that we even begin to become aware of how great His love is.

Only he that loves knows God and is known in the high sense of knowledge, for God is love. Only those in the realm of love, or in the Kingdom of love, really know God and are known of God. Only he that loves is alive: he that loves not is dead, and he that hates is a murderer. The hater is so murderous that his every touch is death. Love is life; hate is death. Love is health, joy, peace, and everything blessed; hate is everything that hurts, blights, and kills.

The very essence of love consists of good will and a desire to help and bless and never to injure. Love works no ill to anyone, but it is always desiring, planning, and willing every possible good. After all, love is the fulfillment of the law. What God grants us is to open ourselves to receive Him, and the immeasurable gifts and blessings of His love and to become channels for the outflow of His love and blessings to all. This receiving from Him and this giving through Him is life.

Happy All the Time

People ask me why they are not happy all the time and why they have so many defeats and disappointments. It is because of closing the channel of receiving and giving. The person in union with the Lord and rejoicing in the Lord, and he who is outflowing always in the Lord's love and kindness is in a state of victory and is going on to greater victory. There is no defeat except in separation from the Lord and in failure to love and to bless. Union with the Lord makes loving and giving divinely natural, and loving and sharing in the Spirit of the Lord keeps and increases union with the Lord.

The Two Laws

St. Paul, who knew so well the tragic failure of life so long as he was a natural man, trying to keep the law, came to know such glorious liberty by becoming a new spiritual man in Christ, wonderfully voices the contrast of the two states (Romans 7 and 8). The holy new law laid upon him requirements which could only be fulfilled by the spiritual man, the man guided and possessed by the Spirit. Only those who are led by the Spirit are in the outflow of God's love, and it is only through love that the law is fulfilled. Love being the gift of the Spirit becomes easy when we yield to the Spirit and become spiritual. To the natural and carnal man this love seems impossible. But when one yields to the Spirit and becomes a channel of heavenly love, he ceases to be a natural and carnal man and becomes a supernatural and spiritual man.

One is a wretched man so long as one part of him wants to obey God and the other part is given over to appetites, lusts, and selfishness. Deliverance comes, as Saint Paul says, through union with Christ. Through this union one comes under the new law of love, the law of the spirit of life in Christ Jesus, and is set free from the law of sin and death. As one lives according to this new law, that is, lives in the Spirit and bears the fruit of the Spirit, even the body is brought in the quickening and transforming glory that raised Jesus Christ from among the dead. The body is not made for lust and appetite, but to be the temple of the Holy Ghost. When the mind and heart are stayed on the Lord and when we are in Him and He is in us, outflowing in joy, peace, and goodness, the whole being is in heavenly places with Christ.

Law Written Within

As far as I am from perfection that is for us all in Jesus Christ, for a year and eleven months I have had the witness of everlasting union with Him. It came about through His loving urges: to be in Him all the time and always to go in love and to do everything in the spirit of love. When I turned to the Holy Spirit to direct my prayers, I was definitely led to pray as follows: to enter into Him and to abide in Him perpetually, never to come out of Him again; to have burnt up in me everything that keeps the heart and mind from being centered on Him and that always keeps us in Him and union with Him first, and to have His nature and laws and spirit written in the depths of my being so that I would do His will by divine inspiration and impulse without conscious struggle or opposition.

Since then, when temptations come there is the conscious desire to keep in union with Him and the prayer to be kept from yielding to temptation. When we prize abiding and fellowship with Him and pleasing Him above the things that bring separation, nothing will be able to separate us from the witness of His love, care, and keeping power. As the Spirit and experience are always teaching, since He is love, in order to keep in the wonder of His love we must be loving, and loving all the time to everyone.

CHAPTER 31

"Creative Love"
January 22, 1933
Macon Telegraph and News

This is being dictated Monday evening, January 16. When I went by to see a local friend a few hours ago, he was on his front porch and said he felt like he imagined one felt who had been raised from the dead. The spirit and glory that raised Jesus from the dead is to resurrect the dead and translate the living, as yielding quickens the mortal body and works miracles.

When I sought to know what I should write about, this came: "Write about my creative love; I make all things new."

As great as God's love and wisdom are revealed in the creation and care of the natural world and natural man, His exceeding great love is seen in redemption and in making all things new and Christ-like. It is by Christ Jesus, the manifestation of God as perfect love, that all things are made as well as redeemed and brought to glory and to immortality. But the wonder of God in Christ as perfect love is not seen except as we yield to His spirit and are brought into union with Christ and become new, loving, glad, and free.

As the natural child had to respond to its parents' love and become loving before it can know their love, so we have to yield to God's love and become loving before we can know Him as He is; as pure, perfect, limitless love and goodness, in whom there is no evil, no hate, and no darkness at all. Only pure goodness and love can walk with and know the real God.

The Fall was and is desiring and choosing a mixture of evil with good. Paradise here or anywhere is pure good without any mixture or knowledge or experience of evil. You cannot eat of the knowledge or the experience of both evil and good and stay in paradise. As long as one is willing to work any evil or harm to anyone, he is out of paradise.

There is no happy deliverance or heaven on earth anywhere until we cease to will even the least evil to anyone. You can't stay glad, happy, free, and in abundant life and in great fellowship with the Lord except in the great refusal—the refusal to be a channel for any evil or harm—and in the great choice—the choice to will and work good and only all possible good to all, to the seemingly bad as well as to the good.

How Love Works

Part of my work is among prisoners and amongst the sick. Just before receiving the Holy Ghost gift and Baptism, and the Lord Jesus came within, it was made known to me that the ultimate and true judgment of life is in terms of obedience or disobedience to the Lord's spirit of love, and not in what seems to be the miraculous and mighty works. It was made clear that men have the gift of love and only pass on the other side because of selfishness and preoccupation. The Priest and the Levite passed on the other side because they were too busy with less important things. It is only as we give ourselves to the most important and the all-important that we are free from this terrible pull of the less important.

The people who are in the greatest need are usually the easiest to help. Great healings come when everything but the Lord has failed. The great deliverances from sin come when the prodigals get to the end of themselves. The men in prison who are most open to kindness and to the Lord are also under the death sentence. All of them are open to kindness, and most of them gladly hear about the love of Christ. The ones who do not come into the great joy of the great salvation are those who either refuse to forgive and love those responsible for their plight, or who are seeking to save their lives by falsehood. When one is willing to forgive all and confess all and turns to the Lord, his release, joy, consciousness of forgiveness and eternal life are sure.

Gregory S. Camp, Ph.D.

Could Come Without Travail

As experience as well as the Scriptures and Spirit make known, people could receive the Lord and enter into the Kingdom of Heaven without much suffering, travail, and tribulation. But it is cause for comfort and thanksgiving that if men resist the spirit of love and the practice of brotherhood, that the very tribulations they bring upon themselves are used to make them more ready to come to themselves and the Lord's way of love. Yet how blessed it would be if society could see and heed and let the Kingdom of Love, brotherhood, and plenty come quickly and come happily.

What wisdom it would be to seek first the Kingdom of God and enter into vital union with Jesus and give ourselves to the finest uses and services. What folly not to do so. But whether we receive the Kingdom without resistance and in great joy, or whether we are forced to come to ourselves and enter the kingdom by great want and tribulation, His Kingdom must come; and when it comes it will be so glorious that all the redeemed will consider as nothing all that they suffered to help bring it.

CHAPTER 32

"Limitless Love For All"
March 5, 1933
Macon Telegraph and News

This is being dictated here in Macon on Friday morning, March 3. As much as I have delighted in the wonderful warmth and luxurious beauty of Florida, and as loveable as are the finest people who live there, it is good to be back in the life and work here that the goodness of God and the friendliness of people have provided for me.

Reasons for Traveling

But as keenly as I enjoy the beauties of God in nature, and the achievements of God in what man too often calls his own achievements, the real reason for all this travelling and incidental sight-seeing is the urge of the Spirit to make known as widely as possible:

1) That Jesus is the most alive and real Being and Person in the universe; that He desires to make Himself everything to everyone.
2) That He longs to baptize every believer with the Holy Ghost and with Heavenly love, fire, power, and glory.
3) That He knocks to come and to reign within and invites us to knock, enter, and abide within Him and the Kingdom of Heaven on earth.

4) That He calls us to go about witnessing for Him and His great love for all.
5) That He wants and enables us to live in His Holy Spirit and holy love all the time and to overcome all evil with good.
6) That it is better and better in union with Christ Jesus and worse and worse outside of this union. Experience as well as the Spirit teaches this.
7) That we have reached the place in history where only the Christ way of love, brotherhood, and cooperation will work.

Until we enter into union with Jesus, until we live in the Spirit and bear the fruit of the Spirit and meet and overcome all evil with good, we are not in the victory, joy, and wonder of abundant and glorious life that He has provided through union with Him.

Opening Doors

I find that people that we call secular (even professional and business men) are at heart far more deeply interested in the Good News from Heaven than in so much seemingly bad news that is happening on the earth. While in Valdosta Wednesday as guests of the Rotary Club there (through the friendly generosity of J.B. Copeland, a leading south Georgia attorney), my old university friend, Henry L. Schoolcraft of Chicago, and myself, noted with particular joy that these men listened to me with far keener interest and brighter faces when I talked to them about the things that the Lord of Life has taught me direct from Heaven and through experience, than to the part of the talk which dealt with the unusual opportunity and danger of the present world situation. No matter how we may seem to deny and resist it, God has made us for Himself and for union with His dear and perfect Son, Jesus Christ, and for heirship and joint services of love with Him.

CHAPTER 33

"The Quest for the Best Life"
(Substance of an address given at Mercer University Chapel, April 28, 1933)
April 30, 1933
Macon Telegraph and News

After spending a little over six very happy years here as a student-teacher, I left Mercer in a love feast of good understanding and fine friendship to seek and find out how far spiritual and mental resources were available for the quickening and healing of the body, as well as for the redemption and transformation of the inner life. The college was good to me in every way: the trustees allowed me to continue my work at the University of Chicago, where I held a fellowship, and also granted me leaves of absence to go to Harvard and to Europe. Every time I asked, they let me go about the first of April.

When I felt that the application of the Golden Rule to them and the needs of my own soul for ideal freedom of quest, even in fields that were regarded as unorthodox, it called for me to put the whole situation before them and to resign. They offered me not only surprising freedom, if I would continue my work, but were ready to offer, it seemed, to keep my chair open until I had time to decide whether or not I would conscientiously return to the college. But as I told them, under all circumstances, the highest thing was for me to resign and for them to accept my resignation.

Years afterwards, when the Spirit had begun to speak through me in foreign tongues as well as in English, I remembered and gave thanks for the sweet way that God had led me. In leaving the Mercer friends and other groups that I had had such worthwhile and happy associations with, I left them in such fine fellowship that the speaking through me said time and time again, "Rata Rara," which interpreted means "a rare portion." The way of utter frankness and good will and love is the rare happy way, the "rare portion."

Authority of the Spirit

Even as a boy it began to become clear to me that the only worthwhile life is in terms of boundless good will and love, that we never win anything except as we win in love, that love has been the one thing that has survived and that causes everything else to survive. As Sidney Lanier puts it so well, "When life's all love, 'tis love; all else is naught." We only live as we love. We murder when we hate, and we are dead when we are not actively loving. Love will someday make a paradise of this old world, and turn every human hell into a heaven. When all else fails, love is just getting ready to win.

The next unfoldment of the Spirit that has increased with the years is that the Good Spirit is our Authority, Teacher, and Guide, Jesus, in going away sent this Good Spirit or the Holy Ghost in great power and authority, and that is in and through His Spirit that He continues and increases His beneficent ministry. When this light broke upon me I was studying a present-day movement that seeks to overcome earthly disharmonies with the divine harmony, life, and love, but that was under a strong visible authority. But never after this precious light of the continuous leadership of Jesus could I call anyone on earth in a religious sense "leader, rabbi, reverend, or doctor." The only true greatness is in being "servant" or "friend" of God and men.

I found whenever there was a marked healing, it came through the Holy Spirit and not through any "argument" or "treatment" that I made in favor of the allness and goodness of God, though it is splendid always to remember His allness and goodness and to drive back the fears and the doubts that seek to deny this. The Lord Himself, the Holy Spirit, and all the fruit and qualities of Spirit heal the whole man.

The Spirit in Control

The next step of the quest brought me to the hope and to the experience that we have the Holy Spirit to the degree of our receptivity and response. The Spirit is even to be given in greater power at the culmination that it was given in the beginning. The greatest Pentecost is ahead instead of behind us.

While I was seeking for the truth about the Baptism of the Holy Spirit, and after the Spirit was working in power upon my whole being, it was made clear in the most precious and authoritative way, that Jesus lived right and taught right and the Good Spirit calls us to live as He lived. The great need is to have Him within as the source, power, and the ability to live as the Spirit calls us to live. I then prayed, "Jesus, if it is possible, come and live within me, and be the life and good principle of your own good life and example that I have found to be true." A little after this I was led to stop seeking and to go to practicing, to go to the prisons, and to sick rooms and to other places of extreme need, not with a responsibility to heal and to emancipate, but to love and bless. I said that night I will go out and tell people that all that I am certain of is that Jesus lived right and taught right, and that the Good Spirit is leading us to go in the way of His sincerity, courage, good will, and love.

But before morning, everything I had ever thought about or could think about was cleared up in a way that produced entire satisfaction and happiness. Revelation after revelation came, and finally heaven seemed to come down and I was brought under the control of the Holy Spirit. I'd asked previous to this time to know the truth about the Blood of Jesus and other deep things I did not understand.

While under the control of the Holy Spirit, heavenly singing seemed to light upon my tongue rather than to come up from within me:

> "Jesus, Jesus, How I love Thee,
> Interposed His Precious Blood"

In and by the wonderful power and glory that took possession of me, I was put, as it were, upon the Cross, and while on the Cross of bliss and glory, Jesus made Himself more real and precious than any other being or person. He breathed Himself within me. I fell on my face as though dead, but as one in heaven on earth that there is no way of describing to those outside of it.

But soon afterwards I came to the wilderness of temptation, something like He was lead into after this descent of the Holy Spirit upon Him. To my shame and His glory, I did not always say or do as He did, but He remained within and remains. Though we are not faithful, He is.

In all of His wonderful and precious dealings with me from then until now, He has been seeking to bring me to the place where I would abide in Him as He abides in me, and where I would be a channel for the outflow and the proclamation of His marvelous love.

The Secret Keys

The secret or keys for entering and abiding in Him and in the Kingdom of Heaven on earth as He had made them known over and over again are:

1) Leave on the outside (repent of) everything that's keeping you on the outside and enter at His feet. You only have to leave on the outside that which is unloving and harmful to you and to others, only that which keeps life from being pure, kind, blessed, holy and heavenly, only that which keeps the outside from being heavenly.
2) If you are so unfortunate after entering into Jesus and entering into the Kingdom of Heaven ever to get out of the experience and witness of this wonderful place (I did it, again and again, but never did He withdraw from abiding within me), repent quickly, ask and knock and obey to get back in. He never refuses.
3) Choose to keep Jesus and the Kingdom of Heaven and the abiding in Him and in the Kingdom first. This will break the power of any temptation.
4) Refuse to do anything but to love and to bless and to announce His love for all.
5) Meet all evil with good and all persecutions with thanksgiving and blessings upon the persecutors.

6) Ask to be wholly sanctified and preserved blameless and whole in spirit, soul, mind, and body unto the whole revelation of Jesus in glory, which if you are ready, will also be your own rapture into the likeness of the body of His glorification. Entire sanctification will bring entire health and wholeness and everything we need.

7) Turn to the Holy Spirit to direct and redeem your desires, thoughts, prayers, and everything, to burn up or to take out all that keeps the heart and mind from being staid on Him.

8) Ask for the fullness of the New Covenant relationship with Jesus and with God, that is, for His laws, nature, desires, will and spirit to be written within the depths of the whole being. It was this prayer, inspired by the Holy Spirit, that seemed to have been the key to the last opened door to me when the witness came of everlasting union with Him. Just as the natural man, as well as animal and plants, by being born of their "parents" and associating with them, grow up into their likeness without conscious effort, so do we, as we are born of His love, Spirit, and likeness. Here it is just as natural to do His will of love and good-will as it is for those born of and deeply under the influence of the old Adam, and to do his will.

9) The life in Jesus Christ, in the Kingdom of Heaven on earth, is free from all responsibility except the responsibility of being in union with Him, and being led by Him and of bearing the fruit of the union.

Same Questions Answered

The Holy Spirit reveals Jesus as God manifested on the plane of our human need. He is God with us. The fact side of orthodoxy seems essentially true, its lack is the Spirit. Liberalism has missed the deeper fact-truth concerning the Christ in His glory and majesty and Deity, but often seems to have a little more meekness and a better spirit than much of what we call orthodoxy. Both need the Holy Spirit; the Spirit will reveal Jesus and the facts of the spiritual world. God seems just as willing to save a liberal as He is to save an unsaved orthodox person. Nobody is fully saved apart from union with Christ and a life lived in His spirit and love and overcoming power.

CHAPTER 34

"Present and Coming Kingdom"
May 7, 1933
Macon Telegraph and News

For four hours last Monday, I heard a group of Baptist ministers, representing eleven or twelve associations, discuss and pray for the Kingdom of God—the blessed presence, government, and peace of God in Jesus Christ and in the Holy Spirit.

As it was said in the Baptist ministers' conference, the reason the world is in the fix that it is today is because the King and Kingdom of God have not been put and kept first. When they are put first there will be no spiritual, moral and economic slumps, and Depressions, and no lack of anything for the spirit, soul, and body. Seek first the very best and highest and you get everything. Seek less than God's best for you and you lost everything.

The Lord has not only work for all, but the best possible work with the best possible pay. The sure pay of the Lord is all necessary things for the body and this life, and everlasting life and treasures and blessedness beyond all we can ask or think. In these kingdoms of selfish competition, the seekers after work are many and the jobs are few. In the Kingdom of God of Christ and the Good Samaritan, the laborers are few and the harvest is white calling for a multitude of laborers. Those who answer His call and go to work in and for His Kingdom now, which is late in the day, get the same wages as those who entered early and have borne the heat of the day. They without us could not be made perfect, and being made perfect in the likeness of Jesus even bodily are the wages received at the close of the present day.

How to Enter the Kingdom

As the Spirit is always seeking to make simpler and more appealing, we enter the Kingdom of God and of Jesus (the Kingdom of Heaven on Earth) by repenting and becoming as little children, leaving on the outside all that is keeping us on the outside, and entering at the feet of Jesus. The key that unlocks the door and all doors is love. We abide and increase in the Kingdom as we abide and increase in love, in Love for Him, in Love for His Kingdom, and in Love for one another. As we choose Him and His Kingdom first, and meet all evil with good, and every temptation to get the mind off Him by choosing to think of Him, we are not only kept in Him, but increase in union and fellowship with Him.

Christ has always been in the world, as the True Light that lighteth every man coming into the world. But when He came in the flesh, as the God-Man and Man-God, the Kingdom and the works of the Kingdom were manifested in a manner the like of which had never been seen before.

During the present dispensation of the Holy Spirit, when it is our urgent call and greatest need to receive the Holy Spirit in Pentecostal power and gifts, and to welcome Jesus within and to enter and abide in Him, it is His will to work and bless in and through us as the Father did in and through Him. The great lack and weakness of most of the ministry and of the church of today is due to the fact that they have not asked, obeyed, and received the Pentecostal and apostolic Baptism and gifts and Holy Spirit, and entered into vital union with Jesus Himself. Without Him and His Spirit and gifts in mighty power, without vital and fruit-bearing union with Him, the church will be more interested in the world and the ministers less and less influential in the church and in society.

The Great Needs and Urges

Therefore the great needs and urges are to repent and believe Jesus and the Gospel, and to receive the Holy Spirit and to welcome Jesus within. We must enter and abide in Jesus and the Kingdom of Heaven and to bear the fruit of the Spirit, and look, pray and fully prepare for His coming in full victory and visible dominion and glory.

Do not oppose or think impossible any coming work or victory of Jesus. Welcome His coming in you, in society, in all the kingdoms of the world, and in the cosmos as the heavenly spirit and leaven. Welcome Him also as the Person of persons, as the King of kings, as the Lord of lords. Welcome Him in every way. He can and will come and work in you, in the church, in the world, and in creation.

He is to appear without when He was made us enough like Him within so that we can stand to see Him as He is, and the seeing Him as He is will mean nothing less than the resurrection of the righteous dead and the translation of the prepared living. He loves us so well that He must have us with Him in His own likeness on the throne of God and of the Universe. But as we yield and respond to His love, we too come to such love for Him that we must see Him as He is and be with Him in every way that the redeemed can be with the Redeemer, friend with Friend, and bride with Bridegroom.

Yes, the coming of Jesus in visible glory with our appearing with Him and being like Him on the highest plane and manifestation of life, bliss, and glory is the necessity of His love for us and our love for Him. It is to be, not only because of its promise in the Scriptures, but because it is promised by His love for us and by our love, longing, and need for Him.

He who came in our likeness, who is now present in the Spirit, as the glorified Elder Brother, Friend, and Bridegroom will also come literally and visibly, and change and everlastingly keep us with Him in His likeness. This has to be so that we can be one with Him in His glory as He was one with us in our weakness and humiliation.

CHAPTER 35

"On the Universe's Throne"
May 21, 1933
Macon Telegraph and News"

About a year ago I heard Professor Edwin M. Poteat of Mercer College, a very able man of keen insight and vigorous statement, quote an English writer to the effect that the riddle of the New Testament is that a young carpenter, wiping the sweat off His brow on a hot July day in a shop in Nazareth, is five years later on the throne of the universe. Professor Poteat's new vital book <u>The Scandal of the Cross</u>, published by Harper and Brothers of New York, is the best answer to this riddle I know of in recent literature.

The other night while I was reading the autobiography of Albert Schweitzer, entitled <u>Out of My Mind and Thought</u>, I decided to take enough time from this rare book to read the introduction and to catch the flavor of Friend Poteat's <u>Scandal of the Cross</u>, and then go with Schweitzer's great book. But I found Poteat's studies concerning the death of Jesus so tremendously worthwhile that I read on that night and the next morning until I had finished them.

Poteat's book rings true to the teaching of the New Testament and of the Spirit. He sees clearly that the deepest truth and greatest power in the universe is centered in the Cross. It is only superlative innocence and goodness incarnated and offered and raised up that have the key to The Book of Life; it is only Love incarnated and going to the uttermost limits and possibilities of love that could ascend to the kingship of our hearts and of the universe.

Years ago when I asked for the truth about the blood of Jesus, the answer came: that He interposed His Precious Blood, that He gave everything, that He went to the fullest limit and possibilities of love. God raised Him from the dead and gave Him all power in Heaven and earth, that through the gift of the Holy Spirit and through receiving the risen Jesus within, by entering into a vital union with Him, we not only receive remission from sin and freedom from our enemies, but we enter into heavenly places in Jesus. Through spiritual marriage with Him we begin to experience everything of His. He who was immortal and had all things emptied Himself in our behalf, tasting death and going to the depths for us that we may put on His immortality and have everything of His, so that we might go to the heights with Him.

Jesus made known to me that when we surrender all and enter into union with Him, we go on the Cross of His glory, where He breathes Himself within us. He went on the Cross of greatest shame and suffering and gave up the Holy Breath or Holy Ghost. He, the totally holy and loving One did this. We who were so unholy and unloving, by believing in Him and yielding to Him, go on His Cross of Glory and receive on this Cross the Divine Breath, the Holy Ghost that He gave and we receive.

It is much more than a legal atonement that He has made for us. It is biological in the deepest and most glorious sense. Through union with Him we are not only set free from our sins and our sinful nature and from all our enemies, but we are adopted into Divine Sonship and enter into joint-heirship with Jesus. Through union with Him we are set free from everything that has separated us from God and are brought back to God as sons. In this restored sonship we have everything.

The One Life

As I have had opportunities, I have told those who believe in Spiritualism that for anyone who believes it is possible to communicate with those who are on the other side, it ought to be easy for them to believe Jesus has the power and the willingness to reveal Himself and to communicate with everyone who will be open to Him. I have also told Spiritualists that since even here in this world none of us are good enough and wise enough to make it without Jesus, how much more the need of Him and His Holy Spirit as guide and shield in the spiritual world.

It is continually being made more emphatic that the highest will of God is for His Kingdom to come and for His will to be done here. As blessed as it is to go to Heaven (and how thankful we should be for the millions who have gone there!), the consummation is for heaven to come here. Heaven is far more anxious to come here than we are to go to Heaven. As blessed as it is to have the soul saved even if we have to lose the body and withdraw from the privilege of living and serving here, it will be far more blessed when we yield sufficiently to Christ for Him to be King and All in all on earth as in Heaven. Those of us who have the first fruits of the Spirit are groaning for the restoration of our bodies, and the creation is also travailing in the awaiting our full redemption, that it may also be redeemed and come into the glorious release of the redeemed sons of God.

The work of Jesus is cosmic as well as personal and social. If we were to in Heaven the great thing ahead now would be to get our resurrected bodies in the likeness of His body and come back here with Him to make this life and this world in the nature and likeness of Jesus. All things are only His by creation and redemption, but are to be His in every sense of actuality.

The Opening of the Spiritual Eyes

But it has been permitted to some blessed people, whether in the body or out of the body (it is not always known), to be caught up into Paradise and get a view of the realm where the Lord's will is done. During the past week, I have heard Friend Bud Robinson, who is very rare, radiant, and heavenly in spirit, tell of the day he spent in Heaven. The essential proof that he has been to Heaven is the fact that he brought so much of Heaven back with him. Heaven, as he reports, is so much like the Heaven that St. John saw that one recognizes it as such. Not only are the Lord and the redeemed there, but the very things that keep earth from being Heaven are not there. There is no sin, no sorrow, no pain, and no death. Bud Robinson says he did not see a single glass eye or crooked leg or any defect of body, soul, or spirit there. These things will not be here when His will is fully done.

Recently I have read two remarkable books reporting what has been seen in visions of the spiritual world. One of these books is <u>The Visions of Sadhu Sundar Singh</u>, the man who seems to have had more of Apostolic miracles in his life and ministry than any other man I know in recent times, and the other book is <u>Itra Muros</u> by Rebecca R. Springer.

Life is One and Deathless

The great truth of these visions is that nobody really dies and that nothing dies. There is a change of environment, but there is no death. As one leaves this world spiritually and morally so he enters the next. The whole effort of everyone over there who are redeemed is to be of all possible help, especially to those coming over in need of help.

But when one goes to the other side unredeemed and sinful, he is so ashamed and afraid that he seeks darkness as a hiding place and the depth of this darkness is hell. But even the very worst sinners are not sent to hell: they insist on going. But where the seed of goodness has been planted, where the Lord has anything to appeal to, where there is any belief in or desire to yield to Him, angels, saints, and the Lord Himself take charge and lead on from light to light, and from glory to glory. Man's freedom is so sacred that it is not interfered with anywhere. But everything is done for everyone that can be done. Sundar Singh says that one of the heavenly ones told him that even the fires of hell are for purification. How like God for this to be so!

The Very Best There

As Sundar Singh tells us, the very best life is the life that loves most and serves best. "They serve one another in love and in the effulgence of God's love and are eternally happy." "A man is as great as he is useful to others, and the usefulness of his life to others depends on his service to them."

Christ is seen as God made manifest; He is the manifest God. God, who is love, is seen in the person of Jesus on the highest throne of Heaven.

Singh says that an angel told him that "since God is infinite, His children who are finite can see Him only in the form of Christ." Speaking of the wonder of the Cross, another angel told Singh that "all inhabitants in Heaven know that God is love, but it had been hidden from all eternity that His love is so wonderful that He would become a man to save sinners, and for their cleansing, would die on the cross."

The Cross is the revealed secret of God's love, power, wisdom, and everything. The superlatively innocent and loving One, who goes all the way of love in life and in death, is raised up to the throne of the universe, and you and I have become one with this wholly innocent and loving One, and are given His Keys that unlock all doors here and everywhere.

CHAPTER 36

"Heart of Law and Gospel"
May 28, 1933
Macon Telegraph and News

(Substance of talks made Sunday May 21 at the worship services of the adult department of Mulberry Street Methodist Sunday School, at the Blackburn Avenue Gospel Tabernacle, a street meeting, and at the Bibb County jail.)

The superlative commands of the law and the prophets are to love God with all the heart, soul, and mind, and to love our neighbor as our self, so in all things we will do unto all men as we would have them do unto us. As Jesus said, on these commandments hang all the law and the prophets.

The Gospel adds to the commandments of the law and the prophets, to believe in and to enter into union with Jesus and to love one another as He loves us. By believing in Jesus, by receiving His Holy Spirit, by living in the Spirit, by receiving Jesus within, by entering into Him and by abiding in Him, the divine nature and the ability to love are given to us. There is born in us, nurtured in us, and called forth in us love and adoration for Him and love for one another. This includes even love for our enemies and the disposition and ability to overcome all evil with good. This is the Christian life and is essentially Heaven on earth. In this union with Him the more you are hated and the worse you are treated and persecuted, the more loving and happier you become. The most persecuted saints are the happiest saints.

Our Ability to Love

Our ability to love which opens us to God and God to us, and thus opens us to Heaven and Heaven to us, is from the Lord Himself. He loves us and wins us into loving Him, into loving one another, and into loving our enemies. Because He is love and has created us for love, we become loving.

According to our love for Him and for one another, we enter into Him, and He into us; the more He enters, the more we love, and the more we love the more we enter into Him. All the love there is, is ready to be ours and in actual experience, as we consent, will, love, and practice loving. The opportunities to love and the calls and urges to love are always at hand. There is no excuse for not loving and every reason for doing so. The essence of the love life, the Divine life, is to will and to work no ill to anyone or anything and to work every possible good. This love life is always kind, always patient, always hopeful, and always rejoicing. There is no failure and no defeat for it: "Love never faileth."

As you didn't know the power of water in a great reservoir until the gates are opened and it begins to flow in great volume, so you don't know the supply and power of love always at hand until you open to Him and His love and consent to let it flow out beyond itself. Likewise, we are not open to His great forgiveness until we are ready and glad to forgive, nor to His great love except as we are ready and glad to love. As our opposition to forgiveness, mercy, and love go and we consent to proclaim and practice His loving goodness, we are flooded with love, joy, peace, and glory.

As P.T. Forsyth says in his very vital book, The Justification of God, the Holy Cross and Resurrection of Jesus brings us to a great and adoring love of Him, into the holy Kingdom of God, into certainty of His final victory in us and in history, and in the cosmos, and gives us the sure witness of Eternity being already present and working and winning in time. As Forsyth also says, "to live in Eternity is our only security in time." He goes on to say "it is Christ, in the crucial action of Christ on the Cross, that overcame the world and created the new heavens and the new earth."

Gregory S. Camp, Ph.D.

Beneficiaries of His Conquest

Since Jesus by His incarnation, death, and resurrection has conquered and redeemed time with Eternity, the natural with the supernatural, the human with the Divine, we through union with Him are already in the deepest reality beneficiaries of His conquest. Through union with Him all things are ours: all things past, present, and future. We inherit His victory over every enemy and are joint-heirs with Him in all of the things of Eternity.

The Cross of Christ is an eternal and a completed victory. As Forsyth says, "it is an eternal act of love, of judgment, and of grace." From the beginning He was "the Lamb slain," even prior to the Cross, "He was always dying and conquering." But on the Cross "He conquered once and for all" and brought forth an eternal conquest which we inherit through union with Him.

Since His eternal conquest over the Cross, our overcoming is the overcoming of everything that keeps us out of union with Him, out of the inheritance of His conquest. The Spirit teaches and emphasizes that we have no responsibility but the responsibility of being in union with Him. In this union, we inherit everything and have everything.

It does not yet appear that we have all things, but it does appear that Jesus Himself, who was made a little lower than the angels for the purpose of tasting death for every man, is crowned with glory and honor and immortality. He has conquered not only everything, but did so in His own experience. He has also conquered for us, but we are only in the beginning of appropriating His conquest in our conscious experience.

There is no more death for us if we believe in Him and live in union with Him. But the appearance of death has not yet disappeared for us. But it is to disappear. There is no doubt about that. In union with Him we have the perfect appearance of it. We have the beginnings of His life working mightily not only in our spirits, souls, and minds, but also in our bodies.

The Key to Everything

So as I have been trying to say, and as Forsyth whom I am quoting from much today says so splendidly well, the crucified and risen Jesus and our union with Him is the key to everything. Union with Him makes us the sure inheritors of all things. "The key to history (and everything) is the historic Christ above history and in command of it, there is no other." He and His victory are here and are coming in great glory. Not only will the world be overcome fully in our experience as it has been in His, but in a deeper sense than we are aware, it is already overcome.

His reign is to be acknowledged and seen here in every sense of reality. "For Heaven," as Forsyth so well puts it, "is not simply the soul lifted abstractly above nature; it is simply the rule of the spiritual; it is nature compelled to serve the redeemed soul. Christ's miracles are parts and even functions of His moral conquest and control of the whole world."

The Glorified Human

In Jesus and in His conquest we have not only the victory of the spiritual in the realm of the spiritual and moral, but we also have the glorified human. This visible, glorified human that we see in Jesus is the beginning of the new creation. In, by, and through Jesus all things are to be made new and perfect. In this newness and perfection we are to have the triumph not only of Heaven on earth, but of earth in Heaven. There is to be brought forth a new Heaven and a new earth which is the marriage of Heaven and earth and the imperfections of earth eliminated.

The way to this consummation is glorious and may be very happy, too. Zion may bring forth without travail as well as with travail. Even the judgments of the Lord, as Forsyth says, are "His great rectifications." Since the victory of Jesus on the Cross, which is an eternal victory, there is no chance for the evil world winning. The only chance it ever had of winning it lost at the cross.

The evil world is a conquered foe. It does not yet appear to be so, but it is so. The kingdoms of this world and all the realms of this life are His and are to be acknowledged as His and be seen as His. He owns all by creation and by redemption, and is to have all things by their own happy consent. By this happy consent on our part, we can be His at once and inherit His conquest and become co-workers with Him in bringing His conquest to the experience of the whole creation.

CHAPTER 37

"The Holy Presence"
December 17, 1933
Macon Telegraph and News

When I asked (the Holy Spirit) what to write about, this came: "Write about My Holy Presence." "Write about everything of Mine," and "Give my love to the whole creation."

His Presence is Everything

In His presence everything is made clean, happy, and free; everything is transformed. No one of himself is holy, happy, alive, free, or healthy. These things come through His presence. In our human experience we are the sum total of our identifications, our affections, our thoughts, our acts, and our associations. For example, Saul of Tarsus so long as he was indentified with the enemies of Jesus, was the "Chief of Sinners," but as soon as he identified himself with Jesus, the highest of all identifications, he became wonderfully like Jesus. So do all of us! If we allow ourselves to be grafted in the heavenly Vine and abide in the Vine, we bear heavenly fruit. As we bear the fruit and submit to the pruning of God, we continue to abide.

Identification and Union

Before I received the Baptism of the Holy Spirit and received Jesus within and came under the immediate control of the Spirit, the highest word used for the highest relationship with the Lord was identification. After the Baptism and the incoming, the phrase that has been used most has been "Union with Me." He has said to me, "Your only responsibility is the responsibility of being in union with Me," "I want you in Me all the time and I give you the keys." And the key of keys is love. Always live in love, always go in love, and always be in a loving and merciful spirit, and you will always abide in Him.

The Christ Cure for the Disposition

One of the best things I have recently heard was something like this: If you are afraid to try the Christ cure on your body, try it on your disposition, and when you get your disposition cured, your body may also be cured. An old Christian Science friend from Chicago said this in a lecture he gave here in Macon last Monday night.

Only a few minutes ago (this is an insert on Saturday morning, December 16) I have a letter from a Pentecostal friend living in Vass, North Carolina who says "I have been seeking for Divine Health for some time, but I see now since reading your article ("My Holy Presence") I need most of all Divine Love." All of us do, and enough of His love and presence is divine health, healing, redemption and everything.

Christ is just as willing and able to heal the body as He is the disposition, but it would not do much good to heal the body without healing the disposition. But as we are willing to yield to the Christ Spirit, the Christ nature, and the Christ disposition, and enter into union with Him, we can much better serve and co-work with Him and glorify Him with whole rather than with diseased bodies.

When we are willing to be "wholly sanctified," we can be every whit whole. When are we wholly sanctified? At every step of our contact with the Lord we are sanctified to the degree of our consecration and surrender to Him, and of our union with Him. We have to be at least partially sanctified to receive the Baptism and gift of the Holy Spirit and to receive Jesus within. But entire sanctification means just what it says: it means entire, constant, and everlasting dedication and yielding to Him; it means glorious union with Him all the time. And it should mean preservation in spirit, mind, soul, and body unto the day of the Lord, unto the day of full victory over every enemy, including death.

None of Us Have the Fullness Yet

The other night when I told a Christian Science friend about the Baptism of the Holy Spirit, the glorious incoming of the Lord, and other blessed gifts and manifestations of His love and presence, I was asked "Is there more ahead?" There is much, much more ahead! When anyone gets the fullness of all the Lord has for him, he will be translated.

This reminds me of what a very witty Frenchman, Blaise Pascal, I believe, told the man who said that he believed he would start a new religion: "Live so perfectly, lovingly, and courageously that you will be crucified, and be so close to God that He will raise you from the dead, and then you can start a new religion."

But since Jesus has already lived this perfect life and been crucified and raised from the dead, the only death we need to die is the death to ourselves, to our sins, fears, doubts, and imperfections. The resurrection that we need comes through perfect union with Him.

The Divine Interchange

Here is the greatest marvel of the love of God in Christ Jesus. The Holy One became like us that we may become one with and like Him. He took and takes upon Himself our sins, death, diseases and our everything that has enslaved us, and gives us everything of His. He took upon Himself mortality and gives us immortality. He took upon Himself our shame and gave us His glory and honor.

In following Him we do not have to suffer everything He suffered. A deep enough yielding to Him will lift one into the place where there is no pain, sorrow, tears, and death. He not only set us the example of the Love way of Life, but He actually achieved tremendously and gloriously for us. The time comes when Zion will bring forth without travail, when nations will be born in a day, and when the Kingdom of God comes forth without resistance in great joy and rejoicing.

"God is Love"

Last Sunday morning I heard our gifted friend, Edwin M. Poteat, say substantially this: "You cannot preach vitally beyond what you have experienced, beyond what you have from the Lord and from life." Sunday night I heard an old Mercer friend, O. P. Gilbert, editor of the *Christian Index*, preach on "God is Love." As he said, the love of God is everlasting and universal. He loved us before He brought us here. He loved us while we were yet sinners. He loves the unjust as well as the just. He loves us into loving.

During the week I received wisdom from all kinds of people. A young man who stopped me on the street the other morning, said, "I used to go to jail. I went three times and decided it was all foolishness, and stopped going!" This reminds me of what Joe Webb at the hospital for tubercular prisoners told me when I asked him what person or human agency led him to the good life, and to consecrate himself entirely to the Lord? He told me what he had done and had been brought into a heaven-his full surrender to Christ. He said it was the Spirit of the Lord that led him to do it. It was the Spirit of the Lord that caused the Prodigal Son to come to himself and to return home. It is the Spirit of the Lord (of course, using human agencies when He has any yielded to Him, as well as working directly when this is necessary and best) that does everything good and blessed.

The Best Food of All

Last night a friend asked me if I could give him the secret of my joy. I told him that we are kept in His peace and joy as we feed on the Lord, as we keep our hearts and minds staid on Him. He replied, "This is the best food of all!" As we feed on Him our whole being is being changed from glory to glory.

CHAPTER 38

"Rare Wisdom"
January 21, 1934
Macon Telegraph and News

This is being dictated on Friday afternoon, January 19, today being the birthday of Robert E. Lee, we are especially reminded of a quality of Christian wisdom that shown out in him above any other human warrior that we have in mind. This wisdom is finely illustrated in the way he settled a difficulty between two of his rather hot-headed generals, Stonewall Jackson and A.P. Hill. General Lee said to these two estranged generals, "The one of you who is least in error will take the first step towards reconciliation." Each feeling himself least in error, took the step. There is wonderful wisdom here: Yes, take the first step. The Spirit and the letter of Matthew 5: 23-24 and of Matthew 18: 15-22 will make anyone a happy and successful peace-maker.

If anyone has anything against you, leave everything, even your religious offerings and services, and go and make peace. If your brother has sinned against you, go to him alone and show him his fault before you dare mention it to a single other soul. Refuse to use your tongue except to bless and make peace, and you will find the rest of the body rather easy to control.

Great Happiness

During the past week I have had hours of such rare fellowship with Jesus, such revelations of His Love and of our glorious inheritance in and through Him, such joy, bliss, and glory, that I am spoiled for anything less. In these hours of deep conscious identification, fellowship, and joint heirship with Him, everything is easy, glad, and free, and it is divinely easy for His love to flow out to everyone. He is always ready for us to have these glorious hours and days, and this glorious Eternity. But we are not ready for them until we choose to identify ourselves with His death, resurrection, and His present and eternal glory, and with His life of limitless love and best possible services.

Death to Sin

To be identified with our risen and glorious Lord, we must be identified with His death, which means our death to sin and self. As Oswald Chambers, in his My Utmost for His Highest, a book much prized and used by the Oxford Group friends, counsels so truly, "Haul yourself up. Take time to be alone with God (with Jesus Christ who is God with us and God's way to us and our way to God). Make the moral decision and say, 'Lord identify me with Thy death until I know that sin is dead in me.' Make the moral decision that sin in you must be put to death." Bury it, and if you see any sign of it coming to life, bury it deeper. Being dead to sin and self and having both put out of sight, we are free to be married to the risen Lord and to bring forth the fruit of heaven. In this new life and marriage, all things of His are ours.

In vital union with Him, we have everything without the responsibility of ministering it or paying taxes on it. In fact, as He makes as clear and blessed "our only responsibility is to be in union with Him." His one new commandment to us that includes and fulfills all the old ones is to love one another as He loves us. Self-effort and self-responsibility, as well as the lack of love, dulls the keen sense of joy and freedom and abundant life that He is ever seeking to impart to us and through us. Religion and religious work apart from Him and His inspiration, spirit, love, joy, spontaneity, and freedom are dull and dead and often nothing more than sanctimonious pretense.

Secret of Healing

There are so many people who need to touch the hem of His garment of power and glory and to be made whole, that I inquired Monday evening for His key or secret of health and healing. The answer came, "Be in Union with Me always," and that "perfect love is the key to this Union." When I asked the key to "every wit wholeness," the answer came, "Be holy, be wholly loving, be wholly sanctified."

Light Given in Dreams

The other night before going to sleep I asked for the dreams of the night to be from Him. And these dreams came, which I hope are prophetic: I was in a company of people and one of the party started to tell something good about me. I left the room to keep from hearing it. The new pastor of the First Baptist Church, Friend Joseph P. Boone was presiding at a large meeting. He made a sincere appeal to his warm personal friends to disregard their friendship and to do what they felt was best for the church, or the cause of the Kingdom. This brought quick approval and applause first from the children, then the adults, then the aged. And finally, I was shown a great program of sanitary and wholesome house-building to take the place of unsanitary, unscreened shacks and crowded tenements. Radios, which cost almost nothing, were to be installed in these houses under government control, and were used as a means of universal education.

Witnessing for Jesus

Monday morning I had the privilege of listening in to members of the Middle Georgia Baptist Ministers association as they witnessed and discussed "witnessing for Christ." Friend and Professor Edwin M. Poteat told how His presence became real to him years ago and has since then been his Companion, Inspiration, Lord, Master, and everything. As he said, in effect, the only way we can witness effectively for Him is to have a vital experience of Him, live in Him, live in His presence and manifest

His Spirit. Words about Him, apart from His presence and spirit and way of life, are as sounding brass and sanctimonious cant.

Friends S. J. Baker and Joseph P. Boone stressed "the great commission and preaching of the word." But, as Jesus commanded and commands, first to "tarry" and "receive power from on high," the Baptism, life, and gifts of the Holy Spirit and after this to be witnesses of Him everywhere.

Even those who receive His Baptism and gifts have to live in the Spirit and bear the fruit of the Spirit and go on to perfection. Those who do not go on to the perfection of love and Christ-likeness, who do not die daily to sin, and thus enter into ever deeper union with Christ, no matter how much they started with, become as severed branches, dry and dead. There is no life except in vital union with Him and in going on to his perfection of spirit, love, and life.

CHAPTER 39

"The Resurrection: Love in Manifest Victory"
April 1, 1934
Macon Telegraph and News

This is being dictated on Good Friday, March 30, 1934. The Inspirer says: "Write about My holy glorious way of life. Write about My glorious way of loving and living. Give My love to everybody and to everything. Abide in Me always. Go to the fullest limits of love and glory." Jesus loved and loves to the fullest and utmost limits and utmost possibilities of love. Today, Good Friday, commemorates this love at its highest heights and deepest depths.

On the night before the most holy sacrifice, He ate His last pre-resurrection meal with His disciples, washed their feet, instructed them, and gave them the promise of the other Comforter and of His own manifestation to them, and of His taking up His abode within them. He prayed for their sanctification and for their union with Him and with each other.

He entered the garden and gave Himself to the ultimate will of the Father, which was to give Himself in death as He had given himself in life for the salvation of the world and the redemption of the universe. He moved on rapidly to the very worst that man at his worst could inflict, and to the very best that the God-man at His best can give in return for man's worst.

It is precisely this meeting of man's worst with God's best and the glory that followed it, that is to triumph because all men, as they glimpse it, are drawn unto Him and to His love way if life. It is by yielding to this drawing, and by giving ourselves to Him and dedicating ourselves to His love way of life that we really celebrate His passion and His resurrection. Any other celebration is unworthy. The death of Jesus calls for our death to our sins, as the resurrection of Jesus calls for our resurrection with Him in His risen life. It is only as we live this new life that we really celebrate His resurrection.

God Raised Him

God to be God had to raise Jesus from the dead. The incarnation and the full offering up of Jesus in death necessitated the resurrection of Jesus and His being put on the throne of the universe. If the agony dedication in Gethsemane (Thy will be done under the most trying and crucifying ordeal of time and eternity), and the carrying out of this dedication in judgment and on the cross had ended in actual failure-as it appeared to end until God showed His hand-this would have been an essentially Godless world, and the universe a mindless chaos. If God could have raised Jesus and failed to do so, He would not have been God; if He did not have the power to do it, He would have been an inadequate God. Thanks and glory be to Him that He held Jesus to the very highest and that Jesus held Himself to the very highest, both revealing God's perfect love and perfect power in seeming defeat on the Cross, and perfect love in glorious triumph in the resurrection.

The way He dealt with Jesus and the way He deals with us, always answering at the right moment and in the best way, gives us a revelation of Him that is wholly satisfying, transforming, and glorious.

The Highest Witness

The resurrection of Jesus not only justifies and glorifies God and gives us the assurance of our own resurrection or translation into His nature, realm, glory, and victory, but it also gives the assurance that God wins in all the realms and kingdoms of this life and all life. As to the fact of the resurrection, it is so right and so like God that it had to be.

The witnesses of the resurrection are the highest and holiest and absolutely the most dependable of witnesses: the Holy Spirit and Jesus Himself. It was Jesus Himself and not the angels or the empty tomb that convinced Mary Magdalene, that convinced two disciples at Emmaus, convinced James, convinced doubting Thomas, and convinced more than 500 at one time. It later convinced Saul of Tarsus, His chief persecutor, and made him His chief witness and Apostle. It is Jesus Himself and the Holy Spirit that He gave and gives who have been the chief and convincing witnesses from the day of the Apostles until now.

The first disciples were in no easy mood to believe in the resurrection. They felt all was lost. It took the highest of all testimony to convince them. The Resurrection was and is fact and not illusion. It is also proved by the good fruit it produced. It transformed the disciples. It gave them a power that upset the world. It gave them courage, good will, and a sanity that only Jesus can give. Illusion brings excitement and followed to extreme limits, insanity and defeat. Only Truth has power to transform, to sustain, to make free, and to make sane.

How Convinced

If you question the testimony that Jesus, the Holy Spirit, and the holy angels gave to the apostles, and all who have been prepared to receive it from then until now, Jesus, if He is risen and alive, it is only natural for Him to reveal and manifest Himself to you, and to take charge of your life. He longs to also Baptize you with His Holy Spirit, fire, and love, to come in and reign within you, and to let you enter into Him and into the Kingdom of Heaven at hand. In so doing, He will so change your whole being that you will desire above all else to please Him and to abide in Him and the Kingdom of God. If you do this in sincerity, He is sure to hear and answer. He will answer in such a glorious and unmistakable way that you will be brought to your face in wonder and thanksgiving. When you are ready to ask and receive, He is ready to answer.

It is not the questioning mind, but the unyielding will that causes unbelief and keeps people out of the Kingdom of God. The one who sincerely asks is sure to be answered. The one who honestly questions is sure to have his difficulties removed. Nothing but your unwillingness to ask and to follow keeps you from the revelation of Jesus Christ and out of the Kingdom of God.

Our Own Testimony

In His dealings with me, He first made known that life must be love to be real life. To be led by His Spirit we have to let our shams and insincerities go, and become nobly and bravely sincere as well as wholly loving. We have to turn away from all lower leaderships to the perfect Leader and leadership.

It was made known to me that we could be Baptized with the Holy Spirit and receive supernatural gifts and guidance. Best of all, it was also made known that to go His way of love, sincerity, and of guidance by the Spirit, that I would need Him within as the source of love and sincerity. Then I asked Him if possible to come and live within and be the life and principle of His own good life and example that I had found to be true. I was led to dedicate to live His love life where it was most needed. Heaven opened and revelation after revelation was given. The power and glory of the Holy Spirit took control and possession of me bodily. The Spirit sang of Jesus and put me in the form of the Cross in the glory of Heaven. Jesus manifested Himself and came within and made known that He is God manifested on the plane of our need, that He is everything. Since then I have failed Him, but He has never failed me. He took up His abode to stay, and is ever leading me to abide in Him as He abides in me. From that great morning until now, I have known that Jesus is alive, and the most alive being of all. Since then I have been a personal witness of His resurrection and His lordship. He desires for all of us to be first-hand witnesses. He also desires to do everything good for us and through us that can be done.

Just last night I heard from a man from Augusta, Georgia who was very radiant and happy in the Spirit, testify that years ago when he turned to the Lord in extreme need, He not only saved him gloriously, but healed him instantly of Bright's disease that almost had him in the grave. Yesterday at the State Farm, prisoners told me of how their lives had been transformed and made victorious. He just longs to come to your rescue, to deliver you and to guide you, and to bring forth in and through you the very best that God has sent you here to be and to do.

What is it About?

As the enlightened chaplain of the State Farm, Friend E. C. Atkins put it yesterday, the whole Bible is really about Jesus Christ, regeneration, transformation, and the wonder there is in Him for us, and the church (which is His body). He came to call, justify, sanctify, and to glorify. As he also said, the account of creation in Genesis is a perfect account of how Christ comes into our lives when all is chaos and darkness and leads us out of it and brings us in to His salvation towards perfection.

Jesus does all of these things through His love, through His word, and through Himself. As the wonder of His blood sacrifice, which the Christian world is especially thinking about today, a little tract came to me on "God's Remedy," which says that healing comes to us without fail as we ask God to put the blood of Jesus on every part of his body as well as upon his spirit and mind. The blood of Jesus and every touch of Jesus makes clean and whole.

Since dictating the above I have received a letter from a Philadelphia friend who says "I was praying last night when all at once the Lord seemed to speak very clearly: the Blood of Jesus cleanses us and is sufficient for all things." Yes, He is sufficient in all things!

The risen Jesus, whose resurrection the Christians world celebrates Sunday, longs to reveal and manifest Himself, and to Baptize with His Spirit and to come within and triumph in and through everyone. His resurrection speaks of life and of victory of life over death, of the victory of His Spirit over what we call matter, and of the triumph of love over everything unloving.

CHAPTER 40

"Keys or Secrets of Union with Him and His Kingdom"
April 29, 1934
Macon Telegraph and News

The urges of the Spirit are: "Be always in Me and give My love to all."

Union with Christ and love and activities of love for Him and for each other and for everybody is His great loving call and enabling for every one of us. He has made us so that nothing short of this will satisfy. This union is our only responsibility, and this love of His flowing out and through us (and it will always flow in as we let it flow out) is the new and all-fulfilling and only necessary commandment.

The keys or secrets to union with Him and for receiving His gift of love and increasing in His love are for us all. But before attempting to share His revelations concerning these keys or secrets, let me speak of some of the victories of faith that I have heard testified to during the past week.

Victories of Faith

Last night at the Oxford Group meeting at the Mulberry Street Methodist church here in Macon, a mother gave this testimony: Her little girl was so desperately ill that the doctors and her friends sought to prepare her for the worst. She prayed, surrendered, and turned it all over to the Lord. He gave her the witness that the little girl would get well. She believed the witness against the belief of the doctors, nurses, and her friends. She was kept in peace and the little girl got well. The faith given her was used of the Lord to give substance or reality to the thing promised or hoped for.

A businessman testified that for a long time his money seemed to go with no income. When he drew a check for his last in the bank he was in such dread of what was ahead that he had a cold sweat. He turned to the Lord's teaching as to faith and prayer as recorded in the Gospel of Mark: *"Have faith in God. For verily I say unto you, That whosoever shall say unto this mountain, Be thou removed, and be thou cast into the sea; and shall not doubt in his heart, but shall believe that those things which he saith shall come to pass; he shall have whatsoever he saith."* (Mark 11: 22 and 24)

Then the man in desperate need said, "The promise is whatsoever thing ye desire. I desire work and a means to live." He offered himself to die to his doubts and fears, and choose to believe that he received what he asked for and needed. Peace and assurance came, and also work and supply. When he gave this testimony some time ago in Thomasville, Georgia, a minister was present without a church and in fear of desperate need. He took the Lord at His word and fought out the battles against doubt and unbelief in favor of trust and confidence. Not only did peace and assurance come, but a call to a church. Another businessman at last night's meeting told of how by turning to the Lord and obeying Him, that when faith and joy came, he was released from financial worries and nightmares.

In the early part of the week I heard Mrs. Everett preach at Friend Allen's Pentecostal Mission on Hazel Street here in Macon, and who, with her husband, is to have a tent meeting at the corner of Oak and Third. She not only told of the triumphant Christ as Savior and Baptizer, but also as Healer. She told of miracles that had come to people who heard the word and promise of faith and believed it, and acted upon it as of greater authority than the testimony the body gives as to its pains and diseases. Another lady told me recently that she was at the point of death and beyond human hope. Her sister prayed for her and got the witness of faith that at the end of the third month she would begin to improve and rapidly get well. Both sisters believed the witness of faith as against the witness of the doctors and neighbors and the desperately sick body. At the end of the third month the improvement came, followed by full healing and health.

The Lord gives us the ability to choose to trust Him and to believe His promises and to do His will, and as Newton Riddell suggests, the very instant we choose according to God's will and best in any situation, His ability, grace, and spirit comes to the rescue to enable us to do what we have chosen. The darkest hour is the very time to trust and pray and give thanks most of all, for as Riddell puts it, "the fact that Christ gives us Himself with all of His virtues, powers, and eternal life is sufficient cause for praise and thanksgiving, no matter what our temporal condition."

Love Source of Trust and Praise

Riddell also says, with characteristic insight, words to the effect that the gift of perfect love is our supreme need for complying with every condition of faith and for working with God. This perfect love which the Lord longs to give to everyone for the desire and the asking for it, believes all things, is always trustful, always patient, gives thanks, and has no failure in it.

The Law of Opulence

As so many people are worried and in straits as to supply of material things, let me share the Law of Opulence as given by Riddell:

> "First, to have the Mind of Christ and work with Him and to His glory in whatever position one is called; Second, to live economically so that nothing shall be wasted, for waste and extravagance are sin; Third, to render through faith the just rewards of one's efforts. Ask and it shall be given you. It is the Father's will that we ask and receive largely, for He has provided a sufficiency for all."

Seek first the will and mind of God and the highest good of everybody. Let go every habit and every indulgence that is not good for you and a good example to others. Use as little on yourself as you can and give in love and in service and in means all that you can. And when you give alms, don't let one hand know what the other hand giveth.

As you put first His will and the highest good of everybody and become a channel for His love and services, everything you need for yourself and to do His will and work for others comes. It is our selfishness, stinginess, lack of faith, self-indulgence, and lack of obedience to the will and wisdom of God and love, and generosity toward people in need that makes us poor. The other day a friend told me of a certain person who by false pride and by giving to the well-to-do instead of the poor, was in financial straits. I believe that there is a proverb to the effect that giving to the rich the things that should go to the poor, tends toward poverty.

Secrets of Union and of the Kingdom

Monday morning I had the privilege of talking at Mercer University on the "Keys to the Kingdom or the Secrets of Union with Jesus Christ." I had meant to make this article an answer on how to enter and abide in union with Him and in the kingdom, but space is almost used up; but let me say this: The Lord so greatly desires to enter into us and bring the kingdom within us, and for us to enter into Him which brings us into the Kingdom, that union with Him is for all of us who desire it enough to bring it about in His own blessed and only possible way. As He is knocking to come and bring within us His spirit, nature, and kingdom, the very instant we want Him to come enough to invite Him, He comes. He abides forever if we desire Him to abide enough to let go the things that cannot stay where He is and reigns.

He also longs and urges us to knock and to enter into Him and abide in Him and grow up into His likeness. We enter into Him by leaving on the outside everything that has kept us on the outside and by humbling ourselves as little children at His feet. The key that unlocks the door and all doors is love. This love is a divine gift and comes to us as we are willing to receive it and to give it.

Knocking, Faith, Love

The Lord is so concerned that we enter into Him that He makes it easy to come and enter. The Spirit is drawing us and enabling us to come to

Him. As we want to get in and ask to get in, the door opens. We just have to leave all evil on the outside, and come in. The gate is narrow enough to keep out everything that has evil and the seeds of evil in it, and large enough to let you in. It is just the right size. If it were any smaller you could not get in, and if it were any larger something would get in with you that would not be heaven.

All Evil Must be Taken Out of Us

This should make clear why it is that God who is love and who is seeking to save everyone and to bring everyone into the Kingdom, has not as yet succeeded except with the wise few. All that causes evil and all the evils that are within one must be repented of and let go in order for one to enter into Heaven at hand, or to come. They very minute you are ready to let your enemies go, the door is opened to you and you enter.

Secrets of Abiding

The secrets of abiding after you enter are very simple: Choose to keep you heart and mind staid on Him. Choose to please Him. Choose to abide in Him; choose not to be drawn out by any temptation. Meet all evil with good; all curses with blessings; all hate with love, all unkindness with kindness, all persecutions with thanksgivings and with prayers for those who persecute you.

After you enter into union with Christ, which is the highest blessedness on earth as well as in Heaven, your highest service is to help others to enter. To get in and to stay in is your only responsibility; and to love everybody and to help them to get in and stay in is your work.

CHAPTER 41

"His Great, Perfect Love"
May 6, 1934
Macon Telegraph and News

When I inquired what to write about, this came: "Write about My great, perfect love and give and live My love to all. Be in Me always; I give perfect everything."

This is a precious anniversary season with me. It was eight years ago, Sunday May 6, when this is due to be published, that the high request and promise were given to me: "I want you in Me all the time, and I give you the keys." The keys are for all who can be induced to use them. The major ones are repentance, faith, confession, humility, and the master key that unlocks **THE DOOR**, and all doors, is love. The master key which is a gift of His love for every one of us as we desire it enough to ask for it and are willing to live it, for it unlocks all the doors of God and locks all the doors against the subtleties of devils and all the forces of evil and death. It also is the key to every heart and every life. It fulfills not only the Mosaic Law, but every law and ideal of right. It is the very essence of the Gospel. Indeed it is the Good News.

Recent Victories of Love and Faith

During the week I have heard precious testimonies as to the power of Christ to heal the body and to transform the life. Three people were healed Wednesday night at the tent meeting on Third and Oak streets, where Mr. and Mrs. Everett are conducting services every night at 8, and every afternoon at 3 o'clock, stressing conversion, the Baptism of the Holy Spirit, healing, and that all are one in Christ. Last night I talked with a gentleman in attendance. He told me that he had been physically afflicted for years. At times it would take him half an hour to turn in bed. He went to the tent-meeting on Wednesday night on his cane. He was prayed for and believed; suddenly his lameness and pains were taken away. He left his cane at the meeting and last night he leaped with the agility of a youngster. He and others told me that the two other healings were equally remarkable, that in one of the cases a crooked bone had been made straight.

The great significance of the control of Christ in the realm of nature and in the body is that it is prophetic of His full control and dominion. He is to reign on earth as in Heaven and what we call the natural is to be set free from its enemies and filled with the glory of Heaven. Every healing of the body is also a work of heavenly love and mercy to the individual, and should draw him into the great desire to be redeemed spiritually and to be one with Christ.

Power of Surrender and Confession

Last night, by special invitation, I went to the Oxford group meeting in the Napier Heights section of Macon. These Oxford Group friends are especially strong on surrender to the guidance of the Spirit and in stressing honesty, sincerity, genuineness, unselfishness, purity and love. They also practice confession of their sins and shortcomings, and give themselves to making restitution.

One prominent man at the meeting last night told how he had been enabled to change other lives by surrendering to Christ and by prayer, and by being changed himself. He also told how supernatural power and presence coming from Heaven had entered his body, and how he had been given grace to love back, where heretofore he complained back and sometimes fought back. He is greatly happy in his new life, is ready to go anywhere, and hopes the way will be opened for him to serve as a missionary.

Stoic as a Youth

Some time ago he remembered that as a boy he had stolen five cents. He took steps to make a larger restitution. He insisted on giving back fifteen cents, going almost to the lengths that Zacheus went. He also told of two other cases of restitution and the joy he got out of coming clean. In one of the cases he had collected twenty-five dollars for a client and sent it to him. But as the letter containing it was returned, he decided as he needed the money and used it. With the new light and obedience he had to find the man and confess and make restitution; after a long search he found him and made the confession and gave him the money. This made both of them very happy.

Others at the meeting told of how surrender and confession had brought release, joy, and gladness and had taken away worry. One lady said that to her religion used to be largely something of fear. She used it as future fire insurance. Now life and religion are a great joy. The fear of death has gone. She said she knows she is not honest yet, but she is seeking to be.

A Cursing Steward Saved

A very prominent man in the business and religious life of Macon testified that he had been saved from the habit of cursing. He said that although he was prominent in his church and a steward, it seemed that he could not keep from cursing. When he was out with one of the visiting Oxford Group friends some time ago, at the time of the general meeting here, he expressed his contempt for two drunkards. The Oxford Group friend responded, "You are worse than they are. You are a sinner and condemning them. They are sinners and are not condemning you."

The sinning steward turned to the Lord and said, "If you will deliver me from cursing, I will go with you." From that moment till now he has not even been tempted to curse. Other things that he did not know were sins have been uncovered and he is seeking to be pure in heart and enter into that victorious fellowship with Jesus that will make him a full overcomer. His cook has seen such a change that she told him yesterday,

"I sure hope that this religion holds out." Of course, it holds out as the friend seeks to be led by the Spirit and be perfect in love, in purity, in unselfishness, and in honesty as Christ is perfect.

Secrets of Going On

By choosing to believe, by choosing to love, to deny self and to put Jesus Christ first, by choosing to abide in Him and to go on to His perfection, every one of us can and will be kept from falling and backsliding and will increase in union with Him. By beholding Him and rejoicing in and choosing His perfection, we are changed from glory to glory into His likeness. As the Spirit as well as the scriptures make known, He desires to give us His Perfect Everything over every enemy, a seat with Him on His throne, and a life of everlasting services, satisfactions, and glories with Him.

Divine Life for the Whole Being

During the week I have been blessed beyond measure by deeper realizations of His love and presence, and by the understanding that came largely through Newton Riddell's <u>Vital Christianity</u>, which I have referred to in previous articles. As Riddell says, in effect, Jesus Christ in a cosmic and universal sense, is the very principle of all life and healing. He created all and is ministering to and seeking to heal every bruised reed, every scarred tree, and every marred and sick life. He is doing His best all the time for the bad and the good, and all that are between them. To recognize Him as omnipresent and as pure love, goodness, and healing is to co-work with Him the more effectively for our own healing and for the healing of the rest.

Messianic as Well as Cosmic

As Riddell saw with such penetrating insight, Christ is not only cosmic, but also Messianic. He personally came into the world as man and revealed the will of God and did the works of God. He went to the cross as our sacrifice, as our substitute, in a deep biological or life sense. As soon as we see this and accept this with heart gratitude and faith, we are set free from condemnation and fear and lifted into the consciousness of the peace and love of God.

Then as we yield to the Divine Spirit and the Divine Love, we are recreated and made new beings in God in and through Jesus Christ. Through this re-creation the Spirit of God makes us new centers for the incarnation of Jesus Christ and we become through Him divine-human beings. Then we are ready for the Baptism of Holy Fire as a perpetual holy flame that burns up the things that need to go and keeps in holy heat the new life in Christ. Fire in the heavenly as well as in the natural realm serves the two-fold purpose of cleansing to the depths and of protecting from every enemy. It also gives the holy zeal of heaven, and keeps one hidden in the holiest place.

In Christ Life

All the foregoing, as Riddell sees so clearly that it must have been given him by revelation, prepares us for the "In Christ" life and consciousness. This life which is literally the life hidden with Christ in God, is in the Spirit, heaven on earth and heaven anywhere.

A little over twenty-four years ago when I asked for the Holy Spirit Baptism, and asked for His best whether I knew what it was or not, I was finally led to ask Jesus to come within, and be the life and principle of the perfect life of love and sincerity that the Holy Spirit is calling all of us to receive and to live. As He is knocking everywhere to come in the whole of our being, when we invite Him to come, He comes quickly.

After the Holy Spirit comes, He remains and increases in His government and peace as we consent and welcome Him to do His will. Then the problem becomes how to abide in Him as He abides in us. This is accomplished by deep death to self that must be daily and constant, and by a rejoicing in Him and by choosing to abide in Him above all else, and by a life given to the activities of love. Since He is love, as we yield to

His love and express His love to all, we are consciously in Him and He is consciously in us. We know Him and are known of Him.

Union With Him

All other glorious works of grace lead up to this glorious union with Him. In this union everything of His is ours. We give Him our sins, faults, diseases, and imperfections to take away, and we give Him everything that is worth saving with which to do His best. Only the enemies are taken away. Every possibility of good in us is perfected and made wonderful beyond anything that we can ask or think. Then He gives us His righteousness, holiness, wisdom, health, abundant life, joy, and love beyond measure. He is leading us on so that we will be ready to receive His resurrected and glorious body and ascend to His throne, presence, dominion, and power to serve and bless without limit.

CHAPTER 42

"Live Me Everywhere"
July 1, 1934
Macon Telegraph and News

Last night when I asked Jesus for His will in a particular situation that had been handled unintentionally to my personal loss, the answer came, "Live Me everywhere, give My love to everything." Earlier in the week it was said, "I give you everything." (He gives everything to all in union with Him) "I give glory and honor and power and dominion and praise." To live in Him everywhere is to love and bless everywhere and to do nothing but love and bless everywhere, in every situation. Love both fulfills and transcends all law.

When in doubt as to what to do, do the kindest and most loving thing, and you will find that this is the will and guidance of God. As long as we try to get things selfishly--even by prayer--we are just beating ourselves against the will of God. When we consent to love and do nothing but love and bless, we yield and swing into the will of God and into union with God. There is no other way to be in union with God who is love, except to yield to His Good Spirit and to His love and go to loving. When we love one another as He loves us, we will be in perfect union with Him, and all things of His will be consciously ours.

Delight to do His Will

On Wednesday it was made greatly precious that we must not only do His will of love and kindness all the time and everywhere, but we must do this will with gladness and thanksgiving for the privilege of doing it. We don't really love anyone until we are glad to do everything for them we can. This is especially true as to our relationship with God. As we love Him we delight to please Him, and we also love everything that is best in ourselves. To yield to Him and to yield to do the very best that He has for us is one and the same thing.

To do His will of love and goodness does not seem easy and possible until you swing into it—until you make the adventure of faith, love, and obedience. Then it is seen to be reasonable and sensible, the blessed, the only thing. The obedience of faith and love brings and keeps us in the presence and fellowship of the Lord. In this presence and fellowship it is divinely easy and happy to do His will of faith, love, kindness and blessedness.

Look and Live by Looking

When reading Oswald Chambers' <u>My Utmost For His Highest</u>, it was brought home with great reality that as we look unto Him, we *ARE* saved. We are saved as soon as we look. The look at once connects us with Him and His salvation, redemption, health, healing and everything. It is not a promise that we will be saved if we look, but is a statement of fact that we are saved *as* we look and that we are kept saved and transformed increasingly as we keep on looking.

To look unto Him, to choose to keep the heart and mind staid on Him, to behold Him in love and thanksgiving, opens the door of Heaven to us, opens the way for the Lord to stream in and shine in. We are transformed by "the renewing of the mind" as we choose to think on Him and to please Him.

Any temptation goes the very instant you choose Him, that you choose His love way, that you choose to be at One with Him. He longs to deliver us out of the hands of ourselves and of all our enemies and bring us unto Himself and into the Kingdom of Heaven; He transforms us, redeems us, and glorifies us to the fullest limits of our consent, yielding, and response. As we choose Him and choose His way of love, we find we are His chosen and His greatly beloved.

Gregory S. Camp, Ph.D.

Cannot Stand the Light

Since Christ is light that works by love, the tempter cannot stand the light. Only the love of Christ can stand the light of Christ. So if you tell the tempter-and mean it-that you will bring to light what he tempts you to think and do in the dark, he leaves you. He prefers to leave you to being told on. You will even stop talking about people unkindly when you resolve and put into practice the Christ way of confessing what you have said to the one you said it about. You will quit anything evil rather than do it in the light.

We are not condemned for what we have done. We are condemned for continuing in the dark, for not bringing ourselves and our sins to the Light. In Him there is no darkness at all. When we yield to Him and become wholly loving there will be no darkness in us, no fear in us, no disease in us, and no death in us. Perfect love sets free from insincerity, shame, pretense, falsity, sin, fear, disease and death.

He seeks to make us perfect in everything, but there is no perfection of Him that is not the perfection of love. We could tell the truth in a way that would hurt, if we did not tell it in love. In fact, there is nothing that is not loving that is really Christlike. Such a good thing as generosity, going to the point of giving everything to the poor, profits nothing except as it is inspired by love and done in the love spirit. So it is with everything.

His Achieved Redemption

Still another thing that has been made especially precious and glorious recently is that Jesus has already achieved perfect redemption and perfect everything for us and the whole creation. So this choosing Him simply opens us up to Him and enables us to receive of Him His marvelous salvation, redemption, love, health, joy, glory, dominion and everything.

He becomes everything to us in experience as fast as our understanding is opened, and as our wills yield to receive from Him and to give out from Him in love and blessedness to all. He is already everything to and for us, but we do not realize Him and what He is to us except as we open up to

Him—as we believe Him, as we meditate upon Him, as we rejoice in Him, and as we do His will of love to all, to the whole creation.

Now in Christ Jesus (in His incarnation, in His loving sacrificial and atoning death, in His glorious resurrection and ascension, and in His omnipotence, omnipresence, and omniscience) we have revealed in the concrete the perfect God and the perfect man and the beginning of the new and perfect creation or universe. What had been seen as an ideal and as a hope has been and is manifested in Him in an actuality.

In seeing Him we not only see the perfect God and Father and perfect man, but we also see what we are to become in actual experience through being in union with Him. We don't see ourselves by looking at ourselves; we see ourselves by looking at and to Him, by yielding to Him, by responding to Him. As we see Him, we see with the eye of faith and spiritual understanding what we really are, the sons of God and the brethren and joint-heirs of Jesus Christ.

Even if you are blind, don't look at your blindness, but look at His perfect light and eyes and sight. If you are sick, don't look at your sickness, but look at His glorious health and perfection. Looking away from the imperfection of yourself and others, and looking to Him changes us from glory to glory into His likeness. The true look to and at Him, this yielding to Him, this doing of His will of perfect love, brings us into His glorious redemption, salvation, marvelous life, health, dominion, and everything.

CHAPTER 43

"Put Up They Sword"
December 9, 1934
Macon Telegraph and News

Of course, the only way to keep from perishing by the sword is to put up your sword and to do it in such a fine wisdom and spirit that you represent the best possible influence for inducing the other fellow to put up his. We must have far more than negative nonresistance. It must be an active offensive of love, of good aggressively meeting and overcoming evil with good. This applies to nations and to all other groups, as well as to individuals. You just have to put off your carnal spirit and put up your carnal weapons and put on the spirit of Christ and His weapons of love, good will, and good sense. You must do this before you can have peace and before you can become an active power in resisting and in overcoming evil, and in winning your enemies to be the true friends. As long as evil is fought with evil, evil is not overcome; it increases. You can't fight the devil with his fire; he has far more of it and is much more skilled in its use. But thanks be to God we have weapons of defense and offense that make us victors over the world, the flesh, and the devil.

Love Forgiveth All Things

A request comes to me to write something on the wisdom and necessity of freely and quickly forgiving every injury, real or imagined. I found out long ago that no matter what anyone said or did, when I finally forgave it,

I was very happy. It showed me the importance of extending forgiveness on the spot. To not do so makes one miserable.

Don't let the sun go down on your foolishness. Don't wait for death or some tragedy or for extended periods of misery to yourself and others, by delaying to forgive; do it all at once! As to how many times we should forgive, the only limit is the capacity of those who offend to repent and to ask for forgiveness. Love your own soul and peace well enough to forgive them and to love them and to do them all possible good.

And since God for Christ's sake has so much forgiveness, it is a little thing for us to show our gratitude for Him and His great forgiveness by freely and quickly forgiving our brother of the comparatively little he has ever done against us. We receive so richly from the Lord because of His grace and because of our great need. In order to abide in fellowship with Him and to keep in the sweetness and peace of His fellowship, we have to give up our stubbornness and go to manifesting His graciousness. Those who are saved by grace are saved to show grace to their fellows.

How to Appropriate God's Health and Redemption

A friend has sent me a wonderful little booklet by Friend F.F. Bosworth, on "How to Appropriate the Redemption and Covenant Blessings of Bodily Healing." It is the best thing of its kind that I have recently read.

So many people write him to pray for them and as to how they can best co-work with God for their healing, that Friend Bosworth has prepared this rare booklet to take the place of long personal letters of explanation. As Friend Bosworth says, the first thing to do after you surrender to God is to know what the Bible so clearly teaches, that it is God's will to heal all of His children (of all their disease) until they finish their course.

When one sees that God not only wills, but longs to heal everyone of His children of all their diseases, he is ready to pray the prayer of faith that heals as well as saves; and as Friend Bosworth says, "Faith is expecting God to do what we know that it is His will to do. And faith, as the scripture says, cometh by hearing the word (the promise) of God." As Friend Bosworth puts it, "just as a little girl's faith for a new dress comes by hearing the promise of her mother to buy it, so our faith for healing comes by hearing

God's word or promise to do it. Both the little girl's faith (for the dress) and ours for healing as well as for redemption comes by hearing."

After we know God's will and promise to heal us, the next step is to believe and act accordingly. Fallen nature is governed by what it sees, by its senses, but "faith is governed by the pure word of God and is nothing less than expecting God to do what He promises, treating Him like an honest being. Faith never waits to see before it believes; it never judges according to the sight or the eyes, or the way the body feels." It gives thanks in advance of any physical evidence, that what it asks for has been granted. It believes that it has received when it asks according to the will of God, and it holds on to this faith against every evidence of the body to the contrary. Just as Jesus at the grave of Lazarus thanked the Father for having heard Him before the miracle had occurred, so we are to believe and give thanks and the signs and the miracles have to follow. If the signs went before, it would not be faith.

Turning Sunsets into Sunrises

For a long time I have known that every tragedy on earth may be quickly turned into a heaven as we turn away from and repent of the evil and turn ourselves to the Lord. The other day in the *Christian Century*, I found this fine phrase, "turning sunsets into sunrises." As we yield to God, everything turns to good. We come to know that everything is working together not only for our good, but for the good of everyone who will let Him work on their behalf.

The one error and sin in my own life that I am most ashamed of is used by Him to be my greatest warning and protection. So it is with everyone who turns his life, sins, and his everything over to the Lord whose judgments of love and mercy unto victory, not judgments of condemnation unto defeat and failure. If you have evil, His will and judgment for you is to be exceedingly good; if you have been impure, to be especially pure; if you have been hard to be very tender; if you have been unloving in any way, to be greatly loving.

John in his blindness wanted to call down fire on the Lord's enemies. The Lord called down John, and instead of calling down fire, He made

John the disciple of love. Saul of Tarsus sought to destroy the church, but instead of destroying him for his false way, Jesus made him His chief witness, prophet, and apostle to build up the church. Peter, in the natural, was weak as water, and therefore the Lord's will and judgment for him was to be a rock and a mighty pillar.

As you will let Him, He will turn all of your nights into days, all your wrong-doing into heavens and make of your weaknesses, sins, and failures, great warnings and fortifications as well as stepping stones for the heavenly ascent. He will do it at once if you will have faith enough to give Him a chance. It doesn't take long for the Lord to do anything, He longs to deliver you out of your sins right now—this very moment—and to bring you into His righteousness, love, peace, and victory.

Achieved Through Union

Another thing that is with me much, is that all life problems and all of our personal problems are so far beyond us that we will always be failing and making a mess of things. When we know and act upon that with Him and in union with Him all things are easily and happily possible for us. So at every step of the way, say to Him, "This is beyond me, but it is not beyond You; You guide me. Give me Your thoughts and Your Good Spirit. Hold me fast and make the best use of me You can."

The thing that is to be brought about by Christ through us--the Kingdom of God victorious in us and on earth—can only be achieved by Christ having His full way in and through us, and by our abiding in Him and co-working with Him. He must bring it forth in us and we in Him. He must do His work in and through us, and do our work in and through Him. It can only be brought about by vital, continuous, and increasing union and fellowship with Him.

Our Only Responsibility

We have but one responsibility and that is the responsibility of getting and keeping in vital union with Him, and in the bearing of fruit of this union. To talk about our many responsibilities and burdens indicates that

Gregory S. Camp, Ph.D.

we are trying to carry our burdens without putting our necks in His easy yoke. In union with Him there are no heavy burdens. In union with Him nothing is even felt to be a burden or responsibility, but everything is seen as a blessed privilege and glorious opportunity.

CHAPTER 44

"The Lord for the Body"
(And the Body for the Lord)
March 17, 1935
Macon Telegraph and News

Disciple of Jesus

Last night my mail brought two letters that referred to the wonder of being an immediate disciple of Jesus, rather than being disciples of disciples. The disciples of the disciples of Jesus are greatly fortunate and blessed in comparison with those who follow their own unredeemed wills and spirits or the unredeemed will and spirits of others. But even a disciple of a disciple of Christ is never quite so vital and free as an immediate disciple of Christ. Of course, all the members of the Body of Christ are to supplement and serve every other member of His Body, as the members of a healthy natural body all pull together and serve each other as one. But the Spiritual Body, as with the natural body, needs to be under the immediate control and direction of the Head.

Especially Anointed

In the Body of Christ, some are especially anointed and fitted for one service and some for another. But those whom St. Paul calls "teachers" are not teachers in themselves any more than those especially anointed for the healing ministry are healers themselves. The Holy Ghost, the Teacher and the Healer, and the Everything of God and Christ simply manifests Himself in His various offices through the members of Christ's Body to profit each by the other, to build up the whole Body of Christ in the likeness of Christ. And in the deepest and truest sense, as Jesus said, no one on earth is to be called Rabbi (Teacher), Master, Leader or Father. He must be the Teacher and the Master and the Everything of every one of us, and we must be just servants, helpers, and friends. It's just the reverse of what it is in the kingdoms of this world, where the boss is the big man. In Christ, the servant and the friend is the big man, and the humbler and better the servant and the friend, the greater the man or woman.

If the Disciple is not Wholly a Disciple

A glorious privilege and blessing of following Jesus directly and of being immediately taught of Him, is that you are kept free from the mixture of human wills and opinions of those who, though the disciples of His, are yet far from being wholly like Him. And the more a disciple of His is led by Him and becomes more like Him, the more insistent he is that you follow him only as he follows Christ, the more careful he is to tell you when he is speaking his own understanding, and when he is speaking by immediate revelation and inspiration. The more you are taught and led and used directly of the Lord, the more you want everyone else to be, and the less you want them to be influenced either by yourself, or by anyone else. Those who want a following rather than want all to follow the Lord are not themselves really following the Lord.

How to Receive from Christ

"How to Receive Healing from Christ," by Friend Bosworth, has been put in a small booklet and gives a wonderfully simple and helpful way the secret of looking away from sin, self, and the symptoms to Christ. And "Take-Eat," a four page tract by Mrs. C. Nuzum, has helped me to realize Christ's body in place of my own. If we yield to Christ, and enter into union with Him, we are not only new creatures in Him, but as Mrs. Nuzum says, "…by faith we must take Jesus to displace all of our old being, spirit, soul and body, and fill the vacancy with Himself…We may take the Lord's health, and strength, and soundness, and eat them by truly believing that these things displace the old." Mrs. Nuzum gives these testimonies of healing that have occurred as people have seen the healthy body of the Lord instead of looking at their own diseased bodies.

One who had an incurable, indolent ulcer took by faith the sound flesh of Jesus instead of her putrid flesh. By the eye of faith she saw only the sound flesh of Jesus, praised God for it, rejoiced before Him, and God gave her perfect healing and soundness. One who had consumption perceived by faith the sound lungs of Jesus, and rejoiced before Him and the Lord gave according to her faith.

The Perfect Body of Christ

The resurrected body of Jesus is in heaven, and is to be forever His individual body, but He is seeking to realize in us His perfected many-membered body on earth. As we look to Him as the Perfect One and look away from our diseases and imperfections, we receive from Him transformation and healing. By receiving Him within and living in union with Him, we can see perfect health and wholeness where we have been seeing our lack of health and wholeness. This is a most telling and transforming truth: to realize Christ as our spiritual perfection as well. He is already our perfect sight and eyes, and everything else of the body as well as everything of the spirit. All we need to do is eat fully and continually of Him and cease to eat of the things that caused the fall, and that has kept us in bondage to self and the body.

Keeping the Body

Before closing let me call attention to "Keeping the Body Under" by Carrie Judd Montgomery in the current number of the *Pentecostal Evangelical*. If we are to be overcomers and eat of the Tree of Life, the bodily tastes and appetites must be redeemed, and the body must be brought under the control of the Holy Spirit who ministers Jesus Christ to us, forming Christ in us, and causing Him to fill every part of our being: spirit, soul, and body

As Mrs. Montgomery goes on to say, the emphasis in I Corinthians 6: 19, is upon the body being the temple of the Holy Ghost. The next verse speaks of the godly and the spirit. But as A. B. Simpson points out, in the earliest manuscripts the words "and in your spirit" were omitted. Perhaps it was implied, but sharp emphasis was on the thought of the body. Therefore glorify God in your body, which is God's. In St. Paul we read *"Know ye not that your bodies are members of Christ?"* (I Corinthians 6: 19) And He even tells us, *"we are members of His body, of His flesh, and of His bones."* (Ephesians 5: 30)

When we crucify gluttony as well as all other false appetites that bring the body into captivity to disease and death, and yield the body over to the Lord, we find that we have only yielded unto Him that which was already His own. Since the body is His by creation and by redemption, it is to be continually offered up to Him as His. Of course, as it is offered up, and kept offered up, He will dwell in it and make it the fit organism through which to manifest to the world His perfect self.

CHAPTER 45

"The Kingdom of Heaven"
May 19, 1935
Macon Telegraph and News

An Hour of Greatest Privileges and Dangers

This is the best hour of history to be alive, provided you are willing to live it according to the light that is available; it is the most tragic to live according to the pulls of the lower nature, and under the influence of the spirit that hates, denies, and destroys. Both the kingdoms of heaven and hades are at hand. The Kingdom of Heaven is as near to you as you are to yielding to the Good Spirit, the Spirit of Truth and Love; the spirit of anarchy and of evil are as near to you, at least in the beginnings, as you are to yielding to the spirit of the evil one.

The Processes of History

The long processes of history are at least budding and blooming. What we call fascism appears to be the entrenched old order of selfishness and privilege seeking to maintain itself with all possible weapons of violence and repression. What is called present day communism appears to be the "class" spirit seeking to set up another form of dictatorship in the name of brotherhood, when it is really being done in the spirit of hatred and with the weapons of the enemy. Both communism and fascism call for the sacrificial spirit, the sacrifice of the individual to the herd, as well as appeal to the idealistic, especially of youth.

Communism seems to be a nearer imitation of what is to be and must be (the brotherhood of the Kingdom of God) than is fascism. Imitations are the most subtle and difficult enemies of the Real. So the race is between Christianity, which is free, voluntary, and produced by Christ's spirit of love and brotherhood, and the despotic, violent imitations.

Of course, the Real wins. The question of how much suffering and tragedy the blindness of men, and especially their leaders, will intervene before Christ and His way of love and freedom are allowed to win remains. We are not made for dictatorships, violence, hate, or bondage. We are made for freedom, for love, and for brotherhood. God has made us for Himself and for our voluntary choosing of Him and His perfect way. The more men pull back from God's good way, the more they are going suffer. The more men resist, the greater the tragedy and doom they pull down upon themselves and others who have also failed to yield to the spirit of Christ.

Education for the New Day

The old education was too largely a training to enable men to get power, money, and control over their fellows. Until recently the educated man found it rather easy to get success in the competitive world. This is no longer true. The only careers open to men of intelligence now are those of unselfish service of men in the spirit of Christ. If you want to serve and to serve unselfishly co-working with Christ to bring the Kingdom of love, good will, and brotherhood among men, which is the current side if the Kingdom of God on earth, there has never before been a better time to get a job. You will find so little competition and there is so much to be done. It doesn't matter how many the workers, there is plenty for each to do. When you get on the path of Reality, nobody is in your way. The Good Samaritan had the whole road to himself, and even if he had helpers, they would not have been in each other's way. Men will never run over each other, or be in each other's way, going to heaven.

How About the Pay?

Anyone who is willing to join Christ to bring His kingdom of love and brotherhood is not only sure of a place in this the greatest of all enterprises, but is also sure of the best possible work for him, with all the equipment and pay he needs. One needs so little for himself when he learns to live sensibly. When you walk with Christ you are sure to receive so much in the way of fatted calves and feasts you cannot fail to cry out, "I am so unworthy of all this!" When we forget all about the pay and give ourselves to the best thing to be done, the pay is best and the surest of all. When you give yourself to get all the pay, the fatted calves, and feasts that you can, the pay is the poorest and the calves the leanest.

Religious Equipment and Emphasis

We have reached the time when nothing short of first-hand contact with the Leader and immediate guidance by Him will suffice. It never would, but it is more apparent now. The disciple of a disciple has always been pale and anemic in comparison with the immediate disciple of Christ. All the men who have made history for God in a great way have been immediately taught and led.

As to the spiritual equipment, the disciple and co-worker of Jesus today needs much, seemingly more than He gave His first disciples before, at, and after Pentecost. True discipleship starts in believing and loving Jesus well enough to leave all and follow Him. Then all of the rest of the equipment follows, if you continue to follow.

Theological Examinations and Creeds

The only theological examinations Jesus gave His disciples were after this manner, and not after the subsequent creed makers, but "Whom think ye that I am? Lovest Thou Me?" Those who did love Him, and those who love Him well enough to keep His commandments and follow Him all the way are not only made new creatures, but enter into vital union with Him.

They receive gifts from heaven, all the gifts they need "to be in heavenly places in Him," and to do the work of helping bring heaven to earth.

One may sign all the creeds from the so-called Apostle's Creed to that one that was offered here in Macon recently by Friend Mordacai Ham, and still belong to the class who says, "Lord, Lord," without doing His precious will and working pure good upon the earth. While the real disciple of Jesus will receive the supernatural gifts from heaven and will be in vital union with Jesus, the distinctive mark of a disciple--that even all devils as well as all men will understand--will be a Christlike spirit manifesting itself as love for the brethren, for enemies, and for everybody. He that loveth with the love of Christ has the real thing, for God is love.

True love for all also means hatred of all evil, and separation from everything that works evil to anyone. We are to owe no man anything, but to love him and do all possible good and no evil at all. We are to owe no society or group anything but to do God's will concerning them.

Jesus Cast Out Devils, and not Disciples

Jesus never ruled out or cast out a single disciple. He cast out devils. His work was and is to get and keep disciples. Unfortunately too many of His disciples, not having sufficient love and power to cast out devils, have sought to cast out and rule one another. When a disciple could not believe that He had risen from the dead, He gave proof that convinced the doubter. When we can't believe without proof, He gives the proof. Jesus was from the beginning the Lamb slain in our behalf. He went to the cross for the very purpose that we might receive not only forgiveness and remission of sins and release from a sinful nature, but also the immortality and glory that He gave up in order to give to us. There is nothing in Jesus that wants to rule out anyone. His whole longing is to get us into and make us like Him and joint heirs with Him.

Disciples on the Way

Of course there are many true disciples on the way who are yet a mixture of the new leaven from heaven and the old leaven from below.

These will sometimes want to call down fire and cut off the ears and heads of enemies, as well as do many things contrary to the spirit and teachings of Christ. However, as they follow on, Jesus will take out of them everything that is not pure love and good will and bring to triumph the longing for the best possible to come to everyone, to come as quickly as possible, and with the least amount of suffering and tragedy.

As Christ triumphs in you, making you new and like Him, you marvel that it was possible for you ever to have had anything other than pity and compassion for the erring and sinning, and for those who in their blindness have hated you, persecuted you, and tried to make it hardest for you to help them. Head your prayer list with those you think are your worst enemies, and just plot and plan how to make it the hardest possible for them to go where no one should go and the easiest for them to come to themselves, to Christ, and to God's best.

Jesus, the Marriage of God and Humanity

Let me say this as to the Jesus of experience and as revealed by the Holy Spirit: He is everything and more than all the holy and inspired men of God have ever claimed of Him. He is "God with us" on the plane of our needs and understanding through the Holy Ghost. He is God manifested as man, and man manifested as God. He is the successful eternal marriage of God and humanity, of heaven and earth. He is the beginning and the head of the new creation, which is this perfect marriage of the best there and the best here. He is the Servant-Savior, the Ruler of both the invisible and the visible creation, whose superlative perfection and perfect love will so draw and grip that His rule by our free, happy choice shall be as a rod of iron.

CHAPTER 46

"Great Happy Days"
August 11, 1935
Macon Telegraph and News

The Blessed One says: "Give My love to all. Will and work pure good to all. Don't be overcome of evil, but meet and overcome all evil with good. Be now in Me. Be everlastingly and eternally and gloriously Mine. Abide in Me always."

Almost Human Satisfaction Here

I have had four exceedingly happy and satisfactory days here at Mars Hill, which is 15 miles north of Asheville. The elevation is 2700 feet and there are mountains in great numbers in this part of North Carolina that are over six thousand feet high. The college here, which is one of the best junior colleges in the Southeast, is being used for the summer terms of Wake Forest and Meredith Colleges. The place is a rare combination of culture and scenic beauty. There is a remarkable spirit both in the college and community. There are no prisoners here, and if I remember correctly the town went as long as seven years without having to send anybody to jail. The present president of the college, R.L. Moore, has been here about 37 years. He came on horseback when there was a small academy named a college. He insisted that it be called an academy. The trustees refused; so in sending out his announcements he simply said this is called a college, but is an academy. The college, which is a real college now, got out of debt during the Depression.

The days that I have been here have given me unusual opportunities for contacting and sharing with some of the finest minds and spirits in the whole Baptist world. Not only has the retreat, which is being held here, been open to me for witnessing, but also the Baptist church and the college. These people have been wonderful to me in every way. Day before yesterday, Friend Walter N. Johnson, a rare genius, took me to Greenville, Tennessee, the town of a tailor shop and other scenes in connection with the Tennessee life of President Andrew Johnson.

Yesterday our very likeable and gifted friends, Professor and Mrs. Edwin M. Poteat, took us to see Craigy Mountain which is six thousand two hundred and five feet above sea level. The physical magnificence and beauty that one finds on these high heights has to be experienced to be understood. If we had this world redeemed and everything happy in it, I believe I would spend a major part of my time climbing mountain heights with blessed people and worshipping upon those heights.

Identify Yourself with the Underprivileged

Some years ago Friend Walter Johnson was essentially flat on his back with bodily infirmities and with need of means to live upon staring him in the face, and with a great burning desire to do what he was sure God had called him to do. A Voice, as it were, and seeming to be the Voice of God said to him, "Identify yourself with the underprivileged and your health and finances will be cared for until your work is done." He got up quickly and got on the job, and neither health nor necessary means for living and doing His work gave has been lacking.

Seek first the Kingdom of God and His Righteousness and everything you need not only for yourself and your family, but also everything you need for doing God's will, will be added unto you. There never was a time in the history of man on this planet when the call was so loud for the privileged to identify themselves with the interests of the underprivileged, for the up-and-outs to come to the rescue of the down-and-outs!

Gregory S. Camp, Ph.D.

Church with a New Pastor

When I was here at Mars Hill at one of these precious retreats about two years ago, an unusual man and Baptist pastor told me that he has served the church so long that he felt the church needed a new pastor. I replied "Why not become a new man in Christ, and be the new pastor yourself?" I am told that he became that new pastor, and that his church members pass that opinion around. They indeed have a new pastor, and news of it has spread rather widely. As I have been saying to the folk here, the dead cannot raise the dead. A dead pastor cannot raise a dead church to life. It takes the living to bring life to the dead. Jesus was and is so alive that He resurrects everybody and everything receptive to His life. He conducted and conducts no funerals. He only conducts resurrections.

His Life, Health, and Everything Contagious

Mr. Robert Ingersoll, the "Great Agnostic," once said, "If God had made the world, He would have made health instead of disease contagious." This is the way God actually made it, provided you receive His perfect health, life, spirit in and by Jesus Christ. Nobody could give a disease to Jesus because His health destroyed disease. Nobody could put any evil on Jesus because His superlative goodness met and meets all evil with good, all disease with health, all death with life. His great longing is to enter so fully into us and for us to enter and abide so completely in Him that we will receive His marvelous health and life. In fact, we will have so much of Him that everywhere we move people will be catching Him and His salvation and health from us.

Can Only Tell the Truth in the Spirit of Truth

A very precious thing that has come to me of late is dealing with people with grievances against each other has been this: You have to get in the Spirit of Truth before you can either hear the truth, see the truth, or tell the truth. As long as one is in the spirit of the hater, and the falsifier, everything is reported incorrectly. You can't stop lying until you get out of the spirit of falsehood and yield to the Spirit of Truth. The devil can't tell the truth, and even when he quotes scripture, he gives it in a false and lying setting. The Kingdom at hand is just as near you as you are to repenting of being led by your own spirit and all other spirits that are less than the best, and being led by the Spirit of the Lord. In this Spirit, you know and abide in God and have your eyes opened to knowing everything as fast as you need to know. It is not knowledge about God that we need, but the knowledge of God which comes through yielding to Jesus Christ, and through abiding in Him and manifesting Him and living His love way of life.

What is the Baptism of the Holy Spirit?

The question that is asked of me here and among other groups who have not received the supernatural presence, control, and gifts of the Holy Spirit is, "What is the Baptism of the Holy Spirit?" This much is certain, that this Baptism comes from the glorified Lord Jesus Christ. It is the first installment of glorification with Him and being lifted even bodily into His likeness. It is a Heavenly presence and a glorious, happy free possession, and control from Above. It is the Lord Himself in Spirit manifesting Himself into His body or church. It brings the glorified Lord into us and brings us into Him. When He is present and has control through the Spirit, He may manifest upon us and through us any of the Supernatural Gifts, such as wisdom, knowledge, faith, discernment, healing, prophecy, supernatural speaking in tongues, and the supernatural interpretation of these tongues. In the early church it appears that everyone who received the Holy Spirit Baptism and glory spoke as the Spirit gave them utterance, and most of them, if not all, spoke in tongues.

When I sought for the Baptism of the Spirit and for God's best, I did not even know what His best was, and was led by the Spirit to ask Jesus, if He could, to come within and to give me the ability to go His perfect love way and His perfect sincere way. I asked for the Baptism, without tongues if He could give it that way, but with tongues if it could only be received that way. When Heaven took possession of me and Jesus manifested Himself and came within, it was accompanied with supernatural speaking or singing in English, and not in tongues. This gift of supernatural speaking in English when I am enough in the Spirit is still present and I get my clearest light this way, or rather I get the light given through spiritual intuition best expressed and confirmed by this supernatural speaking in English. But about six months after the Divine visitation and control, the Spirit began speaking through me foreign words and phrases. He also sometimes gave me the interpretation of what was spoken

Beyond and not Behind

My advice to churches and individuals who have not received the Holy Spirit like the early Christians received Him is to ask, obey, and yield until they do. If they feel that what is called Pentecost today is not really and fully Pentecost as yet, then they should go to praying that they may have today what the first Christians had, and even beyond what they had, as they are made ready for it. The glory of the latter house is to surpass the glory of the former house. The greatest Pentecost of all is yet to be. Jesus' best in every way is yet to be. Jesus is the first fruits of this Best. We come to His best as we believe in Him, yield to Him, receive Him, receive His Holy Spirit Baptism, as we are led by Him, abide in Him, and bring forth the fruit of God. Jesus became like us that He may make us like Him and make us co-workers with Him in making all things like Him.

Instead of drawing back from anything of His, we should gladly yield to and welcome everything of His just as fast as He is willing to give to us. The Baptism of the Holy Ghost which He gives, or that the Father gives in His name, is for every believer. After the Baptism of the Spirit there must be the life and fruit of the Spirit and the entire sanctification of the Spirit. There must be abiding union with Him. There must be the overcoming of all evil with good, and of all things unlike Him with His Good Spirit. There must be to the perpetual rejoicing in Him and the beholding as in a mirror His glory which changes us from glory to glory into His likeness.

CHAPTER 47

"Glory Hill"
August 18, 1935
Macon Telegraph and News

The Blessed One says: "Belong entirely and wholly and only to Me. Do All Things in Love. Go the way of Perfect love. Be meek and lowly and holy."

Since dictating the last article at Mars Hill College, NC, I have had several days at the big tabernacle where the country people go up for a season and live in booths, as it were, that I gave the name of "Glory Hill." The afternoon that I arrived, Friday, August 2, a little girl, looking to be about six, came in and reported that a neighbor little girl had received the Baptism of the Holy Spirit at the children's prayer meeting that afternoon. The men have their prayer meeting out in the woods and the women have theirs, and apparently the little girls have theirs! I am not sure about the little boys, whether they have a separate one or not. At almost any time of the day or night Glory is likely to break out, anywhere on the Hill.

How the Lord Heals

Last year when I was at this camp meeting, a very precious man in the Lord had overworked in getting things in shape for the camp meeting, and had gone through so much during the spring that he had collapsed and feared nervous prostration. He sent for me to come over to see him. I don't remember just what I said to him, but I infer that I told him to look away from himself and his troubles and look to and at the Lord Jesus Christ, and invite Him to come in the whole of his being and reign in it and use it and make him every whit whole. A short time after I left him, he dropped off to sleep, and when he awoke he was in a Vision and saw the Lord standing by his bed. Seeing the Lord, even in the vision, made him every whit whole. The wholeness included his body, of course, and he even pinched himself to see if it was the same body. The newness and the wholeness have remained.

Last Sunday morning when I was on Glory Hill, I started out to the men's prayer meeting and was summoned to go quickly where there was a lady in some kind of physical suffering and need. I found the summer cabin where she was reclining on the bed. She was surrounded by anxious people, observing the condition of her body. I urged her to look away from herself and symptoms, and to look to the risen and glorified Jesus and leave the body to Him to heal. I felt led to tell the observers-of-symptoms rather than the lookers-to-the-Lord (the others in the cabin) that I felt if Jesus were here in the body of His flesh, He would "put all of you out" who look at symptoms rather than to Him. Quickly the symptoms disappeared and the lady was all right.

Monday evening, we went away up toward North Carolina to see a blessed woman who had decided that she had suffered so much she would rather go on to Heaven and get out of it. She is the mother of five children, who seemed to need her much more than anybody needs her in Heaven just yet. After she saw this and began to look away from her body and symptoms to the living Lord, I noticed indications that she wanted to get up. In a short time she was walking over the room, praising the Lord, and a little later, ate the largest supper of anybody there except myself. I don't know if she was completely healed, but something marvelous occurred. If she looks to the Lord and trusts Him with the body, and feeds on Him and not upon symptoms and bodily feelings, the Lord will make her whole.

Glory Deliverance

My friend who was renewed, described earlier, told me many good things as to how the Lord had dealt with him and his family. Before he was sanctified and received the Baptism of the Holy Spirit, he was a great tobacco user, and one day when he was plowing with his mule, he was given, in a vision, letters standing out just above the mule, "Know ye not that ye are the temple of the Living God, and if any man defile the temple, Him will God destroy," and a Voice would say to him: "That's the tobacco." It is needless to say that deliverance came from the tobacco. And 19 years ago, his wife who is now the picture of health, was nearly dead with consumption. One day when he was pulling fodder he received the witness of the Spirit that his prayer for her healing had been answered. He was so sure of it, he did not even ask his wife if anything had happened to her. For two or three days, when he did ask her, she said that she had even forgotten about the trouble. The Lord does this very thing. He not only puts our sins in the sea of forgetfulness, but also gets our physical infirmities out of our consciousness, as well as out of our bodies.

The Lord Doeth the Work

Away back in my early days, when I was feeling after the truth as to how the Spirit does His work and how we can co-work with Him, I had a sense of responsibility to think about the Lord and His perfection, and to try to get my mind off the sense testimony that denies the Lord and His holiness and wholeness. Of course, it is far better to think health than it is to think sickness, and to think the perfection of the Lord than to think about the imperfection of the world of ordinary experience. The night before I received the glorious Baptism and Jesus within, it was made known to me, as I understood it, that all I had to do was to go in love, visit the sick, and visit the prisoners, but without any responsibility of healing them or trying to heal them, and to set them free. Later on, it was spoken to me in the highest kind of way, that my only responsibility was that of being in union with Him. Previous to this, I was told to go in love, and that He would always be in me. I would find that every time I was put deeply in the Spirit, every sense of responsibility would go, except the joyous responsibility of looking to him and of abiding in Him. To be in Heavenly Places in Him is to be like little children, not only free from sin, but also free from the cares that most grownup people have.

Gregory S. Camp, Ph.D.

Jesus Appeared and did the Work

This summer in Philadelphia, I got another witness to the truth that the Lord had been seeking to bring me into glorious happy freedom from every worry and care and from every responsibility except the responsibility of being in vital and happy union with Him. The remarkable little gift here that the Lord has taught, through inspired dreams and spiritual interpretation of these dreams, saw me near to Jesus in His best land, and saw Him send me accompanied by an angel over into the land of confusion. All I had to do was to point people to Him and to share the light of love He gave to me. To all who were ready to be released, He revealed Himself.

How happy and glorious this is! The Lord alone is to be exalted in our day. All we have to do are the simple things that the children and "servants" can do! He's the Teacher; He's the Healer; He's Everything! And you can turn to the Lord, and look to Him and look away from your problems and symptoms, just as well as anybody else can. You don't have to repeat so much prayer of petition, but you do have to look away from yourself to Him; and you do have to forgive everything and love everybody and yield to the Good Spirit of Jesus. If you do this, it becomes easy for you not only to pray according to His will, but also to have the witness that He has heard you and that you do receive what you have asked for. You will find yourself believing so surely that you can laugh at every symptom and every feeling to the contrary.

Participation in Divine Nature

The other morning when I was at Greensboro, North Carolina I read in a book review in *The Christian Century* some sentences like these: The essential conception of the Kingdom of God is that it is a higher order of being in which the Divine will is fulfilled in Christianity, a participation in the Divine nature. Mystery and glory are the words that best express the ultimate reality. Revelation comes by self-surrender and by becoming as little children. It comes by faith through the Spirit; and faith is the frank acceptance of the Divine gift. The Spirit that gives revelation is also the power that responds to it. God in giving to us and gives us the capacity to receive from Him.

More and more, it comes to me that unless you are in the Good Spirit of Jesus, the Spirit of Truth and the Spirit of Love, you cannot know the Truth, hear the Truth, and tell the Truth. So the first thing for everyone out of the Good Spirit is to stop everything else until he gets in the Good Spirit.

CHAPTER 48

"Vital Union with Jesus"
January 12, 1936
Macon Telegraph and News

The Easiest Man to Save

The privilege of meeting and hearing the great Japanese Christian Toyohiko Kagawa has been an enrichment that I trust will increase until the love of Jesus has won out and triumphed. The perfection that he seeks for everyone and that he testifies to gives you the sense that he loves the whole human race. He prays, plans, and works for its good, as good parents plan, pray, and work for their children. Kagawa can only be understood in this light. All of his plans for cooperation and coordination are out of this great heart of love to bring the Kingdom of God to all men and to the whole of life. He literally lives and moves in the prayer and labors of a love that includes the good of all. He is nearer to the universal soul (of Emerson) and universal man than anyone else that I know. He is the easiest man to love that I have ever met, and he calls forth a kind of love that calls us to love everybody, pray for everyone, and labor for everybody's good in every way open to us. Kagawa makes us feel tender and compassionate like I felt when something touched me deeply in the days of my boyhood.

The Lord's Gifts to Each are for All

Among other things that have been brought home to me in a deeper way through these contacts with Kagawa is that any good or gift that the

Lord imparts to any of us are for all the rest of us, too. We receive them by being open, grateful, and humble rather than closed, proud, and resistant. If we are humble and wise enough to receive a prophet of the Lord in the name of the Lord, we receive the prophet's reward. If we are receptive, appreciative, and humble before such a revelation of the Lord's love in Kagawa, the way is opened for us not only to receive the lover's reward, but to be filled with the Lover's Love.

These things we have from the Lord, that Kagawa has not yet received, are for him; just as what he has that we are lacking is for us. As I said to a group of Atlanta friends, how foolish it is to become sectarian and set up walls around something you have from the Lord, when everything of God's is ours if we would only humble ourselves and enter into blessed union with Jesus. We must be open to recognize, welcome, and greatly rejoice in everything and everybody He has given.

The Two Sides of the Cross

Kagawa, for example, seems to know better than any other disciple of Jesus that I know about, the earth-side of taking up the cross daily and denying self, and going Jesus' way of almost unbelievable love. But he does not seem to know yet so much about the wonder of the cross from the glory side as it has even been permitted some of us to know. I had the privilege of telling him something about this other side, and that Jesus will manifest to us and come within us, and lift us up into heavenly places in Him, the same as He did to the first disciples. Kagawa, instead of thinking it was fanatical, or unreasonable, said, "That is great."

There seems to be two fundamental temptations for the followers of Jesus: one being to get on the mount of transfiguration and build tabernacles there, and the other is to be so busy down in the valleys that you never take time to receive the power and glory that He seeks to give.

Jesus wants all of us to be in heavenly places in Him all the time; at the same time He wants us to be living out and manifesting His love as our life's business down in the prisons and dungeons of greatest need. The more we feed and feast on Him, the more we live in the Spirit, the more power we have to do His will in places of greatest need. The more loving we are to all of His children and to all of His creatures, the more blessed the fellowship and union with Him. Neither union with Him nor perfect service to men can come to perfection except in marriage to each other. The commandment to love your neighbor is like the commandment to love the Lord. As Kagawa says, the man that says he can love God and not love God's children is grossly mistaken about it.

In the old covenant the first commandment was to love the Lord, the second like unto it was to love one's neighbor as he loves himself. In the new covenant the new and superlative commandment is to pass on the immeasurable love of God to another as He loves us. We are saved by grace, therefore live in the grace life. Not only do to others what you would have them do to you, but do to others as the Lord does to you.

Grace and Good Works

Our salvation is by the unspeakable love, mercy, and grace of our Lord and Savior Jesus Christ. Any prodigal who will draw nigh home in humility and desiring to do his Father's will, will find himself in the arms, and at the feast of the Father. But to abide with the Father forever, and to stay at the feast forever, everyone must be continuously humble and obedient, and become a co-laborer with the Father in welcoming and in serving every returning prodigal. We are created in Christ Jesus for a life of love and good works, and for nothing else. To perpetually abide in the grace of the Father and to feast at His table, one must devote himself to doing the Father's will of perfect love and perfect service of love. Until we come to a perfect balance of feasting with Him, and doing His will, those who put the emphasis upon doing His will get to the feast; while those whose primary emphasis is on the feast, without doing His will, will come to realize that they will not be permitted to stay at the feast.

There is no way out of this thing but through union with Him and through doing His will perpetually and through being made like him in Spirit. When we live a life devoted to the services of love and mercy, and the Kingdom of God at hand, we enter into the His perfection in every way He is perfect. To have a part in this kingdom we must put off all the unlikeness and put on the likeness of the King. We can't get near the feast without putting on the wedding garment.

Predestined for This Very Thing

Since the Lord has created us for Himself, nothing can satisfy us until we find ourselves in Him. We have to be conformed to His will and affections and love way of life. Everything else will fail us. Everything turns to ashes outside of Him and outside of His will. Nothing has real value except being conformed to His image and will, and that is His happy predestination for us.

When we see our distance from Him, it is seen to be humanly impossible to be like Him even in the perfection of love and unselfishness. But glory to Him, He has not only made us for this, but as we yield to Him, He puts the ability within us; He plants Himself within us. He not only created and called us for this purpose, but he works everything together to bring it about. As soon as we love Him and yield to the call according to His loving purpose concerning us, He lets us know that everything that happens to us or that He permits to come our way, is working for our good. He brings us at times, at least, to the sense that we not only can make it, but that He has us in the places where we have to be to make it.

CHAPTER 49

"Overcome or be Overcome"
March 22, 1936
Macon Telegraph and News

The witness of the Spirit, backed by faith and the obedience of faith, always wins against all testimony that denies the witness of the Spirit. In the glorified Jesus, we have perfect everything; we have in and through Him Christlikeness. This includes dominion over every sin and sinfulness, every form of unbelief and disobedience, and failure to yield. We need to look steadfastly to and at Jesus and His perfection for us. As we look away from the things of the world and death to the Giver of Life and Perfect One, we are changed to the degree of our yieldedness to His Likeness. This goes on and on until we are ready to be transformed, even bodily, into the likeness of the body of His resurrection and glorification. Even now there is perfect healing for everyone who will look away from the things that cause the trouble, and look to and at our perfect Lord, and everything good and blessed.

We are saved by faith, by the right look. Even the children in the wilderness who were bitten by the fiery serpents were all healed when they look away from the serpents and their bites and looked to the brazen serpent that was lifted up as a type of the Perfect Redeemer and Healer. A friend asks why the serpent was used as a type for the Perfect One who was there in Spirit and was to become manifest in the flesh. This may be a partial explanation: In the beginning it was the disobedient serpent that caused the trouble. The Blessed Redeemer is everything that's perfect and blessed. He is typified by the perfect serpent as antidote to the poison of the disobedient one that caused the trouble.

Jesus becomes everything needed for deliverance, healing, and transformation into His nature, likeness, and kingdom. The devil has never been a creator. He is only a usurper, imitator, and one who perverts.

In the millennium the serpent is made innocent, as will be everything that has been so terrible during the period of disobedience, hatred, and carnal warfare. But what a different serpent! The bite is all gone and he's become the plaything of little children. I have a friend who says the serpent will not only be in the new creation, but he certainly gets over into the millennium.

The God of Jacob

Among the last exceptionally good things in Miami was the privilege of listening to Friend F. Crossley Morgan, the son of G. Campbell Morgan. He tells me that his residence is in Augusta, Georgia and he has given up pastoral work to give all of his time to Bible exposition and for the conducting of Bible conferences. I did not get to hear him on the New Testament, but his expositions on of Psalms 46 and Psalms 57 were most illuminating and helpful. He does not use an extra word. He holds to his subjects, and says nothing but which clarified and helped. I never heard his gifted father do anything quite so well. In referring to the phrase "the God of Jacob," he said in effect, there is great comfort here for all of us who are much more like Jacob in his imperfections than we are like Joseph in his unusual perfection of spirit and life. We know that He is the God of one like Joseph, but how comforting to be reminded that He is also the God of one like Jacob!

The Necessity of Overcoming

During the happy hours I have had out here in the country when I have not been listening to the Spirit, are the wonderful things friends had to tell me, and sharing with them some of the precious things that the Lord has given me. I have been reading some choice books, and I have had wonderful minutes with S.D. Gordon's <u>Quiet Talks on Our Lord's Return</u>. The spirit of Friend Gordon is blessed, and he presents the scriptural teaching concerning the Lord's return and the redeemed heart's yearning for it in a way that's softening and melting. It seems to be his best book, but every book of his I have read seems the best yet. Let me share this one thought: Writing of the Lord's messages to the churches in Revelation, Friend Gordon says:

> "The message is an intense yearning plea for overcomers. They (the churches) were in the midst of the very sort of time His Olivet Talk spoke of. They must overcome or be overcome. The forces of evil were making a tremendous effort to overcome them. His coming is intimately connected with their overcoming. It is a tremendous plea, mingling sternness with great tenderness. Even as of a loving father to his son who is beginning to yield to the world's downward tug. It is an intense plea to His followers today to be overcomers in the midst of evil-doers, and those being overcome."

There is nothing that is taught more clearly by life experience as well as by the Spirit than that you'll be overcome unless you overcome, and the only way to overcome evil is to meet it with good. When you meet evil with evil, you are overcome by evil. It is only when you meet hate with love, darkness with light, and every form of evil with its opposite good that you overcome. We are called to the Lord's life of pure good will and good deeds to all. As we yield to this call we come up out of the fall into the Kingdom of Heaven at hand, and we stay in this Kingdom as we look to Jesus and meet all evil with good. To stay in Heavenly places in Him we have to manifest the Heavenly Spirit and give out good and only good to seemingly bad people. You can't meet any evil with evil and stay in Heaven. But you can have Heaven in blessed union with Jesus in the midst of evil about you, if you will only radiate with the Spirit and deeds of Heaven.

Go the Whole Way

The other day while contemplating the threatened dangers at our door, I made inquiry as to how we could best co-work with Jesus to stop hate and war, and all that hurts, harms, and destroys. In order to bring His reign of love and good will upon earth to men and the whole creation, the Answer came: "Go the whole way of perfect, holy love. Be wholly Mine. Abide in Me. Give my Love to all. Meet and overcome evil with good. Do nothing but deeds of pure kindness, mercy, and goodness."

We should be making intercession for all the nations and all the rulers of the nations, and commanding them in the Spirit and in the name of Jesus to love one another, and to repent of all their hates and bitterness. Pray that Jesus and His Love win as quickly and as gloriously as can be!

CHAPTER 50

"The Basis of Inexpressible Joy"
April 26, 1936
Macon Telegraph and News

The Blessed One says, "Humble thyself. Abide in Me, Give all men My great love. Go the whole way of perfect love."

All Things are Ours

Through union with Jesus, we have not only the Lord's joy, but the all things of His that give that joy; and everything of the risen Lord has in it a note of perpetual joy, praise, and thanksgiving. In union with the risen Jesus there is a perpetual inflow and outflow of rivers of joy. The fruit of the Spirit is not only love, but also joy, peace, and all other virtues and graces that are joy-giving. In union with Jesus, one is already in the Spirit, in the Lord's victory, and inheritance, and has the assurance that through this continuous union the victory and inheritance are to become literal, visible, and eternal.

All Things Work Together for Good

The only way to visible and eternal victory and joint-heirship with Jesus is for one who is led by the Spirit, is in vital touch and union with Jesus, and has the witness that everything is working together for his good. He also has the hope and is filled with the desire and prayer that everything shall also work together for the highest good of each and all. When you want nothing but good to come to all, and seek and work for the highest good of all, no evil can enter the heart, mind, and will. That which is encountered from without becomes opportunity, blessing, and the releasing of others, and for the development of your own spiritual muscles.

Has the Secret of Overcoming

One who has the Spirit and secret of Jesus, that loves everybody, even one's worst enemies, and that meets all evil with good, and never yields to the temptation to fight with carnal weapons, is always overcoming, and is never overcome. You just cannot be overcome with hate as long as you meet all hate with love. Neither can you be overcome by any evil as you look to the Lord and choose to please Him, and meet every evil with good.

And if We Should Slip

Anyone who gives himself to Jesus and to His Good Spirit, and love way of meeting all evil with good, should he make a slip, there is always open to him the grace of repentance. And with the acknowledgement of his slip, he finds in Jesus his Advocate and Restorer, and never his prosecuting attorney and accuser. Even the devil, when he finds out that you are going to tell (confess) everything you do while under his influence, will let you alone rather than be exposed. You yourself had rather stop every form of sinning than have to confess it, and make the best possible restitution. Any sinner who will do God's will concerning sin, will stop his sinning.

Grace all the more Abound

Where sin, weakness, and failure have been at their worst and done their worst, they are God's opportunity to do His best and to make His chief of sinners ready to say, "Lord what would You have me do?" The sinner is not only forgiven and washed, and given a new heart, mind, will, and a new everything, but is also made the chief witness, prophet, apostle and co-laborer. The worst drunkard may become the best channel for the release of other drunkards, and the worst everything may become the best witness for the Lord. The best co-laborer to bring release and new life to the worst and neediest in every realm of bondage and need is someone who has been there himself. Everything is turned to good for everyone who turns wholly to the good.

Never without Work, and the Best Work

Everyone who gives up his false will for the Lord's perfect and good will, and who is led by Him and His Good Spirit, is given the best work of all for his own growth and perfection of Christlikeness and for service to others. One in union with Jesus is never without work, the best work, and no one can be happy except in activities that produce happiness. No one can be miserable except in the spirit of idleness, and activities that produce misery. As the friend to whom I am dictating says, "The best work for every man is the thing that is nearest at hand that the Lord would have him do."

Nobody Envies You

Yet another happiness about this work for the Lord is that you have all the room you need, and nobody envies you as you go the way of perfect love and perfect services, where they are most needed. Nobody was in the Good Samaritan's way, nor the Levite, when left entirely free to do the highest will of God. When you are in the will of God nobody is in your way; when you are out of the will of God, it seems that nearly everybody is in your way. Whenever there is mean strife and competition, rivalry is there in the absence of the Spirit and the will of the Lord. In that place, there is the assertion of the spirit of disobedience, the downright foolishness of this world, and the prince of this world. After all, selfish persons and spirits get what they think they want (and find in the end is just what they don't want); everything of God is left open and free.

Don't Have to Beg or Consider Pay

In this heavenly way of wisdom, where you are set free from false desire and pride, it takes so little to meet your bodily needs, and without thinking of those needs, they are always supplied. You just can't put the will, love, wisdom and Kingdom of God first without having everything you really need supplied. The friend to whom I am dictating says "The supply is more than abundant; that there comes in more than you can use yourself; that you can be a generous giver right along while you are receiving." He and his wife have tried this out beyond any others I have in mind just now.

Such Happy Ways of Seeing, Reacting

Those who have the mind and Spirit of Jesus have such happy ways of seeing and reacting, even in the face of situations that those without this mind and spirit worry and go under. They who have His mind and spirit know that Jesus Christ is their present life, health, and healer, even in the midst of so much death, sickness and pain. But at the same time they know that their present sufferings are light and only for a moment, as it were, and are working a greater weight of glory. While they know that through faith in and union with Jesus they have His eternal life and will never see death, and that even their bodies may be clothed upon or transformed rather than unclothed (die), all that is mortal of them may be swallowed up of life. They can nevertheless leave their bodies or tents here with a shout of joy and triumph, because they know that if they go out of their present tents or bodies they go into a mansion or perfect body prepared for them by the Resurrected Lord. If you take away their goods, they can take joyfully to it, knowing that they have something so much better and rejoice in the Power of the Mighty Lord. When they are poorest in spirit, they are most in the Kingdom of Heaven. Indeed, Jesus gives the secret of right reacting in all situations so that one is brought into deeper fellowship with Him, and in the greater victory and glory.

Gregory S. Camp, Ph.D.

So Much Heaven on the Way to Heaven

As a dear old sister put it, she was having such a good time going to Heaven that even if she should be turned down when she got there, she would shout all around the outside of Heaven, telling them how good the journey and quest had been on the way. Of course, the deeper truth is that the one who abides in Jesus, and goes the way of Heaven is sure to enter Heaven. One who finds Heaven already as the most blessed state and way of life is also sure to find Heaven as the most perfect place, as well as state and way of life.

The Best at Hand Now

When Jesus was on earth, the very highest possible will of God was for Him to go to the Cross, "as a ransom for all, to be testified in due time." After He went to the cross and tomb, the very highest of all was to raise Him from the dead—the whole of Him, every atom of Him—and make Him the head of the new creation, with all power in Heaven and earth. And after He had opened the eyes of His friends, the next thing was for Him to ascend to highest Heaven, and the highest throne. After this was accomplished, He had received the Gift of the Holy Spirit with power to be omnipresent, so that He could Baptize, guide, and transform with the Holy Spirit without limit. This work was for Him and His Spirit and Way of Life to be incarnated and victorious in His people, in the creation, and in the whole of life.

As I understand the Spirit, what He is seeking just now with us is to make us entirely humble, receptive, and responsive; to sanctify us wholly and to preserve us blameless in spirit, soul, and body, and bring us forth ready for the great event ahead and at hand—the manifestation of Jesus in victory and control, and our manifestation with Him in His victory and control.

The highest attainment, then, in the days of Jesus was His offering up in behalf of all. Since then, and especially now, the highest is personal preparation for His manifestation and our manifestation in Him in victory over every enemy of man and life. The whole creation is groaning for this very thing, and those of us who have the first fruits of the Spirit are groaning for it too. Nothing short of His perfect victory of love, and a life of perfection of spirit, mind, soul, and body, and nothing short of seeing Him as He is, and being with Him on the plane of His glory, can satisfy. As happy as we are on the way, if we are on the way, we long and groan within ourselves for the full victory, for the redemption of the body.

Humble Thyself

Yesterday, when I asked how I could best help to bring this full redemption, the answer came, "Humble Thyself." When I asked how to be every whit whole, the answer was "Be Wholly Sanctified." The perpetual call to all of us is to be in vital touch with Him, and to be in vital union with Him all the time, and to live and to give His love all the time, to everybody, and to the whole creation.

CHAPTER 51

"The Wonders of Love"
November 22, 1936
Macon Telegraph and News

I find in my mail a letter from a very gifted friend who says, "I am sure you know that I feel as you do about the wonders of love as an instrument of regeneration. Love never faileth." Other things may succeed for a time and in the end fail, and love may seem for a time to fail, but in the end wins. Love gives abundant life and is healing to the body as well as the soul. Those who hate are murderers; those who fail to love, fail to live; those who love really live.

The Antidote to Suicide

A friend writes me that he is tempted to want to get out of life. As I have written him this morning (Saturday, November 14) the remedy for a temptation like this is to become Jesus Christ-centered and away from self-centered. As the ablest man if the past century, Count Tolstoy, found, the thought of God always takes away the desire to put an end to life and brings a desire to live.

At one period of Tolstoy's life, he was so tempted to destroy his body that he would not allow himself to be near any instrument of death. But every time before attempting suicide the thought of God would come to him and with the thought of God there always came a desire to live. So the revelation came to him that since to think about God makes us want to live, and is the antidote for the temptation to want to get out of life, that God Himself is life. With this revelation the temptation to take his life left, never to return.

There is great insight here. God being perfect life always gives the desire to live and to live well. God came as Jesus to give life and it give it abundantly. Jesus never did cause any death. He was so alive that everywhere He went, the dead could not remain dead in His presence. Neither could the sick who believed remain sick in His presence.

It was always His will to heal all who came to Him for healing as well as to save all who were willing to be saved. To get your mind on Him and off of yourself and your fears, symptoms, and troubles opens the way for His healing and saving power to work in your whole being. As I said to a friend this morning, "No one ever sinks as long as his or her attention and affection is upon Jesus; one only sinks as he looks away from Jesus and looks to the waves and the seeming danger."

To be occupied with yourself and your symptoms cuts you off from the great healing power that wants to work in you mightily. To look away from yourself and symptoms and to look steadfastly to Jesus and rejoice in His perfection, opens the way for supernatural life, health, and energy to come from the Lord to you. I don't believe that there is anything with anyone that will not go when the look to Jesus becomes steadfast enough, and when the absorption in Him becomes such that there will be the forgetting of self and troubles of self. Even the lifting of the brazen serpent in the wilderness, a type of Christ, healed everyone who looked away from the deadly serpents and their bites and looked to that which gave life and healing. If the type produced such miracles, how much more the Reality?

It was not a question of how badly or how slightly the children of Israel were bitten; but simply a question whether or not they looked at the serpents, or whether they looked away from them by looking to the remedy. All who looked to the serpents died; all who looked to the remedy and looked away from the serpents lived. Now, it is not how much is wrong with you; all depends upon the way you look. If you look to Jesus and look to Him with affection and desire to be like Him and dedicate yourself to doing His will, there is perfect redemption, renewing, transformation, and healing for you. But as long as you are absorbed with yourself, your troubles and symptoms, you are captive. Still, at any moment, you have the privilege of repenting, of changing your look and direction.

Gregory S. Camp, Ph.D.

Vital Union, All That is Needed!

Vital union with Jesus is all that is needed for His salvation, healing, and abundant life to become ours. He is the True and the Living Vine, the Life-Giving and the Health-Giving Vine. He wants us to be branches of His, and if we look to Him, we are grafted into Him and His Spirit, nature, life, mind, health, healing, and everything flow into us. The branch, while much smaller than the vine, is of the same life and nature as the vine.

Just as the Father was fully expressed in Jesus, so Jesus longs to be fully expressed in and through us. Jesus clothed Himself with the glory of the Father, and the Father clothed Himself with Jesus. Our call and urge is to clothe ourselves with Jesus and His Good Spirit and qualities, and to put off all that is unlike Jesus. As we are willing to do this, Jesus not only enables us, but He also clothes Himself with us. He also wants to do in and through us the works that He did on earth, and greater works than these, because He has gone on to the Father. Since Jesus died for us and rose from the dead, and then ascended on High and received the promised gift of the Holy Spirit, He was given the power to impart the gift of the Holy Spirit to us and to impart Himself to us. He can do more through anyone wholly yielded to Him and in perfect union with Him than the Father did through Him in the days of His ministry in the flesh.

"He Doeth the Works"

While the Father clothed Himself with and as Jesus, it was the Father in Jesus who did the mighty works. So now when Jesus is permitted to clothe Himself with us, whatever He seems to do as us, will be Himself doing the work. I know of several instances where Jesus has done the most precious things for people and for a time it appeared as though a disciple of His was doing these precious things; but later it would be revealed to them that is was really Jesus and not the disciples. As we yield to Jesus and enter into union with Him, we may expect more and more that Jesus will clothe Himself with us and do His blessed works through us and as us.

The Only Responsibility

For a long time I observed that I would load myself up with weights and duties beyond my ability to cope with them, but when I would get to the end of myself, the whole load would be lifted and that I would become light, free, happy, and without a care or a burden of responsibility, except to be in union with Him. Something like 12 to 15 years ago, it was revealed to me with the highest authority and certainty that my only responsibility was the responsibility of being in union with Him. In that union, He does the works. It is the happiest thing on earth for Him to do His blessed work through us. But what a burden to feel that you are called to do things that you haven't the ability to do! We have no ability to do supernatural things except through union with Him, so that He does them in, through, and as us.

The coming of the Kingdom is to be the Kingdom of God or the Kingdom of our Lord and Christ. It will be the Lord and His Good Spirit, love, power, dominion, and glory victorious in us, and victorious in the creation. He has all power to make us in the likeness of His perfection. We have no power to make Him in the likeness of our imperfections. God is in Christ reconciling the world to Himself, and unto the perfection of God, and not to reconciling God to any evil or imperfection.

Since we are to be like Jesus, as we yield to Him and happily go with Him, we need not be disturbed in the least about our own imperfections and diseases. It is our happy privilege to be concerned with and absorbed with Him and His perfection, which perfection is for us and the creation. No matter what we seem to be like now, our predestination is to be like Him. As we love Him and yield happily to His predestination to be like Him in everything, all things are working together to make us like Him.

It is all so Wonderfully Simple

The way the Lord deals with us is in such a marvelous simplicity that babes in the Lord understand even better than the wisest and most prudent. Just last Sunday a friend was telling me that when she was dangerously ill a year ago that her healing started in this way: Friends gathered around her to pray for her healing. Someone sang, "I Once was Lost, but now I'm Found." She said, "I was once sick but now I am healed." With this the friend says the healing power of God struck her body and continued to work until she was healed.

At the meeting Sunday where some of the Atlanta friends, fresh in the Spirit and in their first love were present, one of them said: "When I humbled myself the Lord sanctified me. I feel the Spirit of the Lord on my job and everywhere I go." He will bless us anywhere we are when our hearts are fixed on Him. It is not what we are doing externally that counts so much as the Spirit and attitude we are in.

Seek and do Happily the Very Highest

This morning I found in my mail so many requests that it seemed beyond me to discharge them. When I started to make the effort, it began to flow in my soul to do the highest (and the highest is often to be the servant of the lowest), and to do the highest cheerfully, happily, and as well as I can.

If we give ourselves to do the very highest, we will never be overworked. If we give ourselves to be less than the highest, we are likely to be overworked and over-burdened. Moreover, if we give ourselves to the very highest that the Lord has for us, we are sure to get the very highest and also sure to get everything we need on the way to do it. But if we seek secondary things, we are likely to miss even secondary things and are sure to miss the very highest.

Seeking the Highest, the Basis of Unity

If we seek the very highest, which is blessed union with Jesus and bearing the fruit of this union, we will be drawn into blessed fellowship with all who are seeking the Lord's best. But those who put anything ahead of the very highest, no matter how good it may be, are sure to divide into sects. Only as we are led by Jesus and His Good Spirit will we be in blessed union with Him and also in blessed union with all who are being led by Him and His Good Spirit.

CHAPTER 52

"The Full Will of God"
(For Every Detail of Our Lives, and for the Whole of Life)
January 3, 1937
Macon Telegraph and News

The Christmas season has brought me much good. Today here in Macon, December 29, is as perfect a winter day as I have ever seen—even in Miami, and seemingly as perfect a temperature as could be at any season of the year anywhere in the world. Best of all, the call has been given with new inspiration and authority to bring every detail of life, as well as the whole of life, into the full will, wisdom, and love of God. The Lord has always held me to what seemed to be the highest decisions when He had me caught in a close place. He seeks to bring us to the place where we happily choose and do His will about everything, about the seemingly little things, and the intermediate things, as well as the big things. When we happily choose to do His will about everything, we are no longer under external compulsion, and do not have to get into such close places before we call upon the Lord for His way and deliverance. The wonder of the New Covenant relationship with the Lord is that He so writes His law, nature, and desires within that we go to do His will as naturally as the birds go to the air.

In this New Covenant relationship, all are taught of the Lord from the least to the greatest, not from the greatest to the least, and no one has to be led in a second hand way, but each is immediately led and taught of the Lord, as well as taught and blest by everyone else who is so led and taught. The disciple of a disciple has never been so vital, real, and free as the immediate disciple of the Lord. The day comes, and is now here, when it is the high privilege for all of us to ask for the incarnation and the "inwriting" of the Lord, of His nature, will, and reason so deeply within us, and within the whole of us, that we are no longer divided personalities—one part of us wanting His best, the other parts wanting what is contrary. When we are as one, the whole of us is happily disposed to receive and to do His best and highest, and to glorify Him in everything.

Every Realm to be Brought into Him

Every realm of life, everything of the spirit, mind, body, business, social relationships, and in fact the whole of life, and all the details of living are to be brought into the will, spirit, and wisdom of the Lord; in fact, simply into the Lord Himself. The heavenly leaven is first planted at the point and points of greatest receptivity and conscious need. But its work is to leaven the whole of life. The leaven has the power to change life, but life has not power to change the leaven. Jesus has power to make us like Him, but we have no power to make Him like our unlikeness to Him. God is in Jesus reconciling us to Himself, and to His Perfect Everything, and not reconciling God to any of our imperfections. Light has power over darkness, but darkness has no power over light. Holy love has power over hate, but hate has no power over or against Divine Love.

Pilate thought he had power over Jesus, or at least said he had, but as Jesus reminded him, he had no power except derived power. Jesus had original creative power. Not only does the Father have full creative power, but He has also given the same power to the Son, so that the Son may do the same works as the Father. As Jesus realized, no man had power to take His life. He laid it down voluntarily. Through His laying it down, and the resurrection and the glorification, gift of the Holy Spirit, and the gift of omniscience and omnipotence that were to follow, He planted Himself in every one of us, and in the whole of creation, and brings us and the creation forth into the perfection of His nature and likeness.

Nature Never Opposed Jesus

Neither nature, nor devils, nor diseases ever disobeyed Jesus. When he said to the storm "Be Still!" there was a great calm. When He commanded devils to come out, they departed. When He said for sicknesses to leave, they went. Dead men never opposed Him either. "Hallelujah! Hallelujah!" says the Spirit. When He said "Come forth!" or "Arise!" obedience was sure and instantaneous. Jesus did not conduct any funerals. He only conducted resurrections. Nobody could stay dead in His presence. As Martha and Mary knew, nobody died (or stayed dead) when He was around.

The only obedience to Jesus came and comes from the free wills of men that He wins, but does not compel. It would have to be this way for us to be like Him. He had the power of choice, and always used it to choose the good, the very best. He awaits on the throne of the universe for us to use our freedom to choose like He chose. The Kingdom of Heaven would be here in great power and glory if all of us or even if enough of us used our whole power of choice to chose only good, and the very best for ourselves and all others. Happily for us that by choosing to use our power of choice to choose Him, and choose to please Him in everything, we choose the highest good for each and all in everything. We enter into heavenly places in Him and become co-workers to bring the rest into this union, and to bring His Kingdom, or reign of love in the whole of life. The greatest joy of all will be when the victory is complete and as universal as can be, but what joy there is on the way to perfect joy!

The Contagion of Love and Goodness

One of the keenest joys that I have had yesterday and today came from some visits with a friend whom I met in the Bibb County jail something over a year ago. He first boasted of his unbelief. Then a friend challenged him to listen in to what might be said to him by the Good Spirit and to follow the clearest light and guidance given to him. Everyone who is willing to listen for the highest guidance with the purpose to follow it, is sure to get it.

This interesting man got the guidance (and followed it) to stop lying, and to stop cigarettes, and to stop everything—as he became aware of it—that worked injuriously to himself and to others. He tells me that he never did drink, or disseminate licentious ways, "because anyone who would do this is too big a fool even to make a good crook."

He told me yesterday that the love of one man for him, the man who challenged him to listen to what the Spirit had to say, caused him to so treasure this man, that through this love he had been led on to love the Lord, and to love everybody. There is nothing so contagious as real love and goodness.

The man went cheerfully from the Bibb country jail to a Georgia chain gang. He was sentenced for two years. He showed such a fine spirit and was so dependable that he soon became a trusty and a great help to the warden, as well as an inspiration to the prisoners themselves. His spirit and services were such that he was released a few days ago, and now has work which he is doing with an efficiency and joyfulness that gives me a spiritual uplift every time I call to see him.

He says that in the past when he would try to go straight and to make good, and succeeded in getting a job, when it was found out that he had been in prison or an ex-convict, he was fired. But now, by telling the truth, he finds that people are concerned in helping him. The truth, when told in love, and told on ourselves and to other people, works wonders.

So far as I remember, I have never failed in an effort to get something to do for a man who confessed deeply enough and forsaken thoroughly enough. I have found that it is easier for a man to get a job of this (honest) fallen type, than for one who had never fallen. There is not only more joy in heaven over the repentance of sinners than even over the righteousness that needs no repentance, but on the part of right-feeling people there is also more joy on earth. No man has made the right use of a bad past until he has turned it, or let the Lord turn it, to a great asset.

By Prayer and the Right Spirit

My friend finds that by talking it over with the Lord, and by yielding and manifesting the Good Spirit, victories are easy. Even the man from whom he stole the car that sent him up for two years helped to get him out of the chain gang. A fine friendship has been set up between them, and the former prosecutor furnished the car for bringing him from the chain gang to Macon.

A recent victory that the friend has had was over the desire for coffee. For one day he fought hard against it and enjoyed the exhilaration that comes from overcoming. As the friend to whom I am dictating says, "It is not that the evil is in the coffee, but that there is great reward for every victory over every unnecessary indulgence that one wins through the Spirit." They that are Christ's are not slaves to the desires of the flesh.

Delivered from the Desire to Die

Another very keen joy of the holiday season has been to find a person who tried to get out of life by taking poison, has been delivered, forgiven, and been greatly blessed spiritually. You just can't turn yourself and your sins and blunders over to the Lord without being more blessed than ever. He turns all to good that we turn over to Him, especially when we turn ourselves over to Him.

CHAPTER 53

"New Covenant Perfection"
August 22, 1937
Macon Telegraph and News

Recently in a meeting at Prospect Heights, Pennsylvania, it was stated that the difference between the old covenant that made nothing perfect, and the new covenant that is to make us perfect as He is perfect, is that the Old Covenant sought to achieve ideal justice while the New Covenant is to achieve Perfect Everything through Perfect Love. You cannot be perfect except as you minister or give out Perfect Love and perfect everything, as well as freely receive perfect love and perfect everything through union with the Ascended Lord Jesus Christ.

The law of justice permits evil for evil as well as requires good for good. It is the Law of Reaping as you sow, of getting what you give. This side of it is blessed, but as long as we give people evil for evil, we ourselves by ministering any evil to anybody are kept out the Kingdom at hand. You cannot have perfect happiness, joy, and bliss on any other basis than this.

Even Glimpsed by the Ancients

Joseph among the Hebrews returned good for evil. He had the excellent spirit. Plato among the Greeks saw that the really good man would have to return good for evil in order to be and remain a really good man. Plato also saw that when the perfectly just or good man appeared, he would likely have to go the cross; the life of meeting all evil with good, is the Cross life. Instead of fighting back, you love back. Instead of killing people who try to kill you, perfect love calls for laying down your life, even for them.

How Perfection Works in Us

When we believe in Him, we are born of Him and of His nature and Spirit, and are called to put off our imperfection and to put on His Perfection. When we are Baptized of Him we're given the seal and the first fruits of His perfection. By abiding in Him and bearing the fruit through vital union with Him, we progressively manifest His Perfection. This goes on until we've put off everything unlike Him and have put Him on fully.

We make no progress except as we abide in Him and manifest Him. Every time we minister any imperfection or evil for evil we are dropping back into the old life. It is only as we die to all selfishness and to all that desires and works any evil and give ourselves wholly to hungering and thirsting after the Perfection of God in Jesus Christ, that we make progress. We have to administer Perfection in order to become perfect. We have to give out love and only love in order to become perfectly loving. To give out any hate, even for the worst, is to be pulled out of the Kingdom of Love and its fullness and drawn into at least the beginnings of the lower kingdom.

The Spiritual Thermometer

After the eyes of our understanding are opened and we put first the Kingdom of Heaven, which is at hand through blessed union with Jesus and through bearing the fruit of this union, we're given, as it were, a spiritual or holy thermometer by which we can tell how every thought, feeling, and act increases or decreases our fellowship, joy and cleanliness in the Lord. Here all are taught of God from the least to the greatest. Here all experience becomes educative. Here you learn to cleave to everything that increases union and fellowship with Jesus and His joy and abundant life, and how to shun, repent, and put to death everything that diminishes this fellowship, joy and cleanness.

In the New Covenant, perfection becomes an inner necessity. It is written within us, in the heart, in the mind, in the nature and in the will. The

God from above teaches us and draws us on to perfection; the implantation within draws us, and even the enemy's attacks drive us God-ward.

Out of Hades into Heaven

Recent letters have brought me much joy. A friend that I've known for a long time, not long ago wrote me out of so much temptation and despair that he signed himself "your friend in hades." Just the other day there comes a letter from him out of such joy, hope, and a fine spirit that it might be signed, "your friend in the Kingdom of Heaven at hand."

Another friend writes me how several members of her family have been brought back to the first love and joy of the Lord. A friend who was in the Macon jail a little over a year ago, and has made good in life, writes me about the keen joy he is having in being used to bring people to Christ and to His love way of life. Another friend writes me that he has reached the place where he cannot wear the harness that does not fit him. As I wrote him, all the harnesses or yokes of men are hard to wear, while the harness or yoke of the Lord is easy.

The yoke of Jesus, as Henry Drummond says, enables us to easily pull the loads that we could not otherwise pull. By belonging to the Lord and by being led by the Lord, all things are ours. All the good of all the men of God, and all the good of all the groups of God and man are ours though union with Him who is All, and who is All in All. Moreover, obedience to the risen Jesus is obedience to our own self in the image and likeness of God. Obedience to Jesus is obedience to the Light, to the Perfect life, to the Truth, to God and obedience to the Son of God that has been born and who is growing up to perfection in every child of God. Obedience makes us free. Obedience to anything lower has in it limitation and bondage. Only the Perfect can make us perfect and can free us from the imperfect.

Steps to Freedom

The last visit that I had with a Philadelphia friend and the friends who dine with him, brought me among other things this fine testimony as to how confessing our guilt when we are guilty opens the door to freedom.

Two young men, through lack of work and because of desperate need, yielded to the temptation to take something that did not belong to them. He pled with both of them to get right with God and to come clean. One of them, a university man, said that after getting out of his trouble he might consider this good advice or wise counsel. The other repented and became very happy in the Lord before he went to trial. He told the Lord that if he could better serve Him in jail than out, then the jail would be the better place for him.

When they went to trial, the university man who did not come clean was charged with one offense and received a stiff sentence and a severe reprimand from the judge. The boy who first got right with God and who was happy to go to prison or to freedom as it best pleased the Lord, frankly told the judge that he was guilty of both of the charges brought against him. The judge said, in effect, "I see the making of a man in you, and I'm going to set you free." In every realm, the Truth sets free and all falsehood binds the cords of bondage all the tighter.

The Blessedness of Humbling Ourselves

Another Philadelphia friend recently told us this very helpful experience that he had at the shop where he works. There had been some misunderstanding between him and another man, and he humbled himself and asked the other man to forgive him. The other man broke down and said, "I was more at fault than you were, and you humbled yourself and asked my forgiveness." The good news of the reconciliation spread through the shop, and everybody was blessed because one man humbled himself and asked for forgiveness of another. The one who's least in error should always take the first step towards reconciliation.

CHAPTER 54

"The Single Eye"
(The Eye that is Wholly on the Lord)
September 26, 1937
Macon Telegraph and News

As Jesus says, *"The light of the body is the eye; if therefore thine eye be single, thy whole body shall be full of light."* (Matthew 6: 22)

Drowned, not by Falling but by Remaining

I failed to share in last week's article this fine thing that I heard while attending the Council of the Assemblies of God in Memphis. Friend Howard Carter, the superintendent of the Assemblies of God in England, in his notable address on the blessedness of not backsliding, said, "Nevertheless it is not the falling in the water that drowns one, but the remaining in it."

Happy Macon Findings

When I went to the jail Saturday afternoon, September 11, I found a young man with a shining face. When I asked him where he was born, he said his first birth was in Albany, Georgia, and that his second birth was in the Bibb County jail.

Later, when I went to Bellevue (Macon) and called on a friend, he told me that the night he was healed, his friends thought he was dying; he got his mind wholly on the Lord and found the difficult breathing and pain left him. He had been in the condition that he could not lie down and had to be propped up in the bed. He had suffered intensely and it was very difficult for him to breathe. His healing, he said, occurred about six months ago and since then it has been easy to breathe. When he feels the need of more strength and getting his mind wholly upon the Lord again, as He did on the night when he was delivered from what seemed to be the jaws of death, he finds that seeking the Lord again will bring the needed renewal of strength.

Healed by Faith and by the Spirit

Yesterday, September 12, I was told about a friend who had heart trouble for five or six years and found it difficult to walk to and from his work, a distance of about a mile and a quarter. About three years ago, when he was in intense pain and could not sleep, he told the Lord that if He healed Him, he would serve Him. The pain, he says, was taken away at once and the heart began to get stronger. When he received the Baptism of the Holy Spirit about two years ago, his heart was much strengthened, and he is now able to run without discomfort.

I have a friend who was healed by the power of the Spirit some time before she left Macon, to be especially well and joyous. She said she had had no further trouble. Prior to her healing she had been greatly depressed and her doctor said that she was poisoned from some difficulty in the gall bladder. She had reached the point where she felt that she could not pray. When others prayed for her no faith for healing came, but when someone in her presence yielded to the Spirit and began to praise the Lord, she says that the praises passed over to her and set her mind, spirit, and body free. The Spirit is life and gives life. Those who yield to the Spirit and are led by the Spirit become new and free.

The Control of the Spirit

It has been with me much of late that as precious as it is to be led by the Spirit, it is still more precious to be under the *complete, free, and total control of the Spirit.* Human control enslaves us; divine control sets us wholly free.

When we receive the Holy Spirit, the tongue and the whole body come under the control of the Spirit. The disciples, prior to Pentecost, had been cleansed of the Lord and used by Him; at Pentecost they were possessed by the Spirit. He used their bodies through the Spirit as the Spirit had used His body when He was on earth. Three thousand were added to the church in one day. The disciples became loving enough to have all things in common. In this high tide of love everyone contributed up to the limit of his ability and each one received up to the fullest limits of his need.

The great things that occurred in the early church after Pentecost were under the leadings of the spirit, plus the control of the Spirit. Sincere people may misinterpret and seem to have contrary leadings, but when the Spirit gets control all are made one and continue as long as the control is permitted. The Lord leads all of His people to be one, but it is only when they are under His control that they are actually one. The human mind, seeing in part, even when it is honest, tends to set up divisions. The Divine Spirit, knowing all and loving all, as He has control, makes all one.

Freedom and Vitality

Moreover, all human effort, even under high leading, brings a sense of strain and lacks freedom, buoyancy, and vitality. When it is all in God's hands and under His control there is complete release and freedom from care, worry and strain. There is also great vitality and reality. As long as our wills are not happily one with His they remain enslaved to some false desire, or spirit. When they become one with His will, they are set free from all that has enslaved them and desire what they should desire and get what they desire.

The Best Yet to Be

Under perfect divine control and use all the blessed things that have bloomed and promised are to come to fruition. The Pentecost ahead is to surpass everything behind it. Jesus being Perfect Everything is to bring forth in full redemption perfect everything in us. He is also to bring forth a perfected creation.

The Same Spirit, But Different Kind of People

A friend sends me the Methodist *Christian Advocate* of August 27, with a marked article, "Speaking with Tongues." The thesis of the article is that the speaking with tongues referred to in the Book of Acts, and after Pentecost was different from the speaking with tongues at Corinth.

There was but *One* Holy Spirit given to the early church, but He was given to different kinds of people. Those who received the Holy Spirit at Pentecost had walked with Jesus and been purified by His Word. Those who received at Corinth, at least some of them, had not been purified and had to be purified afterwards. It is like the water that flows from a perfect spring. All who take their vessels to it get the same water, but the water takes the shape of the vessel. If there is any rust or impurities in the vessel, until the water runs long enough to wash it all away, it seems as though the water was responsible for the dirt and is blamed for being dirty. So God, to cleanse us, may seem to some to be responsible for the dirt that He is washing away.

To see this helps us not to call good evil, nor to call evil good. Dirt is dirt and it does not come from the pure water, but from the dirty cup, and enough water makes the cup clean. Everything in us unlike Christ that is exposed and washed out and burned up by the Holy Spirit, is always bad. The Holy Spirit was never responsible for it being in us. He was only responsible for bringing it out from cover and destroying it. The ultimate achievement is in the handling and in the redemption of all things, but things not ready for taming and redemption are to be cast out.

Joseph, under a very overt temptation, ran. David under a similar temptation looked, continued to look, and fell. But thank God, Jesus redeems even the Magdalenes. It is far better to make a good run than a poor stand, to keep away from serpents that you cannot handle. But the highest of all and the end of all things is the perfect love, perfect power, and the perfect redemption that is in, by, and through Jesus Christ.

APPENDIX I

Introduction to "The Way of Love"

The article that follows is a transcription of a talk Rufus Moseley made in Denver, Colorado in April, 1950. Rufus frequently traveled the United States on behalf of Camps Farthest Out (CFO), speaking at their meetings, church gatherings, or wherever he was asked. It was during this period, beginning in the late 1930's until his death in 1954, that Rufus Moseley had the greatest of influences on the CFO movement and its founder, Dr. Glenn Clark of St. Paul, Minnesota. One of Rufus' protégés, Tommy Tyson, occasionally traveled with Moseley during this period, and sometimes transcribed talks for him. There is a good possibility that he transcribed this one. Mr. Moseley's joyous outbursts during his talks were common, and have been kept in the text.

(Rufus Moseley Collection, folder 10, Middle Georgia Archives, Washington Memorial Library, Macon, Georgia)

"The Way of Love"
by
J. Rufus Moseley
Sunday, April 23, 1950

I am profoundly grateful for this opportunity. I would be unworthy of it if I didn't dedicate every minute of it to the best uses. Join me in prayer that of all the things that I may say this evening, I will say the things that will be most helpful to you and most pleasing to Him. Precious Lord, Glorified Jesus, hold us fast to the best of all. Amen.

Full salvation is to be delivered from everything that is negative. Everything that is unlike Jesus Christ where He is now, is to be brought into His likeness. And Jesus Christ, where He now is, is God in full triumph and availability as a personality. He is the Eternal Christ in successful Incarnation, self-offering, resurrection, and glorification. He is the first man we have seen on the throne of the universe. As we go His way, we are to be like Him, and we have a tremendously good time on the way to it! If anyone is in union with Him, He is received within and we overcome and enter into Him and abide in Him; we are essentially in Heaven all the way to Heaven! In Him it is always getting better and better, while outside of Him it is always getting worse and worse.

The first step, if we are going to go the highest way of all, is to do like the prodigal son did, to come to ourselves or to repent and move back where we belong. There is no end to repentance as long as we blunder or sin and make mistakes. It is well illustrated in mathematics: as long as you say two and two are five, you have to repent of it, and the quicker you repent of it the happier it is for you.

The quicker we repent of every unloving thing we do and turn back to love, the better it is for us and the better it is for everybody else. Every time we violate Life, or Love, or anything that God is, we need to have quick recognition and acknowledgement of it. Then we need to go ahead and do what we should have been doing all the time. God is the homeland of the soul. We are no good outside of union with Him. Anything that takes us out of union with Him is sin, and everything that brings us back to union with Him is repentance. So long as we miss the way, the quicker we acknowledge it and get back in it, the happier it is for us and everyone else.

There are Three Degrees of Union with Him

The first is the union of *Interchange*. Whenever a positive and negative meet, whenever great love meets great need, love handles the need and gives the supply. When the prodigal son came home he furnished extreme need. The Father had supreme supply. So the Father takes the prodigal's rags and gives him the best robe; He takes charge of his appetite and gives him the best food. He gives him the ring. He gives him everything. So the beginning of union with the highest is a union of interchange. He takes our diseases and gives us His health and ease. He takes our sorrow and gives us His joy. He takes all of our needs and furnishes the supply. But if we were just receivers only we would never arrive at His likeness. But the great thing about Him is He is the great Giver, knowing it is more blessed to give than it is to receive.

Our next degree of union, if we are to become like Him, will be a *union of fellowship*, a *union of partnership*, or a *union of interaction*. He loves us into loving just as mother smiles a baby into smiling. Here if you want to increase in love, the first thing you do is let Him love you all He wants to love you. We don't love Him in the beginning. He loves us into loving. We love because He first loved us. The next step in becoming loving is to be decent enough to give the love to others that He gives us. This is moving into a union of partnership or a union of interaction. As good as it is to be loved it is still better to love. As good as it is to be forgiven, it is still better to forgive. And as good as it is to be healed it is even better to be used in His healing ministry. In all good things, it is even better to give than to receive. In all evil things it is a great deal better to take than it is to give. *It is a deep law of our being, that whatever we give we become.* It doesn't matter what is turned loose on us if we become wise enough to only give back good, and only good, to give love and only love, to give life and only life. This union of partnership is glorious. He loves through us and we love through Him. He accomplishes through us and we accomplish through Him. In the full achievement of this union with Him, He will bring forth everything in terms of us and we will bring forth everything in His name, or in terms of Him. This union leads to the highest degree of union of all, the *union of Likeness*, or the *union of Integration*.

In this union (union of likeness) we become extensions and contagions of Jesus Christ Himself and of the Kingdom of God. If we have this union we have real apostolic succession. You cannot have apostolic succession without apostolic Reality. If you had what Peter had, even if you had never seen the chair he occupied, you would be his successor. But if you had the chair but didn't have what he had, the thing would have just "petered" out. Apostolic succession peters out unless you have apostolic reality.

I was made decidedly aware of this when I was in Rome nearly two years ago. I knelt with reverence at the stone steps that it is said that Constantine retrieved from Jerusalem. These were the steps said to have been trodden by Jesus when He appeared and was judged before Pontius Pilate. The party I was with was moving on and I got only to kneel on the first step; I knew that if I crawled those steps for a century I would not be walking where Jesus walked. Jesus was walking up to tell the truth and to be judged and then crucified. If I should be willing to walk up to a Hitler or a Stalin and bear full testimony, and do it in love (even if it meant a horrible death), then I would be walking where He walked. You cannot follow Him in externals unless you follow Him in reality. The true worshiper worships Him in Spirit and Truth. We never bring the Kingdom of Heaven in great power until we have union with Him of integration, or a union of likeness. Viewed from another series of steps, it is first a union of seeking to conform to what He is, then it is a union that comes by receiving Him, *"For as many as receive Him are given the power to become the Sons of God..."* (John 1: 12) Next is the union with Him in His Glory; this union comes through the Gift of the Holy Spirit. The deeper work of the Baptism of the Holy Spirit or the Gift of the Holy Spirit is to bring us in union with the Glorified Jesus, so He will be in us and we will be in Him.

A deeper degree of union is the *union of the Overcomer*; the Overcomer enters into Him, stays in Him, grows up in Him and therefore becomes like Him. And a still deeper name for that union/intimacy is *Heavenly Marriage*. The Heavenly Marriage means simply that when we are willing to be wholly His and willing for all we are and have to be His, then He makes it known that He is wholly ours and everything He is and has is ours. This was given when I asked for the secret of (physical) rejuvenation. I had seen some people remarkably rejuvenated. I have one friend who is 95 who started to sing on the radio and television after her 94th birthday.

At the celebration of her 94th birthday, a teacher of voice recognized that the woman in question had a remarkably fine voice, and was a remarkably beautiful woman, too, the most beautiful elderly woman I have ever seen. I have another friend, who by remaining in the Spirit ten hours one day, physically became at least ten years younger. When a doctor examined her some time ago--she is now 66--the physician said she had the structure of a woman about 28. The more you live in the Spirit, the less you grow old, the more joyous you are, the less food it takes, the less sleep it takes, and the less you are fatigued. The more you live like a hog, the more you will have to sleep like a hog, and eat like a hog. I was at a religious meeting a couple of summers ago in the mountains near Pittsburgh, and I saw the brethren were getting their heads down rather near their dinner plates. They asked me to say grace, and I lifted up a prayer that we might look up and eat like birds and not look down and eat like swine.

As the scriptures put it, even in the Old Testament, *"But they that wait upon the Lord shall renew their strength; they mount up with wings as eagles, they shall run and not be weary, and they shall walk, and not faint."* (Isaiah 40: 31) As former Peabody College professor Sam Jones once put it, "They felt as though they could jump the moon and chin a star." As Oswald Chambers says, "Those who wait upon Him are always getting younger, and those who do not, have premature rheumatism and arthritis of the mind and spirit, as well as the body." Old age is largely just holding on to things you should give away. The tongue never grows old because it is kept too active.

Then there is to be *union of literal Bodily Likeness*. Jesus Christ begat us of His own Holy Seed, that in the end we will be His own likeness. This is a tremendous achievement. A new light came to me the other morning as to the difference between making a thing and begetting a thing. If you paint a picture or build a house, it will look like you. You put your mark on everything you do. But when you beget a thing, you put yourself into it, and the thing you beget when it comes to full maturity will be like you. New light was also given to me upon the statement of in John's gospel that Jesus was the Only Begotten Son of the Father. He <u>made</u> the rest of us. We are His children by creation. Jesus Christ is His Son by immediate begetting. Everything that is begotten when brought to full maturity will be like the one who begets it. So if you and I are going to be like Jesus, if we are going to have the triumph of Jesus, if we are going to be on His throne, we have to be begotten of Him. Jesus was begotten in the beginning and provision is made so we can be begotten when we receive Him.

There are three ways:

The Highest way of all is the way of Jesus. It is the way of limitless love. It is the way of doing unbelievable good and not doing any evil at all. It is the way of loving your friends and also of loving your enemies. Jesus is like the sun that shines on the evil and the good; also like the rain that falls on the man who works his crop and the man who doesn't work his crop. But the man who works his crop gets more out of the rain than the man who doesn't. God is all the time doing everything He can for you whether you do much for yourself or not. But you will never be like Him until you join Him in doing nothing but good and all possible good.

All the time when you yield to His Spirit you are born of His love nature, which is all love and nothing but love, which is good will and nothing but good will. You (we) are no mixture then of good and evil. You are in the Kingdom of God, and Jesus is the King of this Kingdom. In Him you are all love and nothing but love. In Him you are all good and nothing but goodness. I mean this new life within you is all this, not that you are yet all this or that He is all this in you. This is the only way I can get meaning of John's statement, "Whosoever is born of God doth not commit sin..." (I John 3: 9) That doesn't mean that Rufus Moseley can't sin; but that Jesus Christ is born within me when I believe in Him and give myself to Him, is sinless. This new life born within me is all love and all goodness and there is no evil in it at all. And this new life, this Son of God within me, when He comes to full maturity, will be like Jesus. This new child of God never has sinned and never will sin, and is put to great humiliation every time we do. That is the only way I can get real meaning that clicks with the experience and clicks with the scriptures that "he who is born of God does not sin."

Our human life is a mixture of both good and evil. We have a strong tendency to love those who love us and have it in for those who have it in for us. Where there is any evil, where there is a knowledge or experience of both good and evil, death is not overcome. We never come to bodily immortality until we give up evil and are willing to receive the good and give only the good. The new creation will be an entirely good creation. It will be a healthy creation, too. It will be an immortal creation. Death is written over everything that is sinful. Death is also written over anything that contains good and evil (compromise). Only life and immortality belong to the pure good. Jesus Himself, as Peter said on the day of Pentecost, could not see corruption because there is no corruption in Him. The life that He offered up is the life offered up for us. The death that He died was the death for us. He could not stay dead. "Blessed be the Lord! Hallelujah! Blessed be the Lord!"

Jesus is now in the realm of limitless Glory where His body is as immortal as His soul, and He will always remain in that realm. You and I become like Him as we believe in Him, are born of Him, and Baptized in Him. We become overcomers as we enter into Him and grow up in Him. We become partners with Him in doing His will. The culmination of that likeness is to be translated or resurrected into His literal bodily likeness.

Some are to receive bodily immortality without ever going to the graveyard. As you have heard me say, I would like it immensely to save myself from witnessing the undertaker looking so sad when he was enjoying the prosperity at my expense. As St. Paul said, "I show you a mystery." Not everybody is going to fall asleep, not everybody is going to die. Those in Christ who have died are not going to stay dead. Everyone that has fallen asleep in Him is going to be resurrected. Full salvation will be to be like Him, not only in love, dominion, and wonder, but also bodily. We then will become partners with Him in making all things in His image. The Jesus way is not only the way of union and the way of limitless love and goodwill, but also the way of meeting all evil with good. As long as you meet evil with evil, you will become evil. You will never be a victor until you meet all evil with good. Then the more evil you encounter the faster you will grow.

Glenn Clark (founder of Camps Farthest Out) has put it well: "All the evil you overcome with good gives a foundation for rising higher. All the evil you meet with evil gets you under evil." If you outflow perpetually with light, love, and joy, and meet all that is evil with the Heavenly, all that has hate in it with love, and all that has sickness in it with health, you will be like a flowing river or an artesian well. But if you meet evil with evil, you will be like a suckhole, drawing everything evil in the neighborhood to yourself. Since we become like whatever we choose to give out, if we give out evil we will never be in Heaven here or anywhere; conversely, when we give out Heaven we will be in heavenly places everywhere, all the time we are giving it out. You will never be in Heaven and love all the time until you go to giving Heaven and love all the time. You are not going to be healthy all the time until you give health all the time. *For you become and enter into the realm that you choose to give.*

So the Jesus way is first of all the *way of repentance*, then it is the *way of union*, then it is the *way of limitless love*. As I have already indicated, the way to increase in love is first to receive His love. Stop resisting His love and let Him love you all He wants to. Then give His love and pray for His love. If you ask anything according to His will, He hears you and there is nothing more according to His will than that you should give up everything that is unloving and go to loving. When you pray for love, you are given as much love as you are willing to receive. When you pray for love you are always praying for His will. This is the confidence we have in Him, if we ask anything according to His will He hears us, and if He hears us, then we know we will receive it. You have no doubt about a prayer to be loving being answered. Moreover, when you are praying for anyone and cannot keep from loving Him, because you are hoping and expecting your prayer will be answered. If your prayer is going to be answered, the bigger the sinner they have been, the better saints they will be. As Gerald Heard has said, "If we could have had anybody that could have forgiven as greatly as Hitler sinned, Hitler may have been converted."

Another way to increase in love is to remove the hindrances to love. How do you remove the hindrances to love? Every time you have done an unloving thing, acknowledge it and ask for forgiveness. When you do that it is just like opening the gate to a milldam: you get a gusher. If your deeds have been unloving, if you have been unloving positively or negatively to anyone, and you acknowledge it to him and ask for his forgiveness, something happens to both of you. You have such a flood of love you are almost tempted to fall out again that you may have the great fun of making up! So anyone who has done unloving things is just at the very gate, the possibility of great joy and a great inrush of love. When the love rushes in, everything else of God rushes in. You know all the virtues belong to the same family. You cannot marry into a family without getting all the family anyhow. If you marry yourself into vices you somehow get all of them. If you marry yourself to Jesus Christ, and in particular if you marry yourself to His love, you get everything of love. In every new situation choose the most loving thing you can think of, and since God is love, the most loving thing you can conceive of will turn out to have been the will of God.

Lastly, and I got this from an anonymous book, remember in every situation how Jesus met situations much more difficult than yours. Also remember what He, through the Spirit, is advising you to do in this particular situation. If you will do this, you will go from love to love and you will go from union to union. For the more union you have, the more love you will have; and the more love you have the more union you will have. You go from union to love and then you go from love to more union; then you go from more union to more love and you are to have perfect everything if you go all the way with Jesus. But the two things you have to have are union and love. They are to be together. In the past people had a tendency to try to have one without having the other.

Orthodox people are particularly under the temptation to say "Lord, Lord" without doing what He commands us to do and enables us to do. Our modern religions and religious sciences are trying to have Love without having the Lover. Our modern world is trying to have the Kingdom without a King, or trying to have fruit without having the Vine. In the dispensation of the fullness of time, we must have perfect Personality and we must have perfect obedience to perfect Love, Light, and Peace. We must have the perfect King and we must have His perfect Love. The two go together and the more of the Perfect One you have, the more you have of His nature and the more you have of His love. The two are really one and inseparable. You cannot go far with Love without having the Lover and you cannot go far with the Lover without having His Love. "Blessed Be the Lord!"

I said to the Glenn Clark group yesterday, of course we know that God is not just in one place, an old man with grey whiskers; we all know this is not so. But if we think about it we will know that nothing can appear in the universe that did not come out of its Cause. The highest thing that we see emerge in the universe is fine personality. The One that brings forth this personality is a Person, an infinite Person. If there is any difference between Him and us, He is a kind of super-person and we are a kind of sub-person. But we have to arrive as real persons. If you cannot see Personality in Him any other way, you can see the personality of God in Jesus Christ. Jesus Christ is the one Man who has arrived. He is the first real man we have yet seen. We have seen certain hints of this in others. As (Ralph Waldo) Emerson says, among us humans you will find one fellow who has a "good leg," another "who has a good arm," but it is only in Jesus Christ that we have seen the real and perfect Man. He is also perfect Spirit, Soul, Body, Truth, and Teacher. He is the perfect Savior, Salvation, Life, and Life-Giver. He is just Perfect Everything. He is perfect fulfillment and perfect balance of all good and perfection. When you arrive at the goal to which God has predestined you, you are going to be as perfect as Jesus is perfect. You will likewise have a perfect soul and a perfect body. You will have perfect dominion.

I noticed that C.S. Lewis, in his remarkable book <u>Miracles</u>, sees that when we arrive where we ought to be, the universe will obey even our wish. When I want my foot to step out there, it does it. If I want my arm to go up, it does. Any healthy body will do what you tell it to do. When we arrive, when we are obedient to the universe, the universe will be obedient to us. We have only lost control of the universe through disobedience. Jesus obeyed the Father completely, and by His obedience He ascended to the throne of His Father. We are promised when we obey Him completely, when we overcome and enter into perfect union with Him, we ascend into His throne just as Jesus ascended into His Father's throne.

I can never be satisfied until I have dominion over myself, and I don't want to boss anybody else. But I do want to boss devils and have dominion over all diseases, and I want dominion over old age! I even want dominion over homeliness! I want dominion over all negatives. I shall never be satisfied until I awake in His perfect dominion over everything. You and I will never be satisfied until we awake at the same dominion that He has. You will not have that dominion until you arrive at the same obedience that He has. When you submit yourself completely to love, all love will serve you. When you obey Jesus Christ, Jesus Christ will obey you, for in union your will and His are one. You can have what you want when you want and what you should want. Nobody really wants except what he should want. If you get anything other than this, you won't like it after you get it.

Then, too, the Jesus way is a new kind of judgment. It is the judgment of love and mercy unto victory and not a judgment of condemnation unto defeat. St. Paul, if he had been judged according to our human standards, would have been guilty of murder many times over. He was a murderer before the fact, accessory during the fact, and accessory after the fact, and on a wholesale scale—and a murderer of Christians, too! Jesus had nothing but forgiveness and opportunity for him. Jesus appeared to Paul and called him to be a witness and an apostle of things He had made known to him on the Damascus Road, and the things He would make known to him on the way. He took His chief enemy and made him His best friend. He took the one that was doing most to destroy the church and put a sentence upon him and gave him opportunity to do most to build up the church. You haven't done His will to your enemy until you have made him your friend. You do not want to kill him. There is too much possibility in him to kill him. The more he has hated you the more he will love you when you win him. We are here to win our enemies and not to destroy them. We are here to love them and not to hate them. We are here to release them and not bind them. We are here to turn all things to good. And so Jesus takes his chief enemy and makes him His best friend. He took Peter who was wishy-washy (a good name for him would have been water) and made a stone out of him.

His will for you, if you have been the biggest liar in the world, is to become the most truthful person; that is His sentence on you. If you have stirred up more evil than anybody else, then His will for you is that you should pray and live down more Heaven than anybody else. His will is a complete reversal of what you have been outside of His will. Where sin abounds, grace shall much more abound. The bigger a sinner you have been, if you give yourself over to Him, the better saint you will be. That doesn't mean that you should go and sin anymore; you have sinned enough to get a good reversal already! If you should go to sinning in order that grace might all the more abound, as St. Paul says, your condemnation would be just. It is nevertheless true though, that when a man like Starr Daily turns to the Lord, he can be more used to bring the Kingdom of Heaven than just a person that is neither good or bad, a king of a negative thing. The worse you have been, if you give yourself over to Him, the better you will be. The harder you have been when you gave Him a chance at you, the more tender you will be. The more you have messed life, when you turn the mess over to Him, He not only unmesses the messer, but He will make an asset out of the mess. He turns everything to good that you turn over to Him. If you are the sickest person of all, His will for you is for you to be the healthiest so you will have a better testimony than those who have never been very sick or well.

Another aspect of His way for us is that you can hate sin all you want to provided you love the sinner whose sin you hate. This is the way you can be angry without sinning. You mothers know if you had a son who was yielding to liquor or anything that destroyed him, the more you loved the son the more you would hate the destroyer. Likewise, the less you loved the son the more tolerant you would be of the booze. So a good life or witness will love the person, and the more you love the person the more you will want to separate him from the enemy who is binding him.

Sam Jones was one of the brightest men I ever knew. His intelligence was largely the keen insight of a good spirit. Whenever the truth is told in good will, and good sense, you have humor. Sam Jones said that he loved the saloon-keeper and only hated the way he made his living. Sam said he had all kinds of admiration for the man, but didn't like the way he made his living off of the misery of families. So you must not hate the sinner, but you must hate his sin. Jesus has pity and compassion on everyone that is bound by the enemy. The more you love the one who is bound, the more you will want to get him set free from his bondage.

He gave His will and willed His joy and His peace to His disciples. He told them to cheer up, that he had overcome the world. You can't touch Him now without getting unspeakable joy. If He could give joy then, what joy there is in Him now! One of the marks of everyone in union with Him is he will be outflowing with love, joy, peace, gladness, healing, and benediction. *He is great Joy. Then He is a great Peacemaker, too!* Let us pray that He triumphs as peacemaker during our time and that we may join Him by being peacemakers. To be a peacemaker you have to be greatly in love with the people you want to bring together. I find this the fine art of peacemaking. For example, if you gentlemen in the front row were not at peace with one another and I were bringing you together (I am glad I don't have to as you are already together), I would get each of you to admit there must be some virtue in the other and then go tell each of you. I would reverse the process of a mischief maker.

The Jesus way is also the way of great joy and wonder right in the midst of the worst that can be on the outside. It looks like we have to have Heaven right in the midst of evil on the outside of us before we are going to be entitled to have Heaven on both the outside as well as the inside. Some of the happiest people I have ever seen have been boys who have committed murder and been forgiven and received the Baptism of the Holy Spirit and faced eternity (on death row) with an unbelievable gladness. One of them went in singing "Amazing Grace" and he looked up and said he saw angels coming after him. A delegation from Heaven welcomed him from the other side. Another one said, "I am in Him and He is in me." Still another said "You could bury me alive and it wouldn't hurt me."

One of the best life stories I picked up along this line I got from the editors of *Sunday School Times*. A missionary in China was caught by some bandits who then demanded ransom for her release. She flatly refused to give it for two reasons: one was the missionaries needed it more than the bandits, and the other was the she did not want to encourage this kind of business. The bandits responded by saying, "We will be back on a certain day and cut your head off." She got ready for it and met the occasion with great enthusiasm. When they were taking her out to cut off her head, she was shouting "Praise the Lord!" The bandits, confused by her reaction, said, "We don't understand you." "Well," she replied, "I am just thinking what a glorious time I am going to have as I am ascending into Heaven and look back and see my head rolling down from the block!" The bandits responded by saying, "If you feel that way about it, we are not going to accommodate you." That is my hope: that we get in so much joy and get so much love that we will win our would-be persecutors, our would-be killers, and get them converted before they have a crime like that on their hands, even if we miss the glory of being martyrs.

There is something about Jesus Christ that if you meet the worst with the best, if you love back instead of hate, and you pray for those who are doing the worst to you, you are just put in a Heaven and a glory that is going to conquer. In the Roman Empire they had to stop killing the Christians, for every time they killed one they met death with such joy and such love, they converted too many non-believers.

The Jesus Way ends up in a glorious triumph. It ends up in a manifest victory. Jesus is already in manifest victory and everyone of us in union with Him to the degree that we are in union with Him already have the spirit of His victory.

Starr Daily thinks possibly the most vital thing that has come out of the way the Lord had dealt with me is that experience that came concerning the Cross. I'll tell you very briefly. I asked about the truth about the Cross, about Jesus Christ's blood and about his death. When the Holy Spirit came upon me and had me, and I think that is the Baptism, He had every bit of me: spirit, mind, and body, and I was singing and singing in the most beautiful English I have ever heard. I had asked Jesus if He could baptize me without the tongues I would appreciate it, but if He couldn't, I would take the tongues.

The Spirit was singing, *"Jesus, Jesus, How I Love You, Interposed His Precious Blood!"* Then my arms began to rise and my body stood up making the form of a cross. The higher I rose the more bliss and more glory and wonder I experienced. Up and up and up. Finally when I stood in unbelievable glory and bliss, on a different kind of Cross from what Jesus had (just the reverse in every point), the Glorified Jesus did according to His promise on the last night. *"He that hath my commandments, and keepeth them, he it is that loveth me; and he that loveth me shall be loved of the Father, and I will love him, and I will manifest myself to him."* (John 14: 21) That verse never meant anything to me before. It was a vague something, but now the Glorified Jesus, not a vision, but the highest reality I had ever known, stood before me. He then inbreathed or infused Himself within me.

Don't you see that is precisely what has been accomplished for us if we enter into union with Jesus through His death and resurrection and the gift of the Holy Spirit? His death means our life, if we get in union with Him now. His resurrection is our resurrection. Because He is in Heavenly places now, if I am in union with Him, I am also in Heavenly places too. Everything He has and is by experience, everything He is and everything He has achieved belongs to each one of us to the degree that we believe in Him, allow Him to Baptize us, allow Him to come and take up His abode within us. To the degree that we overcome and enter into union and enter into Him and abide in Him, it is ours. His death means our life. You see when He was put on His cross it was a cross of agony. The cross He put me upon through the Holy Spirit was a cross of bliss. His was a cross of dishonor. The cross He gives us is a cross of honor. On his cross, he gave up the Holy Ghost, the Holy Breath. On the cross that He puts us upon, we receive the Holy Ghost. On His cross, or the cross where we put Him everything seemed to desert Him. On the cross that He puts us upon, the Heavenly Host is about us. Jesus Christ manifests Himself to us as we are made ready. So He who knew no death, knew no sin, became sin in our behalf that we may become the righteousness of God in Him. He who did not have to die, died that we may live.

What is our cross then? Our cross, as St. Paul says, is to fill up that which is lacking in His suffering that we may bring the Kingdom of Heaven on earth. As long as there is hate in the world, somebody must meet the hate with love: that is our cross. If I meet it with enough love, by giving love where it is most needed, on the inner side I will be in more glory than at any other time. This has been true in Christian experience. It started with Steven, the first martyr. When they were stoning him to death he was praying for the people who were stoning him. He looked like an angel, and of course felt like an angel as he saw Jesus at the right hand of God. Something so tremendous has been wrought out in the universe through Jesus Christ, but you do not enter into the wonder of this except as you enter into union with Him. The young man you are going to marry, if he gets rich before you marry him and then marry him, his riches become yours, too. You might have fallen in love with him when he wasn't worth anything, but if he becomes a millionaire, you are a millionaire, too. Every one of us to the degree that we enter into and abide in union with the Glorified Jesus, His victory over death is our victory over death. His dominion is our dominion. His Heaven is our Heaven. His health is ours. Everything of His is ours.

Just a word on how we can be alive:

I think the reason people are sick as much as they are is that they haven't got enough life to throw off their sickness. There are three ways in particular by which you can have abundant life.

To the degree that you yield to His Heavenly love and give it, you will be all alive. He that loveth is all alive! When even old people, if they fall in love in human way, get alive. Even human love has wonderful rejuvenating power in it. Someone says a boy never washes behind his ears until he falls in love. Now this Heavenly Love which is designated by the Greek word *agape*, means limitless Heavenly love, our word love means a great many different things. This Heavenly Love as Grace is poured out upon us. To the degree that you receive His Grace, the degree we receive His Love, we are all alive. You can hardly be sick if you have enough love.

I was once seemingly dying from appendicitis. "Blessed be the Lord!" That was about 45 years ago. I hadn't a doctor. The dear Christian Science friends were praying for me, doing as best they could and as loving to me as they could be. I woke in a cold sweat. It seemed to be the sweat of death, and I was upstairs alone. My mother was alive at that time. I thought something like this: "Mother is alive and she has had enough trouble and I wouldn't like to die and cause her to have another sorrow, particularly to die without doctor." In the South it is considered disgraceful to die without a doctor; it puts the family in such a bad light. If you die in a regular way, why, you have an honorable funeral; but if you die in an irregular manner, it is very hard on your family and friends. Then I said, "These Christian Science friends have been wonderfully loving and they have done the best they could. It would be just going back on them to lie down and die." It wouldn't help them one bit in a Southern community nearly 50 years ago to die with appendicitis, under a Christian Science "treatment," and without a doctor. As soon as I reacted in love, the Lord of Love enveloped me with love, and Love is Life. Life just shot all over me. The power of death was broken. I didn't have a doctor there to say I was dying, but I believed that was the case. Well, you know, that brought up so much life, I rose up and went to the bathtub and the poison from my body colored the water. I have my appendix yet! Love has so much life! If you dedicate your life to love, it looks like nothing can kill you until your work is finished.

Love is stronger than death. If you are anemic and need life just fall greatly in love with God and everybody. Let the love of Jesus Christ flow in you, through you, and all over you. It will make you alive. The Spirit is life and gives life.

Today I was reading a book by J. E. Stiles on the Holy Spirit, and he made this remarkable observation: when Jesus Christ was here in the flesh, Mary brought forth the body. Now, everyone who receives Jesus Christ and receives His Holy Spirit and lives in the Spirit, occupies the same position. They are the people of the Holy Spirit, the very body of God on the earth.

Highest of all, they who have the Son have life. Indeed, Jesus came that we might have life and have it abundantly. Now He is seeking to come and reign within our whole being that His life may be our life. To the degree of our union with Him, we are alive in Him. Outside of fruit-bearing union with Him, everything dries up and becomes increasing lifeless and dead. So all in union with Him, all who receive and live in Him and in His love, live victoriously and are all alive spiritually, mentally, and bodily. Enough love and deep enough union with Him, and living in the Spirit and receiving and giving His love, will heal all of our diseases and even renew our youth like the eagle.

The more we feed upon Jesus Christ who is our Bread from Heaven, and the more we do His will which is our perfect meat, the more alive we become and we find ourselves changed from deadness to aliveness, from sickness to health, and from glory to ever more glory. Then it adds to your life to be associated with those who are alive and read their witness. When you can get fresh theology, never take canned! Likewise when you can get your natural food fresh from the Hand of God and nature it is much more alive and life-giving. It is much more alive than when denatured and canned.

Above all delight thyself in the Lord Jesus Christ, keep your mind and heart stayed on Him, feed upon Him, live in the Spirit and be perpetually receiving and giving His love. The Jesus Way for us is the way of repentance, seeing, confessing, and forsaking our faults and sins, as long as we blunder and sin. The way of union with God is through fruit-bearing identification, union, and marriage with the Glorified Jesus. He is God's Perfect Everything in full attainment and availability, the way of immediate guidance, limitless love, meeting all evil with good, all hate with love, and all negatives with positives. We must judge in terms of what all may become as they repent and give themselves to Him, so that the chief of sinners becomes the chief of saints, and so those who have most messed up life will be the best partners with Jesus in unmessing it.

The Jesus Way is also the way of loving the sinner while you hate his sins, the way of peace and peace-making, the way of abundant life, health, and healing, the way of great inner peace, joy, and even bliss when men under demonic temptation are doing their worst. The Jesus way culminates in visible, tangible, Manifest Victory and Perfect Everything!

APPENDIX II

After his Baptism in the Holy Spirit in March 1910, Rufus Moseley began to gain something of a reputation in Macon for his whole-hearted--some said excessive--public testimonies of Jesus Christ and of the Spirit Baptism. One old Mercer friend even met with him and sought to "tone down" his enthusiasm. Years later, Moseley himself looked back on this time as one of well-intentioned but somewhat misguided zeal. The article below concerns one such very public demonstration of his fervor. Along with the Macon twin sisters he met and befriended, Susie and Carro Davis, they entered the First Presbyterian Church on Mulberry Street in that city and began to loudly worship in what was otherwise a staid, rather conservative service. They were invited to leave, whereupon they took to the street and began an impromptu street meeting that garnered unkind reviews. Later street meetings had the permission of the Macon police department, but when they grew too large they were asked to break them up. Rufus—by his own admission—resisted this and was about to be taken to the police department when he apologized and was released.

The first article details the initial trouble at the First Presbyterian Church in Macon in December 1911; the second article below is Moseley's response to the trouble he and the Davis sisters had, as well as seeking to correct some public perceptions that the meetings were otherwise more than spontaneous. Another misperception Moseley sought to correct was that he was the "head" of what had become locally known as the "Children of God" or "Holy Rollers" cult. Despite his early enthusiasms, which he admitted a few years later, it is great testimony when one remembers that ten years later the same newspaper that published this story invited Rufus to write a religion column in their publication.

Refused Admittance to Church; Big Crowd Hears Holy Rollers in Street

Professor Moseley and Four Women Followers Center Great Gathering on Mulberry Street—Met at the Door of the First Presbyterian Church and turned Back—Police there, but Not Needed

Macon Telegraph December 25, 1911

Refused admittance to the First Presbyterian Church, where a week ago yesterday they were led out of the church because of the peculiar and boisterous manner of worship disturbing the congregation, the sect of "Holy Rollers," self-styled "Children of God," held an open air service on the steps of the Pythian Castle yesterday morning between 11 a.m. and 12 p.m. to one of the largest congregations without a doubt in Macon. Several hundred people stood all through the preaching and exhortation. The service was punctuated frequently by loud shrieks and deep groans.

The elders and officials of the First Presbyterian church had decided, as John McKay stated last night, "that the peculiar form of worship indulged in by the followers of Professor J. Rufus Moseley, head of the sect here, was not in line with the standards as upheld by the Presbyterian denomination," and that it would be best to refuse them admittance.

To this effect the police were asked to have a detail on hand to enforce the prohibition, but the two plain clothes men who turned up just before church time were not needed.

Denied Admittance

In the company with Miss Carro Davis, Miss Susie Davis, Mrs. W. A. Scott and Mrs. Warfield, Professor Moseley turned up at the church sharp on time. Professor Moseley mounted the steps where he was met by Elder McKay. They shook hands. Mr. McKay informed him courteously but firmly that the form of worship indulged in by Professor Moseley and his companions could not be allowed in the church and that he could not be admitted. Professor Moseley assured Mr. McKay of his kindly feelings towards the Presbyterian Church and announced that he would hold a meeting of his own outside.

With the four women, the leader repaired to the steps of the Pythian Castle where a sort of jubilee commenced which in a short time attracted a great crowd. The women moved backward and forward and sideways, jumped up and down, waved their arms and shouted and shrieked and wailed forth in tongues, strange and unheard of. It sounded like no mortal language at least so far as any citizen of the United States on deck yesterday might recognize.

Heard for Two Blocks

The voices of the outdoor worshipers could be heard for two or three blocks. The police were on hand, but had informed Professor Moseley beforehand he would not be interfered with as long as he held his meetings out of doors and there were no complaints made. After fully an hour of the most strenuous sort of exercises, vocal and muscular, the party left for their homes.

At the time that the party was refused admittance to the First Presbyterian church it was circulated among the spectators—and there were many outside the church expecting some demonstration—that the five "Children of God" had provided for that contingency by a decision to go the First Baptist (Church) in case they were refused at the First Presbyterian and that the police had told them they would also be refused admittance there also. However, they made no move in that direction.

Dr. Dargan stated last night that he had never discussed the possibility of a visit of the Holy Rollers to his church with the officials of his church. He knew nothing of the request to keep them out.

"J.R. Moseley Writes Card Explaining His Principles"
Macon Telegraph
December 27, 1911

J.R. Moseley, prominent in the "Children of God" cult in Macon, generally known as the "Holy Rollers," has requested that The Telegraph *print the following:*

Editor of *The Macon Telegraph*:

I know but few things in modern journalism finer than the consideration that the *Telegraph*, under your management, has shown for the religious convictions and personal feelings of all your neighbors. I have known you to sacrifice good news stories because of this consideration.

But as kindly in spirit as are parts of the *Telegraph*'s article on Christmas day, about our being refused admittance at the First Presbyterian church, and the street meeting that followed, it nevertheless misses greatly both "The Truth" and the "true Truth" about me and the four good women whom I was honored by God, as well as them, of being permitted to accompany. But what we most of all desire to get and keep before the people, is not the truth about ourselves; but the fact that we are witnesses that God, according to the visions of the prophets, the promises of Jesus and the testimony of the early apostles, in pouring out His Holy Spirit today and that message after message is being given of the soon coming of Jesus. (See Isaiah 28: 31; Joel 2: 28-29; Luke 11: 10-13; John 7: 36-39; John chapters 14-16; Luke 24: 48-49; Acts chapters 1-4; and Acts 10: 44-46, 11: 16-17; 19: 1-6).

We went to the First Presbyterian church Sunday morning as we went the Sunday before, because God, through the witness of His Spirit through our spirit said for us to go. Even before this we were told to go to the churches and praise Him and He would put His power upon us.

While our spirits greatly rejoiced, our flesh shrank. Never before had I been called to do anything by and for God that seemed so hard, and the hardest part of it was the seemingly unreasonableness of the command. But before we went the light came that the churches dedicated to Him are God's houses just as much as were the ancient temple and synagogues where both Jesus and his early disciples went to worship.

Even before Jesus entered the temple at Jerusalem, which He called "My House," "the whole multitude of the disciples began to rejoice and praise God with a loud voice." That chapter in Isaiah (the 66th) from which Jesus quoted as His reason for cleansing the temple says, "Also the sons of the stranger that joined themselves to the Lord...Even them will I bring to my holy mountain and make them joyful in My house of prayer—For My house shall be called a house of prayer for all people—His watchmen are blind; they are all ignorant...and they are shepherds that cannot understand."

When Jesus came to Nazareth, as His custom was, He went into the synagogue on the Sabbath day and stood up to read (Luke 4: 16). After He had read from the wonderful sixty-first chapter of Isaiah, and revealed not only Himself and His mission, but also revealed His neighbors to themselves—"all they in the synagogue—were filled with wrath and rose up and thrust Him out of the city."

You see the mistake we have all made, insofar as we are directly or indirectly responsible for it, is in making worship monarchical or autocratic, that is closed, when it should be democratic, or open to all to pray, to give testimony, to read from the Scriptures, to prophesy, or to praise as the Spirit leads. This has naturally led to the kindred error of regarding houses of worship as being ours instead of His.

Friends, when you see this, you will have no fault to find with us for presenting ourselves for worship at any church. And we hope you will have no fault to find with those who believe they are doing God's service in casting us out or turning us away. They are people we like and whom we want to share with us "the glorious liberty" as well as the full inheritance of the children of God. All of us who are led by the Spirit of God are the sons or the children of God (Romans 8). When you understand our motive, you will love us all the better for having in the first instance so misunderstood us. But we are not complaining, as we are finding the reproaches for His sake greater riches than the treasures of this world.

If the authorities of the First Presbyterian Church (and this is the only church we presented ourselves to, or even thought of presenting ourselves Sunday) had known that even a child, coming in the name of the church as a whole, telling us that the church preferred for us not to worship there, was all that was necessary to cause us to withdraw with love in our hearts and prayers and blessings upon our lips—I say if they had known this, they could spared themselves of much that was and is and will be a thousand times harder for them than us.

But it is not the first time. Though we would that it were the last, that the elders and officials of the temple had appealed to the law (where there was not even a pretense of need for it) to do what they were naturally ashamed to do and without divine authority for attempting to do. But, thank God, that the authorities of the human law have always done unwillingly and unhappily and as kindly as expediency would allow the behests of the elders and the demands of the Pharisees. Thus far in our case, we have no more fault to find with the authorities of the law than they with us. They did finely under the circumstances, which were evidently more trying for them than to us.

Not until we were turned away from the Presbyterian Church and the wonderful glory, peace, and praise of God came upon us and Miss Carro Davis began to speak and sing in the Spirit, and the people began to gather about us did we have any definite idea or purpose as to what we would do. The meeting formed itself or was formed for us.

So far as the future is concerned we have no plans, except to try and know and do as best we can God's will; and "whenever, it be right in the sight of God to harken unto you more than unto God, judge ye." It may be the Lord's purpose (I do not know) to give the Presbyterian Church still other opportunities to change its mind. He is plenteous in love and mercy, and we pray that even the great tribulation that is prophesied that must come to pass are to work out the wise and loving purpose of God to bring many to repentance, faith, charity, life, and bliss everlasting.

If we seem to be beside ourselves, it is for His sake. If we are sober, it is for your sake. It is hard to share so much glory and wonder, and yet appear conventional enough not to seem beside oneself to the conventional.

While all of the Children of God have to be led by the Spirit of God as a condition for being His children (Romans 3: 14) insofar as we have even the semblance of a human leader, it must always be the one (not necessarily always the same one, either) whom God seems to give the clearest light and leadings. So far as we had the semblance of a leader Sunday (I mean a human leader) Miss Carro Davis whom God first called to preach His word to the black people of her neighborhood, was the one; Mrs. Wayfield and Mrs. Scott (of our number) received the Baptism of the Holy Spirit before I did, and Miss Carro Davis led us all in zeal and boldness, as well as in quick obedience to the command, "Go preach My gospel."

I am not only not "a ringleader" nor even a "leader of any sect," but am not and never intended to be a sectarian, a cultist, or a "particularist in religion" any more than in politics, sociology, philosophy or literature. In politics, I am an independent; in sociology I am an individualistic socialist and a socialist individualist (looking for a society where Jesus is King as well as Redeemer, and where each produces according to his ability and receives according to his needs). In literature, I am an eclectic, looking for the marriage of the highest truth and the most perfect beauty. In philosophy, I am a totalist (the term so far as I know originated with me), looking for the totality or wholeness of truth and welcoming the good and eschewing what seems to be error from every source.

In religion, I am a Child of God, seeking to be led by the Spirit of truth to the best and to all that God has for me with the blessed hope and assurance that I am now by faith and am to be by actual experience an heir of God and a joint-heir with Christ.

I am a special debtor to the Baptists and the Christian Scientists; and it seems that from almost every religion and philosophy I have seen reflections or rays of that "true light which lighteth every man that cometh into the world." (John 1: 9) I am indebted in a special high way to those who brought to my notice that the promises of Jesus with reference to the other Comforter, the Spirit of Truth, the Holy Spirit, or the Holy Ghost, is literally true and is now being realized by all who rightly ask and tarry for this Spirit.

Together with the Father who sent Him and the Holy Spirit who now represents Him on earth, I am indebted most of all to Jesus, whom the Spirit reveals and glorifies as Lord and Christ and bears witness to His soon reappearing.

J.R. Moseley
Macon, December 26, 1911

ENDNOTES

1. J. Rufus Moseley, <u>Manifest Victory: A Quest and a Testimony</u>. (New York: Harper and Brothers, 2014 reprint edition, 1947), p. 47; Wayne McLain, <u>A Resurrection Encounter: The Rufus Moseley Story</u>, (Minneapolis: McAlester Press, 1997), p. 35. I encourage all to read these two Moseley books.
2. Moseley, <u>Manifest Victory</u>, pp.40-41.
3. Ibid., p. 50.
4. Ibid., pp. 51-52.
5. <u>The Mercerian,</u> May, 1900, p. 37; <u>B. D. Ragsdale, Memoir of Pinckney Daniel Pollock, President of Mercer College, 1897-1905</u>, (Atlanta: Self Published, 1905), p. 102, 216, 220-222; Moseley, <u>Manifest Victory</u>, pp. 59-62. In the <u>Annual Announcement of Mercer University, 1898-99</u>, the classes Moseley taught are listed as: General History, Modern Europe and the United States, Comparative Politics, American Political and Constitutional History, Principles of Political Economy, Psychology, Ethics, and The History of Modern Philosophy. He also taught a short-lived course called Lectures on Pedagogy.

    In the Mercer student publication for 1900, <u>The Mercerian</u>, a paragraph was published stating great regret at Rufus Moseley's leaving. Both Moseley and Kilpatrick, of course, went on to great things. Of Kilpatrick, Moseley reported it as once being said, "The only way you can kick Kilpatrick is up." Indeed, Kilpatrick went on to Columbia University and joined with John Dewey in reforming American education for decades to come, and Moseley became one of the most influential Christian leaders of his day, with an influence that remains to the present.
6. William L. DeArtega, <u>Agnes Sanford and Her Companions: The Assault on Cessationism and the Coming of the Charismatic Renewal</u>, (Eugene, OR: Wipf and Stock, 2015), pp. 160-63.
7. <u>Macon Telegraph</u>, March 27, 1921.
8. Moseley, <u>Manifest Victory</u>, p. 93.
9. Ibid, pp. 88-89.
10. Ibid., pp. 104-105

[11] Ibid., pp. 95; 102-107; J. Rufus Moseley, Perfect Everything, (Greensburg, PA: Manna Books, 1951), pp. 47-52.
[12] McLain, A Resurrection Encounter, p. 106.
[13] Ibid., p. 107-108.
[14] Ibid., p. 105; Personal interviews with Diana Vinson and Fran Williams of Byron, Georgia, October 17, 2015. They are Rufus Moseley's grandniece and great-grandniece respectively, as well as being mother and daughter.
[15] Macon Telegraph, December 25, 27, 1911; See Appendix II at the end of this book for full transcriptions of these newspaper articles.
[16] Moseley. Manifest Victory, p. 130.
[17] Andrew Manis, Macon Black and White: An Unutterable Separation in the American Century, (Macon: Mercer University Press, 2004) p. 127.
[18] McLain, A Resurrection Encounter, p. 112, 128; Moseley, Manifest Victory, pp. 140-141.
[19] The Macon Telegraph and News, July 17, 1938.
[20] Agnes Sanford, Sealed Orders, (Gainesville, FL: Bridge-Logos, 1972), p. 191-192.
[21] Freelance, January 13, 1993, Fredericksburg, Virginia, p. C-2.
[22] McLain, A Resurrection Encounter, p. 23.
[23] Ibid., p. 107.
[24] Before Moseley's death, Tommy Tyson began a lasting friendship with Oral Roberts. They travelled together around the world in ministry, and in the 1960's, along with ongoing CFO involvement, Tyson was part of the fledgling Oral Roberts University. Tommy's impact on the Charismatic Movement was huge, and just as he expressed gratitude for having known Rufus Moseley, so Tommy's protégés have with him. Tyson left behind a wealth of spiritual teaching and a stellar walk in the Kingdom that those who knew him treasure to this day.

Wayne McLain went on to professorships at Kentucky Wesleyan and American University in Washington, D.C. Like Tommy Tyson, he shared in Moseley's golden years and was greatly enriched by the experience. McLain became a Moseley scholar and helped in a great degree to keep the flame and teachings of this man of God alive for future generations. In a letter to Rufus' brother Millard, a few years after Rufus' death, a letter writer describes McLain as this "brilliant young minister whose ministry mirrored that of Rufus Moseley himself."

This author, while having never met Tyson or McLain, feels a great debt of gratitude to both of them.
[25] McLain, A Resurrection Encounter, pp. 222-223.
[26] Found in Rufus Moseley's personal papers in the possession of his descendents, Diana and Emmet Vinson, and used with their kind consent.

ABOUT THE AUTHOR

Rufus Moseley was a pioneering Charismatic Christian, who above all else sought to provide the keys to Kingdom living to all believers. While he belonged to no denomination, he spoke to a wide variety of them across the United States and in Europe. He received the Baptism of the Holy Spirit in March of 1910 in Macon, Georgia, and began a ministry to the poor, needy, those on death row, as well as to the rich and powerful. Whether in prison death cells, at major universities, or consulting with political leaders in Washington, D.C., his message was always the same: the New Birth, the Baptism of the Holy Spirit, and living in vital, conscious union with Christ as a result of those experiences. Between 1921 and 1954, he wrote a weekly religion column for the Macon Telegraph (Georgia) newspaper, in which the immense depth of his spiritual wisdom and the simplicity that is in Christ was given to readers. These articles contain some of the most profound works on living in the Kingdom of God in the here and now that have ever appeared in print, and are testimony to a man who lived a life in Christ that few have attained, yet is available to all who seek it.

The compiler of these articles, Gregory S. Camp, Ph.D., is a historian who has served as a professor, government researcher, museum specialist, archivist, and independent scholar over a thirty-five year period. He first came upon Rufus Moseley's writings in 1974, and in 2013 was inspired to find as many as he could and make them available to the Christian reader. It is his contention that you will find Rufus Moseley as much a blessing, and his writings brimming with spiritual wisdom, as anything you have ever read.